Exploring Self and Society

Also by Rosamund Billington and Sheelagh Strawbridge

Culture and Society: A Sociology of Culture (with L. Greensides and A. Fitzsimons)

Also by Jenny Hockey

Experiences of Death: An Anthropological Account

Growing Up and Growing Old: Ageing and Dependency in the Lifecourse (with A. James)

Death, Gender and Ethnicity (with N. Small and D. Field)

Exploring Self and Society

Rosamund Billington
Jenny Hockey
Sheelagh Strawbridge

First published 1998 by
MACMILLAN PRESS LTD
Houndmills, Basingstoke, Hampshire RG21 6XS
and London
Companies and representatives throughout the world

ISBN 0–333–63222–2 hardcover
ISBN 0–333–63223–0 paperback

A catalogue record for this book is available from the British Library.

This book is printed on paper suitable for recycling and made from
fully managed and sustained forest sources.

10   9   8   7   6   5   4   3   2
07 06 05 04 03 02 01 00 99

Printed in Hong Kong

For all our students, past, present and future

Contents

Acknowledgements

We would like to thank the following who have helped us in various ways: Steve McCorrie and Louis Billington for supplying valuable references for Chapters 6 and 7; Allison James and Andrew Dawson for their contribution of ideas and references for Chapter 8. Robert McCann (who was aged eight at the time) contributed the 'royal' joke in Chapter 7. Thanks to Pam Davies who shared part of the day of the royal funeral with Ros and helped her to clarify feelings and ideas to add to the book. Jackie Smales and other staff in the Learning Support Centre on the Inglemire Avenue campus of the University of Lincolnshire and Humberside deserve thanks for their patience in sorting out Ros's wordprocessing muddles in completing our final draft. We are particularly grateful to Ethel Strawbridge who provided us with the many cups of coffee and good meals without which this book would have taken even longer to produce.

ROSAMUND BILLINGTON
JENNY HOCKEY
SHEELAGH STRAWBRIDGE

Introduction

In this book we have set out to do something rather different from conventional social science textbooks. The book takes everyday life and personal experience as its starting point, whether in the 'private' spheres of the home and personal relationships or the 'public' spheres of paid work and health care. It asks you, the reader, to reflect on what you know, feel and believe about yourself and your social worlds. The book does not require you simply to get to grips with a body of information; nor to learn new facts about being human. Our aim is rather to help you ask questions, to promote enquiry, and therefore much of its content is exploratory rather than factual.

In this respect, the book reflects a discipline of social science which is less sure of itself than it once was. It is an umbrella discipline which no longer deals confidently in 'findings', 'results' and 'analyses' but has now moved on. In their place it has set a series of questions. These challenge our assumptions about 'truth' and about the certainty with which we can make judgements about human society. They suggest that the ways in which we divide up individuals and classify the social world might be somewhat arbitrary. Key ideas such as class, gender, work, public, private, and, indeed, society itself, are explored in this book, but they are not treated as a shopping list of concepts which students must first inform themselves about and then commit to memory. Rather, they are presented as ways of thinking about our selves and our social worlds that we build into theoretical maps or models to help us find our way about. Like all maps, social science theories highlight some features of the social landscape and leave out others. Not only have they changed historically; they are also likely to change in the future.

Once we begin to work in this way, the 'facts of (social) life' begin to take on a different status. As we struggle to understand ourselves and our experiences we come to see just how complex everyday life is and, incidentally just how much of an accomplishment it is to negotiate it skilfully! Crime, illness or sex cease to be just concrete events which take place during a bank raid, after sharing an office with a 'flu sufferer, or after a few drinks at the weekend. Rather, we can begin to understand them as those features of a complicated social world that our particular maps happen to allow us to perceive. Without the maps we currently have to hand in our society, we might begin to live in a somewhat different, albeit similarly concrete, world. Crime might be the consumption of irreplaceable global resources, illness might be the patterning of an individual's genes, and sex might be something which happens on the Internet. What this book will help you to do is discover the ways in which social maps come into being, who might be involved in making them and changing them, and who might be involved in reading them. It will give you insights into the different landscapes that can often exist in parallel, or indeed in tension, with one another. For example, as a recent popular book title suggested: 'Men Are from Mars and Women are from Venus' (Gray, 1993): some feminists would argue that men and women remain in separate spheres, both spatially and in terms of the way they understand the world.

Our intention, therefore, is to persuade you, the reader of our book, to question what you hear, see and feel, to take nothing at face value, but to think about it as the product of a particular map and ask whether the map is one of your choice or someone else's. It is our hope that you will share some of our excitement in seeing the world from different positions, in particular those made possible by social science. Even the most mundane of activities – a visit to the doctor or a family mealtime, for example – can become a focus for new interest and different ways of seeing that can open up new possibilities for action. However, the focus of this book on personal experience and everyday life can, misleadingly, suggest that it is an easy read. This is not so, because social science forces our minds to deviate from the usual track, to see mysteries in our taken-for-granted experience and, while this can be exciting, it is also difficult and challenging. It can also be uncomfortable and disturbing. If you are new to social science, remember that you would not expect to pick up a textbook in another language, Portuguese, say, and read it straight through. Picking up a book in any new discipline is much the same. Some quite hard work is necessary, but we think that getting to grips with social science brings significant rewards that we should like to share with you.

Chapter 1 invites you into a kind of map library. We shall look at the history of some of the maps that social scientists use, and at the reasons why they keep on choosing to draw up new ones, while at the same time glancing back at the more useful aspects of the old ones. Once you have read Chapter 1 and begun to find your own way around this library of maps you will be able to go further, into the later chapters. Here you will find a more focused approach to personal experience which asks you to think about areas such as sexuality, personal identity, health, work, the nation and its relationship with other parts of the world. In each case you will be introduced to the idea that these are areas of life that might seem to have some kind of inevitable shape or quality, but in fact take on their characteristics as a product of the maps we use to manage them.

As the maps have first been laid out for you to examine in Chapter 1, you may initially find some parts of the chapter particularly difficult, and time spent re-reading it, with the help of the Glossary, will pay off later. The Glossary is intended as a sort of technical guide to the contents of our 'map library' and contains brief definitions of the terms we use in this book that are specific to social science. Many of these are only introduced in Chapter 1 and you will find more detailed explanations and examples throughout the book. The meaning of many of the terms is difficult and in some cases there is disagreement among social scientists concerning their meaning. Some of the terms are in popular usage but have a more specific meaning when used by social scientists. It is worth looking up words in the Glossary even if you think you can guess their meaning. You may also need to consult dictionaries specifically compiled for sociology or social science if you want more detailed explanations. You may only fully understand some of the terms when you have read more widely and deeply. You are also advised to look up some of the names and the ideas in other social science textbooks or dictionaries.

Though we are trying to introduce you to the idea of mapping and therefore to show you the kinds of maps that have been produced, this book itself is, of course, only one way of mapping a complicated terrain and you will need to compare it with others. For example, the map we have drawn suggests a widening circle moving outwards from personal experience to the wider world. This reflects for us the pattern of growth from infancy, in the immediate social world, to the adult, more public, world. However, this can be seen as a very Western, and perhaps feminine, map. We have also started from our specific experience as English women writers. We recognise that this shapes our concerns and distinguishes us even from, for example, Irish or Scottish women writers. Indeed, some of these may not identify with us at all, but see us as oppressors! We have worked outwards to make connections or comparisons with differing cultural experiences but it is important to see just how specific cultural experience is and to avoid, as far as possible, assuming similarities and ignoring differences. This approach will appeal to some readers but others may be critical, and it is our belief that such debate is valuable in itself. We often learn best through argument, and social science is an argumentative discipline supplying conceptual tools but not definitive answers. As teachers of social science we are excited by the ways in which our students, like ourselves, find ideas and maps that are challenging and which enhance their passionate engagement in their own social worlds. We hope that you too will find here ideas to stimulate your own thoughts, arguments and actions.

1

Understanding the Social World

Preparing to explore

This chapter, together with the Glossary, will introduce you to some of the main themes of this book and to the questions it will be exploring. The title of the book, *Exploring Self and Society*, was chosen to indicate that the subject matter – the relationship between the social world and ourselves – can be seen as unfamiliar territory that can gradually become 'known' through the process of exploration. Our purpose in this chapter is also to introduce you to some of the equipment that will be needed in order to explore this territory, and some of the preparations that need to be made before setting out on such an exploration. The Glossary, which defines most of the social science terms we use continually in this book, is also designed to help you, particularly in this preparatory stage.

People living in 'modern' societies are constantly seeking answers to questions concerning the nature of their society, the way it affects their personal lives and identities, and how their society differs from, affects and is affected by other societies. Part of this quest for explanations also involves asking questions about how we might alter those aspects of society we dislike, of which we disapprove, or find frightening. The first resources here might be newspapers, TV and other media, but the social sciences in general, and sociology in particular, are the intellectual disciplines to which we turn for a more expert explanation and understanding of social, political and economic activities, and the role of these in the life and identities of individuals and groups. Some aspects of psychology can also be considered as part of the social sciences and are therefore involved in explaining all these aspects of social life.

Before we go any further it is important to define what we mean by the social sciences and say something about their origins and what it is that they study. They are associated with the development of those societies that are defined as being 'modern'. 'Modern societies', 'modernity' and 'the West' or 'Western civilisation' are associated terms about which there is much debate (see, for example, Hall and Gieben (1992) and Wagner (1994)). They are linked to societies that have formed in the north-western quarter of the world over the past few centuries, and are used to distinguish these societies from those, in other parts of the world, defined (by the West) as being 'traditional'. The eighteenth and nineteenth centuries are seen as being particularly important periods of development, and the change from an agricultural to an industrial way of life, coupled with the growth of more democratic ways of governing society are defining characteristics of modern societies. The intellectual movement of the eighteenth century known as the 'Enlightenment' gave definition to the idea of 'modernity' and birth to the range of disciplines, including those we now call the social sciences, which shaped the modern conception of 'knowledge'. Enlightenment thinkers engaged in an energetic critique of all forms of traditional and religious authority – for example, magical or superstitious beliefs. In their place was substituted a belief in progress, reason and science. What has become known as the 'project' of modernity and of the Enlightenment proposed a vision of a world that valued material progress, prosperity, individual freedom and social justice founded on rational rather than religious or magical principles. All this was to be based on sound 'scientific' knowledge rooted in the 'scientific revolution' of the seventeenth century. This project then, of which the social sciences have been a part, can be seen as a normative one – that is to say, it told people what they should do and laid down clear values and ideas. We need to bear these prescriptions and proscriptions in mind because, as we shall see, one of the misleading claims of the sciences and social sciences is that they produce knowledge that is objective or 'value-free'.

When we are trying to explore the society we live in, it is therefore to the social sciences that we turn if we want expert, objective knowledge. We value it more hightly than the opinions and prejudices of journalists or taxi drivers. As we shall see, however, the relationship between these different ways of understanding society is more complex than it might appear at first sight.

At one level, everyone might enquire about the way society functions, and indeed about what makes up or constitutes society and the social.

However, some groups and individuals central to the functioning of modern societies, for example, social workers, teachers, voluntary workers, health professionals, politicians or civil servants, require answers to their enquiries because they are studying and working in areas and on issues that make their questions, and the answers to them, seem important. It is particularly such people who look to the social sciences for some understanding of the society they live in, for an understanding of other societies, and, frequently, for solutions to issues that are defined as problems in the context of their work. Social science can be expected to provide answers to problems concerning the various types of inequality that exist between individuals and groups, ranging from poverty and homelessness, to mental illness, to crime, to political and economic domination over poor countries by rich countries, and to violence and war. The struggle to impose reason, order and justice on what seems like chaos is part of the 'project', the self-imposed task of modernity. However, as we shall see, some social scientists argue that this project is already dead, that we have now shifted from a modern to a 'postmodern' world. They would suggest that social science in the modern sense of a concern with reason and objectivity may well have died with the project of which it was a part. The question of the death of modernity, and with it social science as traditionally understood, is one theme that will be explored and explained in this book. For the moment, however, we shall consider the nature of social science a little further.

As we have already said, there is a distinction between the questions we might ask as ordinary members of society and those we might ask as, say, social workers, politicians, nurses, teachers, statisticians and so on. The social sciences are often seen as being 'concerned with people', and of use in 'helping people'. Professional workers and policy-makers of various kinds look to the social sciences for guidance in finding solutions to problems defined in particular areas. There is an assumption implicit in this that people are both interesting and important in the workings or processes of society. Essentially, the questions we ask about the social world are about the relationship between individuals and 'society'. At a commonsense level we often distinguish between problems we perceive as being located within society, for example, the rate of economic growth and problems we define as being located within the individual, for example, young men who commit violent offences against others. Sometimes we might argue that *social* problems such as the rate of growth of the economy can be explained by what *individuals* do – for example, that people are not working hard enough and are demanding wages that are too high. Conversely, we might argue that the problem of the high rate of violent crime among young men cannot be explained by their individual 'pathology', but by the lack of employment and opportunity caused by a low rate of economic growth. These are different kinds of explanation although, as ordinary members of society, we may not be very concerned about the niceties of this, but simply with 'making sense' of things we see around us that appear to be problematic.

Mapping the social world

Although we shall consider the complex relationship between social science and common sense in various parts of this book (for example, in our discussion of sexuality in Chapter 4), for now we need to distinguish between the commonsense questions which help make sense of society and the questions social scientists ask and attempt to answer. What makes social science different from commonsense understanding of the world? At the beginning of the chapter we referred to the social world as territory to be explored. It is much easier to undertake such an exploration if there is already a map to guide us. The social sciences can be thought of as a set of disciplines concerned with ways of attempting to map the social world, so that we can find our way around in it. As the term 'science' implies, social science maps are the result of systematic explorations or research; they guide our judgements and actions, and point towards further exploration. The Enlightenment dream for 'modern' social science can be seen in terms of the provision of clear maps that represent the territories of society and social relationships accurately. It was hoped that they would give a neutral and objective picture of the way things are. With such maps, personal and professional explorations of problems and relationships could be undertaken more safely, and kinds of difficulty compared, understood and overcome. Picking up on Weber's notion of 'instrumental rationality', Donald Schon, writing about professional practice, has described this as the 'technical rationality' model (1987, p. 3, see also our discussion in Chapter 6 of work as a rational and instrumental activity) that paints a picture of a vantage point of 'high hard ground overlooking a swamp'. We might imagine an explorer, a social worker, say, standing on this hard ground surveying a swampy lowland, perhaps a family with multiple and confusing difficulties. Clear map in hand (family systems theory), the social worker is able see what the difficulties are and help the family to negotiate them safely.

In this view we may have different kinds of map for different purposes – for example, like Ordnance Survey maps and wiring diagrams – and the differing social sciences and specialisms within them produce these. There may be gaps in knowledge and the maps will not always fit neatly together, but ultimately, if the territory is represented accurately, they will contribute to a developing body of firmly-founded knowledge about society and social relationships. It is here that things become a bit more complex, however. Perhaps, unfortunately, what *is* becoming increasingly clear is that we are, for the most part, stuck in the swamps. Social science has not been able to provide the kind of objective knowledge of the world that was first intended. The vantage points from which we try to map the world below are never as high, nor the ground as firm, as we might like. A certain messiness therefore becomes inevitable when we tramp about in the swamps. Our maps are always constructed with limited vision and differ according to our perspective and instruments of observation. We have had to recognise that newcomers to a particular bit of territory view it from a different perspective. They may describe features differently, or find previously undiscovered features, and we often have no way of resolving differences. We shall see that this realisation draws us away from a modern to a more 'postmodern' view of knowledge in general, and social science in particular (see, for example, Billington *et al.*, 1991, pp. 180ff).

This may make us wonder what the social sciences can offer and whether what they offer is of any use. To make up our minds on this point we need to find out more about what being a social scientist actually involves. Social science map-makers ask a range of questions, and at the risk of oversimplifying, these can be seen as requiring descriptions, explanations and evaluations. We shall begin with the first two of these – descriptions and explanations. Descriptions answer questions such as 'What is it?', and 'What is it like?', 'What is happening?', and 'What are they doing?'. Describing is an important part of all sciences, but it is a much more complex matter than it might seem because when we describe something we often begin to explain it as well. For example, it is unlikely that we would describe a car without explaining what it was for, and therefore why it is produced. Explanations are about *why*: 'Why is it like that?', 'What is causing it to happen?', or 'Why are they doing it like that?'. Sciences, including social sciences, place great emphasis on explanations, often at the expense of description, but description and explanation are, in fact, very closely linked. The third kind of social science question is evaluation. Evaluations answer questions such as 'Is it a good thing?' or 'Is it right?'. Traditionally, it has been argued that the sciences should be free from evaluation but it is now recognised increasingly that evaluations are built into the activities of describing and explaining – for example, in terms of what we choose to describe and which explanations we judge to be adequate. The sociologist Max Weber termed this 'value relevance' (Weber, 1978, p. 66).

By now you may be recognising that the conceptual tools of social science are problematic: there can be no straightforward descriptions, no simple methods of explanation, and no agreed rules of evaluation. In the course of this book you will begin to see why it is neither possible nor desirable for the social sciences to be divorced from values, even though this raises many problematic issues. It is important to recognise that, like the techniques of mapping physical territory over the centuries, the social sciences are undergoing continuous change, so that what is considered to be an adequate study of some aspect of the social world is always changing. As society changes, we need new maps. For example, the years immediately following the Second World War had been 'mapped' by politicians and others in Britain as being ones of economic growth, industrial expansion and full employment. This meant that the poverty noted so frequently by late nineteenth- and early twentieth-century commentators had become invisible. However, social scientists exploring postwar affluence discovered, or more accurately rediscovered, the path that revealed the continuing existence of poverty among certain sections of the population in the 1950s and 1960s (Coates and Silburn, 1970). This shows that map-making is a political process; some people have more power than others to go exploring in the first place and are then in a more influential position to get others to publish and accept their maps as the correct ones.

Moreover, the process of mapping may itself change society and individuals. An example here would be the increasingly influential definition of the menopause as a medical problem rather than a natural bodily change for women. This perception has led to ever more frequent discussion of psychological and physiological 'symptoms', increased use of drug treatments to alleviate these, and arguably the creation of a new kind of bodily 'reality' (Miles, 1991, pp. 197–200). Many doctors and their female patients no longer look at bodily changes during the menopause as something to put up with because it is 'just your age'. Similarly, theories and explanations of mental illness have changed substantially since the nineteenth century and what, for example, might have been seen as 'moral degeneracy' is now seen to be a result of biological changes or family circumstances (see, for example, Showalter, 1987).

As well as arguing that theories or maps of the social world change over time, as society itself changes, we also need to to recognise that different and sometimes contradictory theories can coexist. Thus while the individual social sciences have many aspects in common, there are also conflicts and disagreements between them, some concerning the suitability of the conceptual tools to be used and the maps to be consulted for analysing the social world. The example of mental illness just given would be a case in point, in that some social scientists would understand it as a label given to people who fail to fit into society; others would would see it as a product of the stresses brought about by social inequalries and prejudices; and yet others would see it as a defect intrinsic to the individual. A conflict of central importance for this book is the disputed territory of the self and personal identity. Psychology is usually seen as the discipline concerned with this area, yet sociology and social anthropology have a history, both in the past and in recent times, of concern with this theme. A major task in this book is to show how adequate understanding of any aspect of the social world needs, at the very least, to take account of interaction between individual selves and the social, and even to suggest that self and identity are *essentially* social.

Analysing the social world

Here we want to examine more closely the problematic nature of the conceptual tools of social science. In order to explain, social scientists need first to observe and then to describe what they see, but observing and describing are not as straightforward as they might seem. For example, if someone who has never visited an art gallery is shown a picture and asked to describe it, they might note the objects in it, where they are placed, what colour they are, and how 'realistic' they appear. A painter or art historian shown the picture, however, might describe the brushstrokes and type of paint used, identify the style and locate the work in a tradition, including a view about the nature and function of art. Neither of these descriptions is the 'right' one, but each is based on a different set of assumptions about what to look for in a picture. Both the observers are guided by what we can call 'theories concerning what to look for'. Each theory contains classifications and assumptions about the relationships between things. So, for example, we learn to call different colours by special names – burnt umber, yellow ochre, viridian, indigo. We recognise styles and traditions of painting – impressionist, expressionist, abstract – in the same way that we distinguish animals from human beings, motor cars from bicycles and so on. At an everyday level the theorising involved in making sense of the world around us usually remains implicit, but at the level of the natural and social sciences these theories must be made explicit, like those of the painter or art historian who claims special expertise.

This raises the question of what these theories are actually like. As we have said, descriptions and explanations are starting points for social science theories. They have a basis in logically connected sets of assumptions, concepts and hypotheses which inform and make sense of our observations. The set of assumptions underpinning any social science theory will include a view of the nature of society and the *kinds* of theories that are appropriate to describe and explain it. In other words, they will include a view of the nature and function of social science and, in a similar way to the art expert distinguishing traditions which make differing assumptions about the nature and function of art, we can distinguish differing traditions in social science. For example, one tradition reflects the model of natural science that was central to Enlightenment thinking. This is known as 'positivist-empiricism', and it stressed that knowledge could be held to be true only if based on 'objectively observable' 'facts' which could be verified against the experiences of the senses. This was important, as it was linked to the quest for a rational, empirically-based method for creating knowledge based on direct observation of experience. This is known as the empirical method. To be counted as valid, knowledge must also be free from religious dogma and moral values. It is this positivist-empiricist tradition that influenced the social sciences from the very start and made the production of 'objective knowledge' about society so central. The emphasis in this tradition is therefore on supposedly observable 'facts' about society and human behaviour. However, an alternative tradition dating back to at least the nineteenth century has always contested the appropriateness of modelling social science on natural science. This alternative 'human science' or 'interpretative' tradition claims that subjective experience and meaningful action are defining attributes of human beings, and that distinctive methods for the systematic study of these must therefore form the basis of social science. This view contradicts the positivist-empiricist tradition, which tells us that what we feel and what we value must be left out of our conceptual mapping of the social world. If it is not, our maps will be biased and misleading.

We shall encounter these two traditions in various forms throughout the book. However, there are more than these two ways of identifying traditions and classifying approaches and perspectives in social science. A browse through a selection of textbooks will, for example, reveal positivism; functionalism; Marxist theories; varieties of structuralism; varieties of interactionism; and phenomenological approaches. Controversies will also be identified, such as conflict versus consensus theories, and structure versus action theories, as ways of indicating key concerns and differences. In all this it is easy to despair of finding an adequate map of social science theories, let alone of society. In this book, we suggest that an alternative to despair lies in the recognition that life in the swamps, while often confusing, is invariably rich and interesting. While we may not achieve the god-like clarity hoped for by the thinkers of the eighteenth-century Enlightenment, we may nevertheless achieve interesting insights and useful ways of reflecting on ourselves and the problems of living in society with each other. In the rest of this chapter we shall introduce and illustrate some key perspectives, theoretical ideas and issues identified by social science. It is important to remember that, even when making more modest claims for the possibilities of social-scientific knowledge – what some people would call 'postmodern' – the work of social scientists must be systematic and logical. Their use of theoretical concepts allows other researchers to carry out investigations using the same or alternative theories. What we have been at pains to stress so far is that what we observe depends on the assumptions – the theory – we take to the situation. In the same way that the art expert, informed by theory and specialist knowledge, sees a style of painting within a tradition and our person-in-the-street does not, so social scientists see patterns and regularities in social situations and behaviour which the everyday participant does not.

An example will help to underline this distinction between the observation and experience of everyday life and what the social scientist observes. Living in 1950s America, Betty Friedan, university-educated, wife, mother and magazine journalist, noted that, both in magazines and in conversations with other women, a problem had become apparent but no one had put a name to it. She noted a general feeling of dissatisfaction and pointlessness among college-educated young mothers and wives who spent most of their lives fulfilling the domestic feminine role prescribed for them. As an educationalist and psychologist, Friedan began to observe social factors that seemed relevant to, and made sense of, her initial, rather unfocused, observations and experiences. She theorised that there had been an overemphasis on the home and domesticity for women, following the upheavals of the Second World War. This meant that many women had no sense of personal identity and fulfilment. Friedan's feminist book (first published in 1963) setting out her theory and the evidence for it helped many women to make sense of their feelings of dissatisfaction and began what is now referred to as the 'second wave' feminist movement (Friedan, 1982).

Mapping or identifying a theory to explain the 'problem with no name' is a particularly interesting example for several reasons. It illustrates how social scientific theorising and systematic observation may result in social change. It also illustrates how social scientists may be both participants and observers. Friedan was able to understand some of what she read and what women were saying because this matched her own experience. This also shows the complex interaction between what sociologists call *social structure* and *social action* – that is, the question whether individual lives are largely determined by the structures of the wider society, such as class or gender, or whether society is something the individual actively creates. On the one hand, social structural factors, including specific beliefs and values surrounding femininity and motherhood, limited the activities and affected the identities of a whole generation of women. Ultimately, however, they developed an alternative consciousness directed at changing the situation. Our activities as individuals and groups are shaped by the society in which we live, but we are also powerful social actors who may change this society.

We are all social theorists

The structure – action debate is a theme running throughout this book. It can be seen as the central problem for sociology as well as an issue for other social science disciplines. This debate concerns the question of the relationship between individuals and the society in which they live. This question involves theories about social interaction, between individuals and groups, the situations in which they find themselves and why, and also about the nature of 'society' and the nature of 'individuals'. As we saw earlier, attempts to answer 'why' questions involve the notion of reasons. For example, to say that in the 1950s American women were restricted to the role of full-time housewives and mothers, implies that this was caused by a rigid set of rules prohibiting their work outside the home. Society shapes and constrains the lives of its members. However, to argue that at this period, following the disruption created by the Second World War, Americans valued higher education for both sexes but also became more attached to values emphasising the security of home life and domesticity, implies that women and men both made choices about the social roles they filled.

Many psychological theories that attempt to explain how and why individuals act as they do in the social world are based on some notion of the individual's inherent biological and psychological properties. This creates problems for other social scientists, who begin from the premise that the social world constrains and shapes what we do. However, there are many other theories from psychology that take a different approach. So, for example, Kelly's 'personal construct' theory assumes that people constantly act upon the world rather than reacting to it and that 'we have "alternatives" available to us with which we try to make sense of (or construe) each other, ourselves and the world swirling around us' (Fransella and Dalton, 1990, p. 3). This theory assumes that events and social situations are subject to many different constructions and understandings, but that the specific social and cultural contexts in which we develop as people – our families, schools and places of work – influence and limit the possible ways in which we construe the world.

Kelly developed his theory to help people to construe their worlds differently in order to overcome particular recurrent problems they faced. Rather than seeing the social world as something objective or fixed, he believed that our subjective thoughts and feelings could have a profound effect upon the way we experience the social world. To help people alter their personal constructs about the world he suggested that we see ourselves as scientists who are constantly testing out theories and conducting experiments to test hypotheses about the world. All our behaviour as people in society can thus be seen as a series of experiments. Much of this is not at the level of consciousness, but is implicit in what we do. For example, if I sit on a chair I am in fact predicting, (or testing out the theory) that it will hold my weight. If I ask, on the telephone, to speak to the bank manager, I may implicitly assume that a man will answer, but my 'theory' may be disproved if a woman answers, and I will thus be thrown off balance concerning the loan I wanted to negotiate. My alternative here, in future, would be to change my 'theory' and assume that bank managers may be men or women. Although this example concerns individual activity, if several people change their hypotheses it has implications for the expectations we hold about gender roles at work.

Debate concerning the extent to which individuals and groups are able to act autonomously within social constraints has been part of sociology from its beginnings in the eighteenth century. More recently, Anthony Giddens, synthesising insights from previous theories, has argued that society consists of structured and patterned elements, together with the relatively autonomous activities of humankind. He places social actors or 'agents' – that is, human subjectivity, at the centre of social life, because, he argues, as conscious human beings we have the inherent capacity to understand what we do while we are doing it; in other words, we practice reflexivity.

In Giddens' view, reflexivity – the capacity to reflect upon ourselves and our actions – is made up of two types of consciousness that operate throughout social life: *practical consciousness* and *discursive consciousness*. He also recognises the existence of the *unconscious,* as discussed by psychologists (Giddens, 1984). Much of social life takes place at the level of practical consciousness. We 'go on' with social life because we understand tacitly how to do it, without needing to spell it out, except to small children who are still learning how to 'do' social interaction. This routine of everyday social activity constantly reproduces the structured, predictable properties of social life. However, it is through human action or 'agency' that social life is also altered and changed. Thus it is the fact that human actors reflect upon what they do, and indeed on social interaction in general – they use discursive consciousness, that explains why we do not simply go on 'doing' social life the same way for ever. However, the patterns and regulations of social structures affect both the public and the private dimensions of our lives. Concepts such as 'social script', 'hidden curriculum', 'institution' and 'organisation' are used by social scientists in various contexts to indicate that social life is not simply random, but patterned and regulated. This structured activity can be seen as part of the process through which individuals, social institutions and whole societies reproduce themselves. Although difficult to grasp, we should think of this activity 'as a *durée*, a continuous flow of conduct' or behaviour. Continuity of social life presumes reflexivity, that human actors constantly reflect upon and monitor what they do. Such reflexivity is possible only because there is continuity of social practices yet it is precisely this reflexivity that is necessary if social life is to change in any way (Giddens, 1984, p. 3).

Emphasising human agency is an approach to the social world which stresses subjectivity – the way in which the individual, the human subject, experiences the world – rather than perceiving the social actor as an 'object' for investigation. Using the concept of 'social action' to analyse why people in society act as they do, the sociologist Weber was concerned with human agency and choice; with the social, rather than with individual psychology. Social scientists need to understand why people act as they do in social situations and Weber argued that in order to find out what motivates 'social actors' we need to examine the meaning and significance of these actions for the actors themselves (Weber, 1978). In Chapter 6 we take up Weber's point and discuss the motivations of social actors in the context of work.

Constructing the social world

Our discussion of the development of second wave feminism illustrates how 'discursive consciousness' creates social change based on the subjective experience people have of the world in which they live. Friedan not only experienced 'a problem with no name', but also reflected upon it. Discursive consciousness is reflexive; it examines itself in a continual monitoring of what is occurring. It can be seen essentially as a type of theorising about social interaction which is built into the fabric and institutions of social life itself. The discursive consciousness of social actors means that society is constantly subject to scrutiny, to criticism and therefore to potential change, at the same time that social patterns are continually being reproduced. Giddens refers to this as the *duality of structure*, indicating that human society is a systematic, and not a random process, and at the same time dynamic; it is also constantly changing.

So far we have argued that, as social agents, our constant monitoring of and reflection on social life means that we are all social theorists. It is perhaps useful at this point to see the social sciences as disciplines which have the formal task of making more explicit and systematic the built-in reflexive processes of social life – that is, theorising or mapping the social world. There are, then, similarities of some kind between our everyday theorising and understanding, and the academic disciplines of social science. As Weber pointed out, we can only understand human motivation and social action based on it because we are human our-selves and capable of entering into the emotions, actions and meanings of others; of being empathic. He called this the *verstehen* approach, from the German word meaning 'understanding' (Weber, 1978, pp. 77ff; Eldridge (ed.) 1971, p. 28). This is clearly very different from the positivist–empiricist tradition, which seeks to eradicate links between the observer and what they are observing, in the name of objectivity. Some professions with a knowledge base in the theories and insights of social science explicitly use the human capacity for empathy as part of their professional practice; counselling and psychotherapy, and perhaps teaching are obvious ones. The approach clearly belongs in the interpretative tradition and relies on our intimate knowledge as participants. Giddens uses the term 'hermeneutic' in this context (Giddens, 1984, pp. 1–2). The term first gained currency in the early nineteenth century in relation to the study of problems of interpretation of meaning.

The structure of the social world

Giddens' emphasis on what he terms the 'duality of structure' of the social world – its capacity to be both systematic and dynamic – is an attempt to move away from a position that dominated sociology for many years and is still influential. This is the conceptualisation of social worlds as structures that have deterministic effects on human activities, a position which results in what has been called the 'over-socialised view' of humankind (Wrong, 1961). As stated already, a basic assumption of social science is that there *is* some pattern to be found, some regularity and order to social life. As participants in social life we assume this too. Although an over-deterministic model of social structure takes insufficient account of human agency and the meaningful character of social life, some notion of social structure continues to be a useful device to explain the continuous and ordered aspects of the social. There has been, and continues to be, considerable debate, particularly amongst sociologists, about how this structure is conceptualised and the way the actions of individuals are affected.

The nineteenth-century sociologist, Emile Durkheim, attempting to establish sociology as a scientific discipline in its own right, emphasised the existence of social structure as a determinant of human thought and activity. Society, he argued, exists *suis generis*, in itself. It exists outside individuals, and 'the science of society', sociology, must explain social events and behaviour in terms of society's existence, rather than, for example, in terms of individual psychology.

Durkheim's emphasis on the reality of social structure has led to accusations that he reified society – that is, he saw it as something concrete and separate from human beings. This is to misunderstand the point that, in a sense, society *does* exist outside each particular individual. We are born into an ongoing society, which continues to exist when particular individuals die or leave. Thus society is something more than the sum total of its constituent parts. Durkheim's concern to give social rather than individualistic explanations for social life can lead to a theoretical position where social actors appear to operate simply as social puppets. His emphasis on society as constraint and structure, however, alerts us to the fact that activities and phenomena which may appear to be highly individualistic, such as suicide, or a belief in god, are rooted in the nature of society itself. Moreover, it positions individuals firmly as actors in society, making it impossible to conceptualise human behaviour and thought as occurring outside the social. When we think of our personal identities as women and men, mothers, fathers, lovers, sisters, workers and so on, however unique these may be, they are still social identities.

A further dimension to Durkheim's view of social structure is that the different parts of the structure are integrated into a whole, and the relationship of the parts to each other and to the whole is a functional one; each part has a purpose in maintaining the overall equilibrium of the structure. An important part of the structure is the system of values and norms – that is, the ideas and expectations that guide our activities. Durkheim's term for this was the *conscience collective*, translating, rather inaccurately, from French as 'collective consciousness'. In the twentieth century, Talcott Parsons developed and elaborated Durkheim's structural–functionalist theory of society, laying great emphasis on the importance of a central value system and the way in which we are socialised into the norms and values of society, with the family and education playing a key part in this process (Parsons, 1951; Hamilton, 1983). Like Durkheim, then, Parsons was asking how society functioned, rather than what it meant to its individual members. His theories are an attempt to answer this question and as such they influence the way he describes and explains the social world around him.

Social anthropologists adopted Durkheim's structural–functionalist approach to observing and analysing non-Western cultures, in societies like those of Africa and India that were subject to Western colonial rule. There are many criticisms to be made of such an approach, but applied to non-Western, sometimes non-literate cultures, it did focus the observer's gaze on activities and customs very different from those in the West, yet recognisable as purposeful aspects of the total functioning of the culture. One of the limitations of this approach is that it assumes all aspects of a society or culture have a function, and that the society is cohesive and integrated, and therefore that conflict is absent.

So far, we have used interchangeably terms such as society, the social, the social world, and sometimes culture, implying some entity called 'human society' or 'human culture'. Historically, however, sociology and other social sciences have distinguished different *types* of society or social structure and we frequently talk of different or 'other' cultures. The basis on which we distinguish one society or culture from another depends both on our purpose and on our value position. So, for example, Western Europeans writing about traditional African or Asian societies used to describe them as 'primitive' or even 'savage', to indicate that these societies and their inhabitants were in some way 'underdeveloped'. It was assumed that they needed to 'progress' along the lines of Western societies, which were often unquestioningly regarded as 'advanced' and superior. Indicators of superiority and inferiority were variously identified as technology, literacy, kinship systems, belief systems – including religion, and other factors such as the existence of a money economy. Today, social scientists either use terms indicating more measurable differences between societies and cultures, such as per capita income or levels of education, or take pains to understand different cultures in their own terms. Before exploring some types of society in more detail, however, we need to examine a different notion of social structure from the structural–functionalist one we have discussed.

Writing, like Durkheim, in the nineteenth century and, like him, concerned about the conditions of life in newly industrial societies, of which Britain was the prime example, Karl Marx classified societies according to the type of productive system on which they were based. He called this the 'mode of production'. This classification was an integral part of Marx's work on the nature of social structures and the process by which they change, a process he called the theory of *historical materialism.* Although this may be an unfamiliar term, it is quite straightforward once we understand Marx's basic assumptions about social life.

Marx thought that what distinguished human beings from other species was that they are producers; they have to produce in order to live, even if production consists of using very simple tools to obtain or grow food. So all societies, according to Marx, have a material, or 'real', structure based on the way in which production is organised. This is discussed in more detail in Chapter 6. In Marx's view, the economic structure, the foundation or base of a society, largely determines its other features. That is, the 'superstructure': the types of relationship that exist; the legal and political system, and the overall culture, including the system of beliefs and values. Beliefs and values are reflections of the social relationships created by the economic system and they represent power and interests rooted in the processes of production. Marx uses the term *ideology* to describe this cultural consciousness. According to this theory, societies change historically according to the way in which their material structures, and therefore their ideological systems, change. This is what we have already referred to as *historical materialism* – historical change based on real (material) economic factors (see *Preface to the Critique of Political Economy*, Marx, 1950a, pp. 328–9; Lee and Newby, 1983, pp. 113ff).

Unlike the structural–functionalist approach, this model of social structure does not assume that the social system is fully integrated or stable. Built into Marx's structure are tensions or contradictions, the result of which is that each society, each 'mode of production', contains within it the seeds of inevitable change. The contradictions or antagonisms Marx sees as the motor of social change are rooted in the social relationships that stem from the necessity for human beings to produce, to labour, in order to live.

Durkheim singled out the increasing social division of labour as the unique feature of industrial societies. By this he meant that each social institution became more specialised and different in function from others. Rural self-sufficiency gave way to more specialised urban occupations. Durkheim argued that it was this increasing specialisation that made social actors interdependent and ensured social integration (Durkheim, 1984). For Marx, however, this division of labour involved a fundamental inequality between those who laboured and those who owned the factories and machinery in what he termed 'capitalist' society. Expressed through what he called class antagonisms, Marx saw social change arising out of this inequality. Again, in contrast to Durkheim, who saw the social actor as essentially the outcome of social structure, Marx saw human actors as the agents of social change, although he saw the real material world as the overall determinant of social relationships and consciousness. Human beings became conscious of the injustices involved in class relationships stemming from production, and set about overturning them. This is expressed in one of the most famous quotations from Marx:

> men make their own history but they do not make it just as they please; they do not make it under circumstances chosen by themselves but under circumstances directly encountered, given and transmitted from the past. The tradition of all the dead generations weighs like a nightmare on the

brain of the living. (*The Eighteenth Brumaire of Louis Bonaparte*, Marx, 1950b, pp. 225)

We shall return to the important topic of the consciousness of social actors later.

Although not all models of social structure deal satisfactorily with how societies change, or the extent to which social actors are agents of this change, the notion of social structure allows us to classify societies according to sets of specific characteristics that have interested social scientists since at least the nineteenth century. Classifying societies according to specific criteria not only allows us to investigate their characteristics more closely but also to compare one society with another.

Types of social structure

It will be apparent already that the terms *industrial society* and *capitalist society* are often used interchangeably with *modern society*, and that they refer to the most recent historical past and, more controversially, to the present. More specifically, by industrial society we usually mean the type of society that developed in Western Europe and the United States of America from the eighteenth century onwards, characterised by an economy increasingly based on mechanised manufacturing industry conducted by specialised labour processes and centralised in large-scale factories. A range of other characteristics are usually linked to these technological and economic factors, including centralised government, the rule of law, and a democratic political system. There is sometimes an unwarranted assumption, carried over from nineteenth-century social evolutionary theory, that to become an industrial society is the aim of all societies. In Chapter 8 we shall see that the relationship between industrialised societies and those that are not is an extremely complex one.

As a description, the term 'capitalism' implies some of those factors that characterise industrial society, but also indicates the specific economic basis of industrial production – that it is based on the rational accumulation and reinvestment of capital, a process theorised by Weber. Capitalism also involves the fact that some people own and others do not own capital, which Marx thought crucial in explaining social processes. As a form of economic and social organisation, capitalism has an impact beyond the boundaries of any particular society, country or nation. Industrial and capitalist social organisation are very powerful forms and it is to this type of society that others are compared. Historical change can be theorised as the transition from one type of society to another. We should remember, however, that while industrial and capitalist societies are the most modern, the spectrum of world history includes many other types of society which existed for much longer than those with which we are more familiar.

In this book, many of our examples of social life and identity are from Western societies, or from other industrialised societies. We shall also refer to the traditional, small-scale or non-literate societies studied by social anthropologists. Such societies have been profoundly changed through contact with and encroachment by Western industrial societies, but traditionally were organised as 'tribes', or 'bands', or ethnic groups. Many were hierarchically organised with an overall ruler, but in others, political life operated at the level of the extended kinship group, although recognition of the boundaries of tribe or ethnicity might also be important. Such societies today are generally incorporated into larger nation-states, many of which are variously termed *Third-World*, *under-developed* or *developing* societies, to differentiate them from Western societies. A more recent way of referring to the contrasts between Western and non-Western societies is to speak of the North and the South, but it is difficult to find terms that are not value-laden and do not imply that Western society is superior.

Although we have implied here that capitalist or industrial societies are the most modern, we have already noted that some writers have detected a shift away from these types of society. They have variously used terms such as *postindustrial, postcapitalist* or *postmodern* to indicate this. Such terms attempt to categorise and encapsulate the ways in which industrial capitalism has changed in the last decades of the twentieth century. Some of these are concerned with changes in the economic structure, including the way in which work is organised and the transformation of technology, particularly the development of new technology based on the microchip.

We have noted too that as well as changes in the organisation of work, 'postmodernism' also refers to cultural and ideological shifts which question Enlightenment notions of knowledge and the search for overarching explanatory theories (see also Billington *et al.*, 1991, ch. 10; Storey, 1993, ch. 7; Hall and Gieben (eds), 1992). Since these include the theories we have discussed above, we can now see more clearly that the question posed by postmodernism for social science concerns the viability of its more all-embracing claims. Thus, many of the traditional ways of looking at society that social scientists have developed are themselves undergoing change. This issue will be discussed throughout the book and we shall focus our thinking around it in the final chapter, reflecting on the need for our map-making to be on a more modest scale.

Returning to the categories or types of society we have just discussed, we can see that they are really shorthand terms which provide reference points to help social scientists map the world. They are what Weber termed 'ideal types'. These are models or maps which describe the essential features of what we are examining but are not complete descriptions (see Lee and Newby, 1983, pp. 175ff). Importantly, they select those aspects which help us to answer our initial questions about society, whether they are to do with its functioning, with social change, or with the meaning of social action. 'Ideal types' differ from one another just as maps do, and, like maps, they are designed for a particular purpose. For example, a road map will pick out routes we can drive along but does not show the local topography of an area, but a large-scale Ordnance Survey map for walkers *will* show these features. Similarly, an 'ideal type' construct designed to explain the difference between different types of economy, is not useful if what we want is to look at the differences between different types of religious belief system.

It is important for social scientists to be able to categorise different types of society. If social structure has some effect on who we are and how we see ourselves, then the implication is that people's sense of self and personal identity varies in different types of society. For example, as we shall see in Chapter 2, much of the emphasis on the development of the individual rather than the collective is a relatively recent, Western notion. Different types of social structure provide the actor with different opportunities and constraints.

Similarly, an awareness of different types of culture is a useful tool for the social scientist. In this book we shall often use the term 'culture' interchangeably with 'society'. Although frequently used in this way, the term 'culture' refers to social patterns and regularities in a more experiential way than the term 'society' does. Our use of the concept indicates that culture is a *lived* experience; it is what people practice and what people believe in a society. A society may contain many cultures, some of which are in conflict with each other, and to some extent participation in these alternatives by an individual may be a matter of choice. Such a view moves us away from the Durkheimian and structural–functionalist notion of some overarching culture that functions both to create the individual and to integrate society. 'Post-modern' culture, it is argued, contains no overall integrating vision, but encourages cultural eclecticism and relativism, issues we shall pursue in following chapters.

Aspects of social structures

The concept of social structures is important, we have argued, as a tool to help observe, explain and analyse what is taking place in society. As we have also pointed out, there are patterns and some degree of regularity to what is taking place, although social actors as individuals or groups may intervene and alter these processes. Our intention now is to examine some of the concepts developed by social scientists attempting to make sense of these structured social processes.

The origins of sociological theory and some other social science disciplines lie in the desire to solve what are defined as problems within industrial and perhaps, now, postindustrial societies. By the late nineteenth century, in Western Europe and the USA, many of these problems were associated with poverty, poor housing and other failings of urban industrial life. Although many people accepted, and still do accept, inequalities of wealth and income, education and other 'life chances', much of the policy-making of peacetime Western governments during the first half of the twentieth century concentrated on providing the basics of welfare for the whole population, including health provision, education and housing. In the late twentieth century, however, many Western societies appear to have entered a period of policy-making designed to dismantle this attempt – for example, the introduction of private health schemes, private pensions and fees for higher education.

The contribution of social science to the analysis of social problems has been to focus on explanations for the social inequalities and social divisions perceived. Durkheim has been criticised severely for theorising that industrial society is one in which there would be some kind of consensus and minimal state regulation. Interdependence would be created by what he called 'the social division of labour', and occupational associations or 'guilds' would reduce conflict at work. He apparently did not recognise, as both Marx and Weber did, that social consensus was unlikely, and that social inequalities based on economic factors could not easily be abolished.

In discussing Marx's model of social structure, the importance of inequalities based on social class and the power and conflict involved in class relationships has been emphasised. In capitalist societies, Marx distinguished two major class groups: the owners of capital (the capitalists); and the proletariat, who sold their labour. Weber, too, theorised economic inequality as the basis of social class, but did not see conflict as being inevitable. He also developed other concepts which referred to 'social stratification', the hierarchical organisation of society. Weber explained that social status, the 'honour' or prestige accorded to certain individuals and groups, might be separate from their class position, which is determined by their 'market situation'. By this he meant the skills or other kinds of resource that gave them economic and social advantages. For example, these might be good looks, a particular type of education, or highly-valued social skills. He also conceptualised political power as something that is not necessarily associated with social class or social status. If society is structured then it is common sense that individuals have structural positions, and both Weber and Marx were theorising the basis for these (Marshall *et al.*, 1988).

The social sciences and many professional activities based on them, including market research and the collection of official statistics, categorise the population on the basis of social class; that is, individuals and groups are assigned structural positions. However, 'official' class categories, while bearing some relationship to the concepts developed by Marx, and particularly to those of Weber, use occupational categories as indicators of social class. The rationale behind these categories is that occupation determines income and life-style. There are many difficulties with these categories, not least that they lump together dissimilar occupations as well as often assuming that the social class of women is determined by the occupation of their husbands or fathers. Recently, sociologists have pointed to the fact that the occupational structure is stratified by gender: men and women are concentrated in different occupational sectors (Abbot and Sapsford, 1987). These official class categories also exclude more subjective and experiential dimensions of social class and class culture.

In many of the areas investigated by social scientists, class has been seen to have important determinant effects for individuals and groups: for example, on educational achievement; rates of mortality and morbidity; and attitudes to work. In this volume we shall use the term 'social class' in a general, descriptive way, implying some of the meanings we have discussed. Where necessary we shall use the term in a more specific sense, which we shall make apparent.

Recently it has been recognised that there are other major social divisions which are not encapsulated by the concept of class. These centre on gender and 'race', and may interact and intersect with social divisions based on class, so that an individual's structural position will be at the intersection of all these divisions. For example, a young, black, working-class woman will be in a different structural position from an old, white, middle-class man.

By gender we mean social differentiation, inequality, and sometimes discrimination and prejudice, based on perceived differences between the two sexes. It is the perception of differences between women and men, and the meanings attached to them, rather than differences themselves, that are of social significance. Many aspects of social life have a gender dimension. For example, we have already mentioned social class and occupational categories as being 'gendered', and we shall also refer to culture as gendered. It is important to recognise the gendered nature of society and social action (which the founding *fathers* of social science signally failed to do) because it is a major source of social identity.

Like gender, 'race' is also a social category and provides the foundation for inequalities based on perceived biological distinctions. Historically, much effort has been spent in classifying different 'races' and attempting to prove a scientific basis for racial differences. Although there are notable exceptions, most social scientists today do not see 'race' as a scientific category, but rather as a social and evaluative notion, frequently used by 'white' people to refer to 'black' or Asian people. We shall discuss this in more detail in Chapter 7. Identifying people as belonging to a different race is to perceive them as 'other' and the origins of racial discrimination in Western societies lie in the 'discovery' by Western explorers from the fifteenth century, of societies in Africa, North and South America and Asia, of which they previously had no knowledge.

Whatever the disagreements between different theorists concerning the basis of social class, there is some consensus that it is economic in character. Similarly, there is some agreement that there is an economic basis to 'race' and racism in Western societies. The historical details vary, ranging from slavery as an economic system in the southern USA; mass immigration to Britain to meet post-Second World War labour shortages; and the complex system of apartheid in South Africa. Alternative or additional social science explanations of 'race' and racist feelings are that values and beliefs are developed on the basis of contact with the 'other'. To avoid the problematic nature of the term 'race', the term ethnicity is sometimes substituted, to refer to cultural differences between groups. However, it can be argued that the notion of ethnicity as a more 'neutral' term might be seen to overlook the issues of power and oppression involved in racism (see, for example, Billington *et al.*, 1991).

As members of a society we are assigned structural positions on the basis of an additional range of social categories – for example, age, disability, employment, health and so on, and these categories may also be the source of social inequalities. Like social class, we shall frequently refer to gender, 'race', and ethnicity, and also to age and disability as social categories that have consequences for, and are embedded in, the social and personal identities of individuals.

Social formations

The association of industrial or capitalist society with the notion of political democracy, which we mentioned earlier, introduces the separate but related concept of the state. Many theorists, including Weber, have demonstrated that industrial capitalism required the existence of the modern, centralised nation-state for its development. Like many other features of 'modern' societies in general, the state has a relatively brief history. Our conceptions of the modern state, again, stem from the Enlightenment period in Europe. One of the marks of modernity was the forging of a conception of society as 'an entity open to human agency, whose workings are in principle open to our scrutiny' (Hamilton, 1992, p. 55). Along with the belief that the world was comprehensible went the belief in the capacity of human beings to change it.

Historically, various forms of state have existed, but it is the form that began to emerge in Europe from about the sixteenth century that we know as the modern state. This is a legal and political form of society which includes an administrative system separate from the ruler's household, and capable of administering a territory within formally-defined boundaries. Increasingly, administration is bureaucratic and, as Weber discussed, made up of a hierarchy of officials and governed by legal codes and regulations. The modern state, it is argued, has power that is distinct from the power of hereditary rulers and from the power of ordinary citizens. Modern states, of which there is more than one variant, are characterised by clear territorial boundaries, an impersonal structure of power, control of the ultimate use of force (the existence of armies, for example), and the designation of legitimacy on the basis that the state represents the interests of all its inhabitants (Hall, 1992, pp. 87–8). The term 'nation-state' refers to the power of the state over a particular territory which does not necessarily contain inhabitants who share the same ethnicity or culture. This is further discussed in Chapter 7.

The existence of the modern state as the territory and political entity in which we as citizens live and to whose laws we are subject has a range of implications for the way in which our structural positions and personal identities are formed. Alongside the concept of the state, with its formal and public apparatus for administration and government, the concept of 'civil society' has developed. By this is usually meant the areas of social, domestic and cultural life that are organised aside from the state, although the enormous power of the state may affect them indirectly. Social scientists have a range of theories of the state, which vary in the weight given to the direct and indirect power of the state apparatus, and therefore to the relative autonomy of civil society.

Historians and others have examined nineteenth-century European societies and commented on the increasing separation of the public and private spheres of life associated with industrialisation and modernisation (see, for example, Zaretsky, 1976; Davidoff and Hall, 1987). Some feminist writing from the 1970s onwards has, however, emphasised that this separation is more apparent than real. Insistence that such separation exists, they argue, conceals both the direct and indirect power of the state to affect its citizens in the private areas of their lives – for example, in their domestic and married life (Pateman, 1987). Other theorists argue that many 'private' areas of life are coming increasingly under surveillance. For example, Foucault would include here sexuality, which we discuss in Chapter 4, and through the 'clinical gaze' and discourse of modern medicine, our bodies too, which we discuss in Chapter 5 (Foucault, 1981; Turner, 1987). Nevertheless, the idea that social life may be lived out in private as well as in public has considerable explanatory value for the relationship between individuals and social structure, although there may be important overlaps and intersections between the two spheres, and between social life and individual identity.

Consciousness, discourse, subjectivity and identity

Earlier in this chapter we mentioned various types of 'consciousness'; we referred to 'culture' as an aspect of consciousness and of experience, and also used the term 'ideology'. In addition, we referred to ideas, beliefs and values as aspects of social life. In the following chapters we shall use the term 'discourse', sometimes interchangeably with ideology. The assumption of human consciousness, experience and reflexivity emphasises the centrality of human 'subjectivity'. This list of terms or concepts we have linked together is by no means random, but the relationship between them is not easy to unravel.

Without wishing to enter into the arguments of philosophers, we shall take as our starting point for analysing social life the view that it is the consciousness of human beings that makes social life possible and alters the world. As we have seen, Giddens distinguishes different types of consciousness involved in social processes. Durkheim, Marx and Weber, too, although divergently, emphasise that the way in which we understand, interpret and are conscious of social life is part of that social life itself. To greater or lesser degrees, in the work of all these theorists we find the assumption that ideas, beliefs and consciousness are at once part of and shaped by the social, and that these aspects are subject to social scientific research – in particular that branch of sociology known as the sociology of knowledge. Here, we want to concentrate on the controversial and complex notions of ideology and discourse that will frequently be referred to in following chapters.

Marx wrote:

> It is not the consciousness of men that determines their being, but, on the contrary, their social being that determines their consciousness. (Marx, 1950a, *Preface to a Contribution to the Critique of Political Economy*)

This famous quotation sets out quite clearly Marx's theory concerning the relationship between consciousness, ideas and beliefs, and the material structure of society (see previous section). It focuses our attention on the importance of the social actor, on social interaction and social relationships, and on perception or consciousness as the consequence of these. The statement also implies subjectivity, that ideas and beliefs are based on the social experience of individuals and groups, although this experience itself is determined, or at least structured, by the 'material reality' of social and economic constraints. These constraints include the fact that some groups are in a more powerful position and thus able to impose their ideas on others through a variety of means, including control of the mass media and the education system.

'Ideology' is the term used by Marx to describe this social consciousness. It is a theoretically problematic and contested notion in social science, but here we shall attempt to give a 'working definition' as a guide to how we shall use the concept in later chapters. Ideology refers to the link between consciousness and conflicting 'interests' that are based on our real 'material' position – for example, as members of a social class, a gender, an age group and so on. An ideological set of beliefs and values is a view of the world that works in favour of some and to the disadvantage of others. It does so by, in some way, concealing a conflict of interests. For example, the ideology surrounding the differentiated roles of men and women in Western societies constructs women as carers and nurturers, which is to the advantage of men, who receive this care and who are not expected to provide it for others. For women, it may mean exclusion from paid work and independent leisure. Both men and women perceive this as a 'natural' difference rather than a social construction; that is, they 'naturalise' it. This makes it difficult to challenge and contributes to the maintenance of stable, though oppressive, social relations. So, in general terms, ideology helps us to make sense of the world, often by naturalising what exists. Further examples would be that it is 'inevitable' that there are vast inequalities in wealth and income between different groups, because some people are 'naturally' more able than others. There is a danger that we see ideology too simplistically, as some kind of conspiracy by powerful groups against others, but many studies – for example, of the mass media, of work and organisations, or of gender and race relations, indicate the very complicated ways in which ideology can be seen to operate.

While Marx drew attention to the power of ideology in maintaining social order by concealing conflicting interests, our understanding of how this works has been greatly enhanced by 'structuralist' approaches to the study of language. These approaches owe much to the early work of Saussure (1974). He argued that languages cannot be understood in terms of separate elements such as sounds and words, but must be approached as structured systems. Separate elements only have significance by virtue of their relationship with other elements in the system. This is easy to see when we consider the meaning of words indicating or denoting family positions: for example, 'sister' only has meaning in relation to 'brother, and 'parent' in relation to 'child' and so on. According to structuralist theories, it is the structure of language that determines the lines along which we divide up and make sense of our experience. The notion that language exists prior to individuals, who are born into, say, an English-speaking culture, is similar to Durkheim's view of society existing *suis generis*. The emphasis here, however, is on

the the structure of language and its centrality in constructing consciousness, rather than on social structure as conceived by Durkheim.

The work of the Marxist writer, Louis Althusser, who has greatly
influenced recent understanding of ideology, is often referred to
as 'structuralist'. His definition of ideology is very much like a map.
He sees ideologies as systems of symbolic representations that exist in
their own right, like languages, and work at a deep level through
structuring the consciousnesses and personal identities of individuals
(see Althusser, 1971). These ideological maps allow us to recognise
ourselves as men, women, churchgoers, or whatever, all of which are
social constructions: we learn to say 'I am a girl', 'I am a boy', 'I am
white', or 'I am black'. We see ourselves and the rest of the social world
through these categories and it is difficult to think or feel outside them.
As a Marxist, Althusser is nevertheless conscious of the tendency in
structuralism to 'reduce' the whole of social life to the level of symbolic
relations. He resists this, insisting on the 'material' basis of social life
and the reality of structures of oppression, such as class and 'race'.
While he argues that ideology is to some extent a relatively autonomous system which has real effects on the rest of the social structure, he
retains Marx's notion that ideology, as part of the superstructure of
society, is 'in the last instance' determined by the material, economic
base. Althusser argues that if we think of language as a system of
symbolic representations, we can begin to understand how, as language
users, our consciousness is socially structured. However, he also draws
our attention to the way ideologies are embedded in real, material
practices, the social interactions and rituals of everyday life which are
fundamentally structured by the productive life of a society. Moreover,
Althusser uses Pascal's instruction to 'Kneel down, move your lips in
prayer, and you will believe' to make the point that ideas derive from
the material practices rather than the reverse. This is a good example as
we can easily see how a young child, who is taken to Church, goes
through the motions of prayer and so on long before the rituals have
any meaning. By the time the meanings are understood the practices
are taken for granted and the child recognises her/himself as a Christian.

Structuralist theories of language and Althusser's theory of ideology
are very helpful in conceptualising the ways in which individual consciousness and identities are constructed socially, but they are less able
to show how people can have novel ideas and initiate actions to change
the structures they are born into. They are prone, like other structural
theories considered earlier, to the criticism of portraying human beings

as 'over-socialised'. Equally, languages and ideologies tend to be taken as unitary systems. All speakers of, say, French, are seen as speaking the same language, and a whole range of variations is overlooked. Similarly, the complexity of ideological systems in a society can be overlooked and an over-simplified view of a 'dominant ideology', representing the ideas and interests of a unified 'ruling class', constructed (Abercrombie *et al.*, 1980). Life is never as simple as our most attractive theories, however. More recently, the concept of 'discourse', which can perhaps cope better with complexity, has frequently been used in social science to replace the concept of ideology. The notion of 'discourse' is particularly associated with the work of Michel Foucault, which is usually defined as poststructuralist and sometimes postmodern (see Foucault (1974) for an extended discussion of discourse; and Burr (1995) for a good introduction).

A discourse is a systematic set of beliefs, ideas or knowledge and practices specific to particular social situations or locations: the discourse of gender, of medicine, and so on. Foucault emphasises the power inherent, not in social structural arrangements distinct from consciousness, as Marx does, but within discourses themselves, particularly in professional discourses. So, for example, the scientific discourse of modern medicine gives a great deal of power and control over people's bodies to the medical profession. Discourses are frameworks which produce and limit subjectivity – meaning, experience and identity. So, as in structuralism, language is central in the construction of persons, but Foucault, like Althusser, holds on to the materiality of social life through the notion of practices. The concept of discourses also recognises the plurality of meaning systems in a society, and the contestability of meaning. So discourses are sites of conflict and struggle. Foucault argues that within any discourse there is always the potential for developing an oppositional discourse. An example here might be the discourse of holistic medicine, which has developed alongside and in opposition to modern bio-medicine. Although Foucault himself appears to ignore gender in favour of sexuality, which we shall discuss in Chapter 4, if we define gender as a discourse, we can see that a range of oppositional discourses also exist – for example, the 'new man', or the independent woman – which contradict and raise possibilities for action other than those within the dominant discourse (Foucault, 1979; Macdonell, 1986).

It is easy to be confused by the similarities and differences between the notions of ideology and discourse. T. Purvis and A. Hunt provide one attempt at a synthesis, arguing that both concepts are useful, but that ideology is concerned with the 'external' aspects of how lived experience (such as gender or 'race') intersects with social structure (the material constraints), and discourse concentrates on the internal features of social and communicative practices. Some discourses, however, are ideological because they have a connection with the wider systems of inequality of interests in society (Purvis and Hunt, 1993). For example, we can argue that the bio-medical discourse concerning women's bodies is ideological, because it is part of and reinforces the structural position of women primarily as childbearers and carers, with its emphasis on defining the female body in terms of reproductive functions and perceiving menstruation and childbirth as medical problems. In this attempt we can see Purvis and Hunt continuing to struggle with the conceptual tensions between structure and action, and consciousness and material reality.

Emphasis on the experiential aspects of the social and the symbolic nature of social interaction, consciousness and communication, and the concepts of ideology and discourse, enable us to focus on how the practices of social life create the subjectivity of human actors. This emphasis, together with a stress on the fragmentation and changeability of social life, is characteristic of 'postmodernism'. Rather than enduring, overarching theories, postmodernism advocates the limitation of knowledge to small-scale temporary theories, and it questions the earlier attempts of writers such as Durkheim and Marx to develop more general theories to explain the whole of social life. Although Weber thought social science explanations could be only partial and open always to reinterpretation and further research, by placing subjectivity even closer to the centre of our focus on social life, postmodernism moves us even further from the preoccupation with structural explanations of much social science.

Conclusion

In this chapter we have introduced a number of themes and issues, and a range of concepts we shall use in later chapters. All these are defined in the Glossary at the end of the book, and you will find it necessary to keep referring to this. We have looked at social science as a way of mapping or guiding the explorer through the territory of the social world, and in doing so have seen that there is considerable argument and disagreement concerning how to read the maps, the best route to take, and the most useful tools and equipment for the exploration.

We have emphasised the utility of assuming that there is some structure, predictability and coherence to social life, much of which continues simply because of these characteristics. This predictability and structure can also be seen to organise and constrain many aspects of individuals' lives and identities. In contrast, we have also examined the notion of human consciousness, agency and subjectivity, which places the social actor at the centre of the stage, introducing the possibility of a *range* of interpretations of the social world, and of flexibility and changes in the structure.

In the following chapters we shall attempt our own exploration of multiple social worlds by examining a number of questions concerning the way in which the self-identity of individuals is both constructed through and constructs the processes of social life. We shall look specifically at the processes of personal identity and at the social transitions made by individuals as they negotiate their passage through the lifecourse. Emphasis here will be on the social construction of 'roles', such as gender and old age, and on the problematic and sometimes unstable notion of personal identity. We shall also examine the nature of knowledge about ourselves and the social world, and question the assumption that it is either 'subjective' or 'objective', seeing it rather as a social construction, which includes our experience of the social and the personal.

Issues concerning identity and the self, raised in the first two chapters, will be addressed through examining a number of areas chosen to clarify some of the specific cultural and social processes that make up or constitute human experience and action in the social world. These areas are intended to illustrate the processes rather than to provide a definitive account of them.

The chapter on sexuality will challenge some commonsense notions of sexuality as an essential human characteristic, focusing instead on sexuality as a socially constructed discourse with consequences for social and personal identity. We shall also begin to explore the contradictions between the notion of a socially constructed sexuality which nevertheless belongs to the 'private' sphere of social life. Similarly, the discussion of health and illness will take up the theme of the social construction of 'mind' and 'body', and the various professional and lay (or commonsense) discourses which contain inherent issues of power and control. We shall look too at the way health and illness, and their social interpretation and management, become important aspects of the social identity of individuals. The experience of work and organisations are also important aspects of the way in which individuals develop a sense of self. We shall also point to the fact, however, that formal definitions of work and organisations are insufficient to explore the way in which social actors 'work' at 'doing' social life. We shall show that work is gendered, that it intersects the boundary between the public and private domains of social life, and that it is as much about 'being' as 'doing'.

We shall then examine the wider implications of the social for the identity of individuals and groups by exploring such notions as 'community', 'nationality' and 'ethnicity', where we shall see that such notions have both an historical focus and a strong ideological function. In the penultimate chapter we shall move further from the individual to look at the idea of 'globalisation', asking questions about the nature of modern societies and their relationship to each other in a world where modern communications and technological systems appear to blur previous historical distinctions between 'self' and 'others'. Such questions turn our attention to inequalities of power on a global scale, and take us back to some of the issues first raised by the founding fathers of sociology.

In the final chapter we shall make more explicit some of the conceptual problems and tensions raised by the areas we have explored, relating this discussion back to the issues we have introduced in this first chapter.

In this volume, overall, we shall attempt to explain the complex ways in which individuals develop separate, yet social, selves and identities by drawing on the work of social science as we examined it at the beginning of this chapter. This includes both its foundation of structural analysis as well as its competing concern with interpretation and the agency of social actors.

2

Personal Identity

'Home is where the heart is'

Having introduced some of the general themes relating to our exploration of 'self' and 'society', we shall focus our attention in this chapter
on the 'self' and consider some of the issues involved in understanding
the nature of the 'self'. 'Person', 'self', 'personal identity', 'selfhood',
'individuality' and 'individual' are all words used by writers with an
interest in this area, and the specific meanings of these terms will vary
according to the perspective of the writer. For example, the notion of
'self' is sometimes used to imply the existence of a core entity which is
untouched by social experience, while 'personal identity' often refers to
our own sense of who we are. Here, we are particularly concerned with
the questions suggested by the very different experiences of personal
identity found in differing cultures. We lean towards the view that not
only is our experience of who we are deeply affected by culture but so
also are theories about the nature of the 'self'. Indeed, some cultural
experiences throw into doubt the very idea of the 'self' as it exists in
some Western theories.

The connection between the English sense of self and the houses the
English live in is noted by Nigel Barley. He comments that 'of all
known peoples, the English are by far the most insistent about actually
buying and owning the houses they live in' (1989, p. 51). Why, he was
asked by a group of Indonesian hill tribespeople visiting England,
should anyone spend so much on owning a home they could never
be in because they had to be out working to pay for it? Barley's answer
was that English personal identities are very much tied up with the
home, in contrast to those of Indonesians, who were more identified

with their ancestors and with their glorious ancestral houses than the modest houses they lived in.

The private house can in some ways be seen as symbolising the private self; it is a container with clear boundaries which shut out the public world. Home ownership is not just for the rich: increasingly, it has become something for every English person to aspire to: 'the Englishman's home is his castle'. It is interesting that ownership is linked to house *purchase*, and to identity and belonging: 'myself', 'I own it', 'it is my own home'. Of course, the English ideal is not one of houses occupied by single people, but by families. The private individual is not isolated but is a member of a family, and the ideal English family consists of a sexual couple, bound together by romantic love, and their children. Nevertheless, within the family, each person ideally is valued as an individual for her or himself rather than for any particular talents, characteristics or roles. Private houses are designed to accommodate such private families. Each house is lovingly individualised, often by the owners themselves, who may spend large amounts of time, energy and money consulting magazines, visiting 'DIY' stores, designing, extending, decorating and furnishing so that their houses and, more recently, their gardens, express their personalities.

Forced entry and burglary are often described in terms of violation and rape, powerfully expressing the way the house symbolises the integrity of the individual. Boundaries are marked with fences or walls and homes increasingly protected by burglar alarms and dogs. The private world of the family, inside the house, is safe; the public world outside is dangerous and threatening, and we are reminded of Christopher Lasch's characterisation of American families supposedly providing a 'haven in a heartless world' (Lasch, 1977).

Interestingly enough, although this separation of the private individual family world from the public social world seems 'natural' for many modern Western people, it is culturally and historically located. It also presents us with a paradox that seems central to the way we experience our selves. Those of us who have grown up in modern English or similar Western families will have learned to prize our individuality, our autonomy and our personal responsibility. We may have established families of our own and be proud of the homes we have created. However, looking again at the experience of living in English private houses, we can begin to see just how public the private world is.

Examining the houses in an English suburb, Barley notices how structured they are. They begin with front gardens which must be kept in good order but never sat in; it is only permissible to sit in back gardens. Front doors, often elaborately furnished, open into a hall and various public rooms. Rooms are segregated according to functions relating to human bodily functions, such as eating, washing and defecating. Dinner, for example, will only be served in a bedroom if someone is ill. Access to rooms is regulated, so access to the sitting-room implies more formality than the kitchen, and lavatories can be used by visitors with permission. Bedrooms, where the most private sexual functions are performed, are considered to be the most personal rooms, and people knock on bedroom doors. The ideal is for each individual or sexual couple to have their own bedroom, and for new couples to have a new house. Bedrooms are individually furnished or decorated by their inhabitants, but it is never difficult to identify which member of a family owns a particular bedroom or what are their age and sex. It would be difficult for one English suburban family to feel at a loss in the house of another. However, should they visit a Japanese house in Tokyo, the story would be quite different.

This helps us to see just how public and culturally regulated our private lives really are and, what is more, although we may pride ourselves on our individuality and difference, our desire for approval strictly limits us. We can, for example, be acutely embarrassed by the manifest disapproval of our taste in wallpaper shown by a potential house buyer. Perhaps this can also help us to recognise just how oppressive images of 'ideal' suburban families can be to English people who, from choice or necessity, live out their identities differently.

The myth of the self-contained individual

The view of human beings as self-contained individuals whose uniqueness is there from the start, 'an essential core' carried deep inside themselves, is ingrained in Western thinking, although, as we shall see below, some feminist theorists have identified it as a masculine view. It is linked with notions of possession or ownership of its capacities and abilities, as well as being expressed in the ownership of homes and other possessions. It is also seen as being bound in a bodily container clearly separated from other similarly bounded selves:

> Some thirty inches from my nose
> The frontier of my Person goes;
> And all the untilled air between

> Is private *pagus* or demesne.
> Stranger, unless with bedroom eyes
> I beckon you to fraternise,
> Beware of rudely crossing it;
> I have no gun, but I can spit.
>   (Auden, 1976)

We have seen that it has been one of the central problems of social science and psychology to grapple with the issue of the relationship between the self and society. The problem has been seen as one of formulating theories that conceptualise the links between them, and the ways they influence each other.

The way the question is posed suggests two distinct entities. Self and society are often opposed, with the latter imposing constraints. When Shakespeare tells us 'All the world's a stage, And all the men and women merely players'; we can feel with him the sense of hollowness connected with being cast into socially-defined roles to act out pre-determined plots and relationships (see Strawbridge, 1993). We want to break out and 'do our own thing'. In the words of the popular song, we aspire to the epitaph, 'I did it my way'. The goal of much modern counselling and psychotherapy is to rescue the 'repressed' inner core or 'true self', which is frequently likened to a 'free child' – spontaneous, expressive and good. Social relationships are perceived as overlaying this true self, which originates within the individual, with a false, often damaging, form. So other people, particularly parents, and 'society' are seen as threatening the core self from the outside, limiting and damaging its uniqueness and potential:

> They fuck you up, your mum and dad.
> They may not mean to, but they do.
> They fill you with the faults they had
> And add some extra, just for you.
>   (Larkin, 1974)

Paradoxically, however, we feel most 'at one with ourselves' when we have a role to play, when our sense of identity is confirmed in our relationships with others, and we have a recognised place in society. In Britain, as in the USA, in many Western European countries, and increasingly in the Third World, unemployment does not just mean financial hardship, it also undermines our sense of identity and value. In cultures that celebrate heterosexuality, coupling and families, homosexual, lesbian and single people can similarly struggle for a sense of identity and self-worth. The more we seek the inner core or true self, the more we find our culture with its expectations and patterns deeply embedded.

Our most intimate relationships, where we expect to be valued for ourselves, are clearly structured by social expectations, as we have seen in the way English suburban families arrange their homes and home life. In this context, it is easy to see how the foundations of identity can be destroyed by homelessness. The image of marriage, central to home life as the place where romantic love is enshrined, is held in some of the traditional 'fairy tales' which assure us in childhood that, following their trials and tribulations, the prince and princess will find each other and 'live happily ever after'. Even the way in which we experience the body, that 'natural' defining boundary of the self, is culturally influenced. Eva Hoffman tells us how, as a fourteen-year-old Jewish immigrant from Poland in the 1960s, her body was reconstructed into that of a Canadian teenager. Polish ladies, who had been in Canada long enough to be 'well versed in native ways', shaved her armpits, plucked her eyebrows, tried various shades of lipstick on her face, initiated her into the 'mysteries' of using shampoos and hair lotions and putting her hair in curlers, and suggested to her mother, 'in an undertone', that she should start wearing a bra:

> My mother obeys. I obey too, passively, mulishly, I hold my head rigidly, so that my precarious bouffant doesn't fall down, and I smile often, the way I see other girls do, though I am careful not to open my lips too wide... Inside its elaborate packaging, my body is stiff, sulky, wary. (Hoffman, 1989, pp. 108–10)

The essential or core self is then elusive, even the unconscious, according to much modern psychoanalytic thinking, is structured by language and culture. The difficulties in conceptualising both the core self and its relationships with society can perhaps best be seen as a function of the way in which the problem is posed. Instead of conceiving of self and society as separate but interacting entities, some theorists have preferred to think in terms of 'social selves' or 'subjects'. We agree that this is a much more productive way of looking at the self and shall explore it further. At the same time, we must bear in mind the point made in Chapter 1, that some classical sociological perspectives, critical of the notion of a pre-social or essential self, have been accused of proposing an 'oversocialised' view which fails to theorise individuals adequately with a sense of identity and the genuine capacity to choose and be responsible for themselves and their actions (Wrong, 1961).

It will be useful to try to establish some distance from what, after all, is for Westerners a very seductive and seemingly 'natural' way of thinking and of experiencing 'ourselves'. The self-contained individual is a powerful myth central to the way we perceive the self and our relationships, and central to Western political concepts and to the separation of the public and private or domestic spheres. Nevertheless, the anthropologist, Clifford Geertz, tells us that:

> The Western conception of the person as a bounded, unique, more or less integrated motivational and cognitive universe a dynamic centre of awareness, emotion, judgement and action organised into a distinctive whole and set contrastively both against other such wholes and against its social and natural background, is, however incorrigible it may seem to us, a rather peculiar idea within the context of the world's cultures. (Geertz, 1993, p. 59)

Some perspective may be gained by considering briefly both the historical development of this modern Western notion of the individual and some of the very different ways of conceiving of and experiencing the self in other cultures.

The discovery of the Western 'individual'

There is some agreement amongst scholars that the notion and experience of the self as an autonomous self-contained individual is the outcome of an historical process. Studies of early Greek texts of around 900–800 BC when, it is argued, the *Iliad* and the *Odyssey,* attributed to Homer, were written, find a very different view. There is no word equivalent to our 'person', though the vocabulary is rich in words which express a 'community of being', for which we have no equivalent. The human body is presented not as a unified whole but as an articulated combination of limbs, many actions are depicted as products of external forces, rather than being under the control of agents, and various components of mental life, such as dreams, are perceived as objective and external realities (see, for example, Dodds, 1951 and Snell, 1982). So when did the self as we understand it take shape?

Sociologists have, often critically, linked the doctrine of individualism, located in seventeenth-century political thought, with changes in property relations, the organisation of the market and the genesis of capitalism. We have already noted connections between the notion of ownership, property and the self. N. Abercrombie, S. Hill and B. S. Turner summarise the differing and complex ways in which Marx, Durkheim and Weber were all critical of the self-interested 'isolated' individuals of 'economic individualism', while holding distinctive views on 'moral individualism' linking personal identity and the potential for self-realisation of valued individuals into community and social responsibility (Abercombie *et al.*, 1986, ch. 1). C. B. Macpherson, in his influential examination of the political doctrine of individualism, says that fundamental to seventeenth-century individualism is the notion that 'the individual is essentially the proprietor of his own person and capacities, for which he owes nothing to society' (1962, p. 263). Moreover, since

the individual is human only in so far as free, and free only in so far as a proprietor of himself, human society can only be a series of relations between sole proprietors, i.e. a series of market relations. . . . Political society is a human contrivance for the protection of the individual's property in his person and goods, and (therefore) for the maintenance of orderly relations of exchange between individuals regarded as proprietors of themselves. (p. 264)

Charles Taylor similarly lays emphasis on the eighteenth century when he identifies a 'new moral culture', the Enlightenment, radiating 'outward and downward from the upper middle classes of England, America, and (for some facets) France'.

In making the transition to new societies and strata it is frequently transformed; so that what we end up with is a family of resembling moral cultures, or certain civilisation-wide traits with important variations among nations and social classes. Thus . . . the modern self-enclosed family is often quite differently lived in different classes. (Taylor, 1992, p. 305)

Nevertheless, although lived differently, common themes can be identified. It is a moral culture which, among other things: prizes autonomy; gives an important place to self-exploration, in particular of feeling; features personal commitment in its visions of the good life; and has a political language which leans towards egalitarianism and subjective rights. It stresses, therefore, both the ability and obligation of human beings to define themselves and their relationships among other human beings. So the notion of the autonomous, self-contained individual has been widely linked to the development of those British, Western European and North American cultures that have been described as 'modern' in the post-Enlightenment sense. They are liberal democracies with capitalist economies, and the seventeenth and eighteenth centuries are often seen as the crucial period in this development. Other theorists have, however, taken a longer view. A. Macfarlane, for instance considers English society to have been essentially individualistic throughout the feudal period (Macfarlane, 1978). His controversial thesis attacks the view of medieval England as a peasant-household economy with tightly knit organic communities and non-individual property relations.

Taking us even further back, Colin Morris nicely introduces his discussion of the historical development of the modern Western concept and experience of individual identity with the verse by W. H. Auden quoted above. He argues that our sense of ourselves as 'people with frontiers', divided from each other and having an inner being of our own, has its origins in the eleventh century (Morris, 1973). The development of Christianity with its distinctive confessional tradition oriented to the conscience of the individual is seen as central to an evolving inward-looking subjectivity, the separation of an individual from a collective sense of identity, and an increasing valuing of individuals. Morris's evidence includes the increase in the autobiographical content of published works such as the confessions of St Augustine, the growing popularity of collections of letters and other literary forms which indicate an interest in individuals, and the development of portraiture giving attention to individual characteristics.

This all seems very confusing, so where does it leave us? Abercrombie, Hill and Turner convincingly argue that both long- and short-run theories can be recognised as contributing to our understanding of the modern conception of the individual. As well as historians such as Morris, sociologists, notably Weber and later Parsons, have located the origins of a uniquely 'Western civilisation', to which the discovery of the individual is central, in the Judaic-Christian tradition. In contrast to the Jewish notion of a community of God's chosen people bound together by blood and descent, 'the Christian community emerged as a de-tribalized group of individuals bound together by faith'. Christianity was a Jewish movement that developed inside a Greek culture. The complexity of its community with diverse ethnic origins favoured the emphasis on the individual soul. Moreover, it further developed

> inside a Roman context, where Roman legal notions of the *persona* began to merge with Christian emphases on the soul. In other words, there was a fortuitous combination of a particular aspect of Roman legal theory and Christian theology to produce the notion of a subjective personality with rights and obligations. (Abercrombie, Hill and Turner, 1986, p. 50)

It is also argued that the particular character of the European Christian confessional tradition played an important part in the emergence of the 'modern' personality as a self-reflective consciousness with an emphasis on individual conscience. This facilitates a form of social control, through internalised 'guilt', said to be characteristic of individualistic cultures as opposed to more external forms of social control through public 'shaming', common in collective cultures. Foucault, some of whose ideas we shall consider elsewhere, also lays much stress on the history of the Christian confessional. He argues that it has given rise to a culture that is peculiarly autobiographical and in which we are all compelled to confess and explore our interior lives (see Chapter 4, where Foucault's work on confessions and disciplinary power is discussed).

This tracing of the slow emergence of the individual as a separate identity does not negate the significance of the enormous changes in the sixteenth and seventeenth centuries. It can be argued, with some justification, that the Protestant Reformation, changes in property relations and the rapid development of capitalism, together with political and philosophical individualism, combined to accelerate enormously the growth of the highly individualistic cultures characteristic of the modern West.

'Selfhood' in differing cultures

Exploring the sense of selfhood in three different cultures, in Java, Bali and Morocco, Geertz asks how the differing ways of referring to the self and of characterising people fit into the more general form of life of each culture which is manifest in its symbol systems. In Java he discovers two quite separated 'realms' of self. An inside self, or *batin*, is the felt realm of experience, 'the fuzzy shifting flow of subjective feeling', considered to be identical across all individuals and which, therefore, effaces individuality. Similarly an outside self, or *lair*, comprises behaviour including external actions, movements, postures and speech. The goal is to be *alus* (meaning pure, refined, polished, exquisite, ethereal, subtle, civilised, smooth) as opposed to *kasar* (meaning impolite, rough, vulgar, coarse, insensitive, uncivilised) in each of these independent realms. They have to be put separately into proper order. The inner world is stilled of emotion through spiritual practice, while the discipline of etiquette structures outer behaviour. Geertz describes the powerful difference he perceived between this conception of selfhood and his own notions of 'the intrinsic honesty of deep feeling and the moral importance of personal sincerity', when he saw a young man, faced with the sudden death of his wife, who had been the centre of his life, struggle to 'be smooth inside and out', to 'flatten out' his emotion by mystical techniques and greet everyone with a set smile and formal apology for his wife's absence (Geertz, 1993).

Balinese culture is, by contrast, structured by an intricate ritual life in which all aspects of personal expression are stylised. It is not the individual as such that is important but rather his or her assigned place in the patterns that are played out in Balinese life. People are not construed as unique individuals with private fates but as '*dramatis personae*' characters with prescribed parts to play, or representatives of generic types.

Selfhood in Morocco is different again. It is defined by co-ordinates that position an individual in relation to others in terms of such categories as region of origin, tribal membership, language, religion, kinship, occupation and so on. A person is contextualised but not defined in terms of attributes or qualities. So in terms of interactions and relationships, individuals may be 'pragmatic, adaptive, opportunistic, . . . a fox among foxes, a crocodile among crocodiles', without risk to their sense of identity (Geertz, 1993, p. 68).

As in the case of Eva Hoffman, discussed above, it is sometimes the pressure to become part of an alien culture that can impress upon us the crucially differing ways that people experience their selfhood. Dorinne Kondo is a Japanese-American anthropologist who went to Tokyo to study the relationship of kinship and economics in family-owned enterprises, and found her Western ideas about the relationship between self and social world 'exploded' (Kondo, 1990, p. 9). This came about through her deeply personal experience of being 'both Japanese and not Japanese'. Most of the Japanese people Kondo met had a basically biological definition of Japaneseness and, seeing her as racially Japanese, met her cultural incompetence with exasperation and disbelief. Their response was to set about making her as Japanese as possible, and she found that 'comprehensible order in the form of "fitting in", even if it meant suppression of and violence against a self

I had known in another context, was preferable to meaninglessness' (p.12).

Kondo's transformation involved a fragmenting of her identity into 'Japanese', 'guest', 'daughter' bits which entailed duties, responsibilities and interdependence, and conflicting 'American', 'researcher' bits which meant independence, mastery and decisive action. A key moment occurred when, out shopping, she glimpsed her reflection and recognised a typical young Japanese housewife. She sensed the collapse of her American identity and this led her to emphasise both the differences between cultures and between various aspects of identity: 'researcher, student, daughter, wife, Japanese, American, Japanese American . . . In order to reconstitute myself as an American researcher, I felt I had to extricate myself from the conspiracy to rewrite my identity as Japanese' (p. 17). Kondo then did not remain on the 'outside' in researching Japanese identity but experienced the difference between her own Japanese and American identities 'from the inside'. Her Japanese self was constituted through social obligations, 'living my life for others', and maintaining good relationships irrespective of inner feelings. Kondo was thus confronted by a profound challenge to her Western assumptions

> about the primacy of the 'individual' and the boundedness and fixity of personal identity. My neighbours, friends, co-workers and acquaintances never allowed me to forget that contextually constructed, relationally defined selves are particularly resonant in Japan. I was never allowed to be an autonomous, freely operating 'individual'. As a resident of my neighbourhood, a friend, a co-worker, a teacher, a relative, an acquaintance, a quasi-daughter, I was always defined by my obligations and links to others. I was 'always already' caught in webs of relationships, in which loving concern was not separable from power, where relationships define one and enable one to define others. The epiphanal moment when I realised the lack of importance of any personal self apart from social obligations . . . simply crystallised the themes already so much a part of life in my neighbourhood. (Kondo, 1990, p. 26)

Some Western feminists such as Gilligan (1982) argue that American women have a more relationally defined sense of self than American men. She argues that the self-contained individual is a masculine myth enshrined in American psychology, which defines developmental norms in ways that judge women's moral priorities, for example, as being generally less adult than those of men. This is because women, more often than men, will place a higher value on

maintaining relationships and caring for others than on general principles. Although such work suggests some similarity with Japanese
priorities, Kondo contends that the experience of American women
(her own included) remains solidly within a linguistic and historical
individualism. Japanese selves are fundamentally inextricable from
context in a way difficult for Westerners to grasp at all. This is brought
home by a striking, and for Americans highly problematic, feature of
the Japanese language. That is the plethora of ways of referring to
oneself. The word 'I' cannot be used in a context-free sense in Japanese
and it is therefore difficult to form a sentence referring to oneself
without also placing oneself in relationship to others. Status, intimacy,
distance and context are all conveyed by the word chosen and a mark of
maturity is the ability to refer to oneself appropriately in differing
relationships. Identity and context are thus inseparable and the distinction we make between them in English is virtually impossible in
Japanese, where the sense of self is more fluid, open and shifting within
the complex of social relationships.

Theorising the 'self'

We can see, then, that how people experience their sense of self varies
significantly with historical changes and from one society to another.
Theories of the self are ways of conceptualising and mapping these
experiences. Such maps can help us make sense of ourselves and some
of the problems we encounter in living by relating individual experience to the experiences of others and to a wider social context. One
thing we must remember in exploring such theories, however, is that,
while they can provide usable concepts and maps, they have themselves
been developed by people who are historically and culturally situated
and they reflect the preoccupations of particular times and places.
Indeed, the Western academic distinction between sociology and psychology, separating 'self' and 'society', is itself one that reflects our
preoccupation with the 'self-contained' individual discussed above. It is
a distinction that seems to be becoming less useful as, even in the West,
we are developing theories of the subject which dissolve this separation.
Nevertheless, to us, a psychology without an unambiguous 'I' appears
to be a contradiction in terms.

More than this, the normal Japanese experience can be perceived as
being deeply disturbed from the point of view of Western theories.
'Attachment' and 'object relations' theories, for example, acknowledge

that intense relatedness with others is crucial to the formation of a self. However,

> The foundation of the self in early social relatedness may lead to great difficulties for the individual if he is never able to escape from this way of being, and in adulthood to depend upon the attributions of others for a definition of the self may be extremely corrosive even if some sense of separateness has been established. Betty Friedan (1982), in discussing 'the problem with no name', which she saw as afflicting able and intelligent women who after marriage allowed the image of themselves to be restricted to what she calls 'occupation housewife' as defined by others, demonstrates with a plethora of examples the deeply damaging effect of the attempt to live in accordance with an image of the self which is derived almost completely from the other. (Morley, 1984, p. 23)

As Western women, the authors can feel, along with one woman in Betty Friedan's book, the intense frustration of 'always being the children's mommy, or the minister's wife and never being myself'. We can sense too the desperation of the woman who feels she has no personality, being 'a server of food and a putter on of pants and a bedmaker, somebody who can be called on when you want something. But who am I?' (Friedan, 1982, p. 19). This confirms Kondo's view that, even though we may have more relational 'selves' than is common among American and English men, like them we desire to be autonomous beings, each with a clearly identified sense of 'I'. We must nevertheless recognise that a Japanese woman may perceive her developmental tasks and feel fully mature in a profoundly different way, when she is able to portray herself as accommodating to duties and the needs of others. There are 'fundamentally different cultural ideals about what it is to be human, a woman and an adult' (Kondo, 1990, p. 33).

Recognising this presents great problems in theorising the self. We can see that what is normal, healthy and mature in one culture may be abnormal, sick or immature in another. It will also present us with problems if we are, for example, professional social workers, counsellors or psychologists, applying our theories in work with people from differing cultural groups. Our problems become incredibly complex if, in addition, we are concerned to identify and challenge oppression, for we must be careful not to perceive oppression from a purely Western view of equality and self-realisation.

Bearing all this in mind, how, then, can we theorise the self? Even this question only makes sense in a particular context and the theories that we draw upon in this book are modern or postmodern Western theories. They are not universally applicable but offer something to us as Western women struggling with the predicaments of our lives. The theories that we find most useful emphasise the fundamentally related nature of our being in the world with others. As women we are also concerned to make some sense of our own felt oppression in ways that help us to connect with the oppression of other people placed in categories that define them as inferior and force them to live in positions characterised by discrimination maintained by differences in power. Concepts and theories that help in these ways have tended to be sociological and have often written out the self in ways that seem to accord more with the Japanese experience than with that of women who sought to articulate 'the problem with no name'. Like the women in Betty Friedan's study, we desire some sense of self as an 'I', an independent, autonomous being. We shall later consider how it might be possible to fully realise our social being and yet retain an 'I'.

Roles

The concept of 'role' mentioned above is one that has been found very useful by Western theorists trying to bridge the created dichotomy between 'self' and 'society'. Roles are subjective and integral to our personalities. The roles we play become part of our identities, how we see ourselves and how others see us. They are at the same time objective, outside, part of culture and social structure, handed down across generations. We get our roles 'off the peg', with the cultural 'scripts' attached. The complexity of the task of becoming a socially competent person, someone who fits in, feels at ease with others and relates to them in socially acceptable ways, is perhaps more visible in Japan, where there is no unifying 'I' to conceal it. Nevertheless, when we consider the vast range of roles and relationships a woman may cope with in a fairly ordinary day: daughter, teacher, friend, mother, wife, author, cook, counsellor, manager and so on, it can seem quite daunting. Each role has its subroles and boundaries, and may overlap other roles. A wife may play cook, lover or friend to her husband, but must take care not to play teacher or counsellor to him!

Seeing identities in terms of patterns of roles and relationships connects them to social expectations. It also draws attention to the way they are constructed out of social action. It is people who create or change roles, and however strong social expectations may be, people are continually rewriting the scripts. Moreover, we can see how some of our roles are worn lightly and cast off with ease – those connected with a job seen just as a source of income perhaps, while others such as daughter, friend or author are more intimately linked with our sense of identity. Each role, then, is played according to a basic script and situated in a set of culturally defined social relationships. American marriage has, for example, been described as 'a dramatic act in which two strangers come together and redefine themselves' (Berger and Kellner, 1979, p. 30). They have been provided with a taken-for-granted image of marriage by their society and anticipate stepping into their taken-for-granted roles. Nevertheless, there is some room for interpretation and negotiation. Conversations are conducted, about in-laws, friends, children and the like, in which common definitions and meanings are sought, and couples work to define their shared meaning of 'family'. This highlights the centrality of the creation and mainte-nance of meanings in human social life, and the importance of lan-guage in this process.

Cultures comprise patterns of belief, values, attitudes, expectations, ways of thinking, feeling, moving, using objects and so on. They can be defined as 'symbolic systems' like languages which, 'structuralists' tell us, exist as structured systems independent of their use by particular individuals. Indeed, our ability to speak and be understood depends on the existence of languages as structured systems of meanings. They are internalised as we learn our native tongue and this is integral to the process of 'socialisation' through which we become social identities with recognisable roles to play. We have already seen just how public our private worlds are and, as studies of language, culture and socialisa-tion increasingly inform each other, we can understand how this happens.

The concept of role therefore can be very helpful in linking personal identities with social life. It can nevertheless feel quite unsatisfactory from a Western point of view, as to see personality constructed in this way seems to dissolve our sense of 'I'. The focus is on the social order and the way it is maintained by social actors. Erving Goffman, for example, perceives this as being achieved by individuals suppressing their own desires so as to maintain a working consensus (Goffman, 1971). He describes the process as one of 'impression management' and sees the problems of individuals presenting themselves to others as 'dramaturgical' ones, akin to those of actors on a stage who must make their performances convincing to their audience. Although Goffman distinguishes between the self as a character and as performer, his interest is in the performer, who trains in the skills of a social actor, learns parts, courts success and adulation and risks the shame of failure. Peter Berger, placing more emphasis on the internalisation of roles and the construction of identity, nevertheless describes the self as, 'no longer a solid, given identity that moves from one situation to another. It is rather a process, continuously created and recreated in each social situation . . . held together by the slender thread of memory' (Berger, 1973, p. 124).

All this can be very threatening, and from a different perspective R. D. Laing has connected the insecurity of experiencing the self as tenuous and unreal, lacking in solidity and threatened by relationships, with the development of schizophrenia (Laing, 1965). He views every individual as having an inherent self which is the core of its being, a directive centre, the origin of action and a reference point of experience. This self nevertheless needs validating in relationships. Laing sees schizophrenia as an attempt to defend the self against invalidation. Tragically, the defence, by a withdrawal from relationships, itself leads to the decomposition of personality. While our historical and cross-cultural reflections lead us to reject the notion of an inherent core self, we can experience the desire for an 'I', which has some integrity of being, and the fear of its absence or loss. Is it possible, then, to acknowledge the validity of the deeply social and relational view of personal identity conceived as a complex of roles and retrieve a sense of 'I' which does not rely on the notion of a pre-social essence? We shall return to this question but, for the moment we shall stick with the ways our identities are socially constructed and consider in particular the dimensions of power and oppression in their construction.

Power in the mirror of society

We do not wish to oversimplify theoretical issues, but we are here more interested in drawing on theoretical concepts to make sense of our experience rather than deepening theoretical understanding for its own sake. In this context we can say that if 'role' is a useful conceptual bridge between personal identity and society, it is also of value in helping us to make links between differing theoretical perspectives. We have noted that seeing identity in terms of a complexity of roles tends to dissolve any sense of a coherent self, an 'I'. This position is more or less explicitly taken by a wide range of 'structuralist' and 'poststructuralist' theorists who prefer to use the term 'subject' rather than self. The subject is contrasted with the self by being 'decentred', produced socially, in relationships through the systems of meaning within language and culture (see, for example, Burr, 1995). Marxists, post-Marxists and feminists have found structuralist ways of thinking useful in understanding how power relations are reproduced. These kinds of theories are often termed 'anti-humanist' precisely because they deny the self as being the essential core of identity.

The work of the French Marxist philosopher, Louis Althusser, has greatly influenced work that connects the formation of the subject with the social reproduction of power relationships. In his essay on ideology, he examines how ideology functions to reproduce social relationships (Althusser, 1969). Writing as a Marxist, he is particularly concerned with those relationships crucial to production. A society or 'social formation' is understood as a structure whose fundamental character is determined by the economy and in which the most fundamental power relationships are those of class exploitation. Whether or not they agree with Althusser in this respect, many theorists have found his work on ideology to be of immense value in understanding the ways in which power relationships are reproduced through the construction of the personal identities of 'subjects'. Althusser does not specifically use the concept of role but he does employ the metaphor of an 'authorless theatre' in describing society. He conceptualises ideology as a system of symbolic representations, structured like a language. It works by constructing individuals as subjects and calling us out to play our parts. It is as if a mirror is held up to us in which we recognise ourselves (see also Lacan, 1949). This mirror of society is rather like the mirror in the fairy tale which tells us who is the fairest of us all, and as we recognise ourselves as male, female, Christian, English, black, white and so on, we locate ourselves in positions in society and take on appropriate attitudes, beliefs and feelings. As we take on our identities, so we participate in reproducing the social structure. Inasmuch as our social positions are structured by relationships of inequality, discrimination and oppression, these will be experienced as integral to our identities and have a 'natural' feel. For example, it is difficult for women and men in our society not to experience gender inequalities as being in some way 'natural'. This is a central way in which ideology obscures the nature of exploitative social relations, making their reproduction possible.

It was again an important insight of Althusser's that ideology could not function to reproduce real social relationships if it did not adequately represent them. Ideology is not false, but functions in a mythical way, constructing, in our imaginations, important relationships in a way in which they can be lived in our everyday lives and which disguises their exploitative nature. Like roles in the theatre, identities are scripted and acted. Althusser would say that they are embedded in material practices. This is important because of the connection it makes between the symbolic structure and the ways in which identities are practised in our actions upon the material world and in our relationships with each other: 'By their deeds shalt thou know them' (Matthew ch. 7 v. 20). So far we have said that a system of symbolic representations is like a language, and this analogy has been very important in the development of our understanding of ideology. However, more recent work has been influenced by the idea of discourses and the study of myths and metaphors. We shall explore some of these notions further, for example in relation to the sexual dimension of identities. At this point it will be more useful to examine a little further the impact of oppression on identities.

Monologues and the suppression of the 'other'

Many people who have eventually recognised themselves as 'oppressed' have described their experience of being invisible except as a negative image. Ralph Ellison, for example, shows black Americans being rendered invisible by being represented only through white eyes, lacking a positive identity of their own (Ellison, 1976). Toni Morrison takes this further and shows how, in white American literature, a negative presence of African-Americans becomes:

> the vehicle by which the [white] American self knows itself as not enslaved, but free; not repulsive, but desirable; not helpless, but licensed and powerful. (Morrison, 1993, p. 52)

She describes the way in which white literature constructs the African-American as a 'serviceable other' whose existence serves the needs, interests and desires of the dominant group. Similar observations can be made about the construction of 'woman' in relation to 'man', 'disabled' in relation to 'able-bodied', 'homosexual' in relation to 'heterosexual' and so on. Each person who inhabits an identity defined by a dominant group as inferior or abnormal serves the interests of that group by providing them with a construction of what they are not (see also the discussion of a 'serviceable other' in Chapter 9 below).

People in many oppressed groups can be compared to colonised people who learn the language and history of the coloniser. Frantz Fanon writes powerfully about his personal experience of colonisation:

> Every colonised people... finds itself face to face with the language of the civilising nation; that is, with the culture of the mother country... The black schoolboy in the Antilles, who in his lessons is forever talking about 'our ancestors, the Gauls', identifies himself with the explorer, the bringer of civilisation, the white man who carries truth to savages – an all white truth. There is an identification – that is the young Negro subjectively adopts a white man's attitude. (Fanon, 1970, pp. 14 and 104).

The notion of colonisation can perhaps provide us with a powerful way of seeing oppressed identities as it conveys well a sense of being taken over from the inside, and all successful processes of colonisation involve the imposition of language and culture. Paulo Friere has described in some detail how in learning the language of the dominating culture, oppressed people lose their own voice and are imprisoned in a 'culture of silence' (Friere, 1972). The process of liberation and decolonisation involves a struggle by oppressed people to find a voice in a language of their own. Friere's adult literacy programmes with people in Brazil and Chile demonstrate clearly that education can never be neutral, but is always about domination or liberation. Feminists too have written much about this struggle to find a voice and an identity when the only words available are those of masculine language. So oppression works in the very heart of personal identity and this accounts for the difficulties that oppressed groups have in overcoming their internalised homophobia, racism, sexism or some other form of self-hatred. The slogans 'Glad to be Gay' and 'Black is Beautiful' are, first of all, self-affirming messages.

We noted earlier the significance placed on the Enlightenment for the development of the self-contained Western 'individual'. Edward Sampson has linked the construction of oppressed groups as serviceable others to this same culture. Central to the Enlightenment was a concern with political democracy based on the notion of human equality and the universality of the humanity underlying all difference and diversity. For fair and universal standards to apply, identities warranting special treatment must be ignored and everyone must be judged only in terms of individual merit. The familiar American myth of a cultural 'melting pot' is one expression of this. Sampson argues that, although we commonly see all this in terms of the celebration of the individual, it can better be described in terms of the active suppression of the 'other'. Modern cultures can be seen as 'monologic', consisting of only one voice, and this one 'universal' voice has slowly been shown to be that of dominant social groups, primarily white, Western and male.

Who am 'I?' Dialogues constructing selves

We earlier posed the question as to the possibility of reconciling the fundamentally social nature of identity with the desire for a sense of 'I' that we three authors certainly retain as Western women. The work of George Herbert Mead suggests an answer and directs our attention to the significance of 'self-consciousness', consciousness which always includes, at least implicitly, a reference to an 'I'. He distinguishes the 'I' from the 'me', or socially-acquired identity, and the 'I' becomes conscious of the 'me' in the course of development. Mead tells us that self-consciousness is fundamentally social. It can only develop in relationships with others and an individual's experience of self 'is one which he takes over from his action upon others. He becomes a self in so far as he can take the attitude of another and act toward himself as others act' (Mead, 1962, p. 171). Our mistake is perhaps in trying to conceptualise the 'I' as an 'entity' or essence rather than as a 'capacity' to reflect. In Robert Landy's words, as

> a central intelligence that frames the personality. If at the core of the human personality is not a thing, a godlike self, perhaps we can conceptualise a dramatic process – that of impersonation, the ability of the developing person to fashion a personality... the concept of role implies not only that the world is a stage and the people are players, but that the space between reality and imagination is the source of creative energy. (Landy, 1993, p. 30)

The development of a 'self' can then perhaps be seen as a project for which the fundamentally social, reflective capacity, the 'I', can become responsible. As we become more aware of how our personal and social histories shape our lives we can release our creative potential both to fashion our roles and relationships and to struggle against the socially structured relationships of power that constrain and oppress us. For while we are fundamentally social beings realising ourselves in social relationships, we are also cast in roles in which we live out existing structures of oppression. These can be conceptualised as written into a social and cultural 'text'. Drawing on the work of Michael Bahktin, Sampson describes this text as monologic (Sampson, 1993). In other words, the text represents a dominant voice, a monologue seemingly the work of a single author. This notion of monologue is in some ways over simple and reminiscent of the notion of a dominant ideology. It nevertheless offers a powerful metaphor of oppression, and Sampson sees voices of resistance embracing diversity and reasserting themselves by calling for a move beyond the Enlightenment or modern view of 'equality as sameness' towards 'equality through diversity'. He finds the promising beginnings of a way of theorising this postmodern movement in Bakhtin's stress on the conversational or 'dialogic' quality of human nature. Human beings are not to be understood in terms of internal processes but rather in terms of the processes or dialogues that occur between them. Dialogues, unlike monologues, involve differing but equal voices. One of the central themes in postmodernism that has attracted the interest of feminists, black theorists and others concerned with oppression and its effects on identity, is that of difference. The struggle to recognise and celebrate difference is a key issue in the politics of identity and it can be seen as a struggle towards genuine dialogues, in which differing voices are heard and in which each participates in the ongoing construction of the other. We shall take up this theme again in the last chapter of the book.

Conclusion

To summarise, in this chapter we have explored the experiences and ideas that challenge some of the notions relating the 'self' and personal identity which can feel very natural to us as Western writers. We have considered briefly the social and historical circumstances within which these notions have developed, and seen that people with different cultural experiences have very different perspectives. We have also looked at how a more social conception of 'self' and 'personal identity' can help us to understand how the construction of identities links into and helps to perpetuate the structures of power and domination in society. As women writers we are very encouraged by the liberating potential of some of these ideas. We find in them ways of naming, conceptualising and confronting our own experiences of discrimination and oppression.

3

Transitions through the Lifecourse

Being and becoming

As the previous chapter shows, personal identity, or the formation of the self, is the product of experience and interaction. We become the people we are through our experience within the family, at school, among our networks of friends, and in the workplace. It is through interaction with others that we come to know who we are and who we are not. Our responses to those around us and theirs to us make us into the people we know ourselves to be. How the self undergoes changes across the lifecourse is a related question which the present chapter will explore. This will involve looking at the relationship between the ways in which our bodies alter with time and the ways in which our social identity can be transformed. The role of accounts, stories or scripts is important here, providing a way of linking these kinds of changes, whether they are accounts told in anticipation of change or in retrospect. Often they create a sense of transition by emphasising the way in which the individual changes in relation to those around them. Using the ethnographies provided by social anthropologists, we can examine the way these scripts become acted out or transformed into ritual practices. Though much of this material focuses on more traditional societies, it provides a theoretical framework – the concept of a rite of passage – which also allows us to understand how lifecourse transitions take place in contemporary Western societies. Through examples, we shall examine the way bodily change and social transition come to relate to one another. In so doing we cannot ignore arguments which stress the lack of any shared pathway through life for people in present-day post-traditional societies, and we finish the chapter by examining the question of choice and how the possibility of choice might shape the way in which we experience transitions.

First, let us be more specific about what we mean by lifecourse transition. Though the term lifecycle has often been used to describe the stages through which human beings pass between birth and death, the newer term lifecourse has been coined as a way of acknowledging the less rigid patterning of lives in contemporary Western societies. While 'cycle' implies a rigid set of transitions which determine the age-based status of the individual , 'course' points towards the range of possibilities through which the individual negotiates their passage. By using the term lifecourse, therefore, the chapter takes a broad focus, including both the gradual transitions, such as adolescence, and the more rapid transformations which take place, for example, when a bereavement occurs. To be human is therefore not only about learning to be a male child or a white shopkeeper, but also about learning to become someone who is different from the person we previously knew ourselves to be. That changed self might be someone who is older or unemployed, someone who is disabled, someone who is a father or a wife, or someone who is a student.

Thus, we can ask how the transition from being a person who is able-bodied to a person who is disabled comes to take place. When Jenny Morris broke her spine in an accident, she was no longer able to walk (Morris, 1991). Becoming 'disabled' was, however, another matter. Changes in her body and changes within her social identity did not mesh smoothly with one another. While medical professionals readily categorised her as disabled, the identity through which she and her family knew her was less easily transformed. Former social self and present physical self were in tension with one another.

If we reflect on the passage of the individual through life, experiencing bodily changes, the development or loss of their abilities, and the shifting patterns of their social relationships, we are confronted with questions about how that experience of transition or transformation comes into being. We have already recognised possible mismatches between the private experience of the self and the identity which others read off from one's body. This point is further exemplified in the experience of a contributor to Jo Campling's collection of disabled women's writings:

> On leaving hospital and finding the mantle of 'disabled' placed firmly upon my unwilling shoulders I entered a world which was alien, absurd and ultimately defeating. My weak grasp on my identity was no match for the

massed forces of society who firmly believed themselves to be 'normal' and myself just as firmly 'abnormal'. (Campling, 1981, p. 48)

This statement reflects a model of the individual as someone who can look at 'society' as a separate entity, as something that exists independently of them. It raises a theme that is central to this chapter, and indeed to the whole volume. As social scientists, how should we think about the 'I' of the author who experiences her 'social' self as a mantle or overlay, imposed upon her by an external world? Implicit within her statement is a notion of the 'I' as something private and separable from the public sphere of the social.

This chapter will examine some of the ways in which the relationship between the individual and society has been understood, recognising at the outset that the notion of the self and society as separable entitities itself represents a particular theoretical position. Durkheim, for example, worked from this premise in developing his view of society as something that existed over and above the sum of its individual members (Durkheim, 1982; see also Chapter 1 of this book). If we compare his work with that of a sociologist who works from an interactionist perspective we find, by contrast, a view of 'society' as a fluid entity that exists very much within the unfolding of a myriad of individual exchanges (see, for example, Blumer, 1969). When we try to provide a single sociological account of lifecourse transitions, we are therefore rather like the rail passenger in a stationary train struggling to explain the sense of movement as another train, framed in the carriage window, begins to pull away. What is moving and what is fixed? Are passengers and trains one and the same thing? Or are they separate things, and if so, what is their relationship to one another? Some theorists have viewed society as something permanent through which a succession of individuals appears to pass; others cast doubt on the notion of society as an independent entity. It is these kinds of perspective which this chapter will examine critically.

In exploring questions about the nature of the self and its relationship with the nature of society, the human body is often seen to represent a 'natural' sphere of some kind, a surface upon which society traces its designs. We must ask, however, whether what we think of as our 'biology' can really be seen as something separate from the social domain. Many lifecourse transitions – into parenthood, adulthood or retirement – are events or processes seen to be intimately bound up with changes in our bodies. In a physical sense, passage through the life course will tend to mean that we grow larger, become fertile, age and die. In human societies these bodily changes are often associated with transitions in the way we are positioned within society. For example, as Jewish boys mature physically their growth is made social through a *bar mitzvah* ceremony, which signals a transition from one social category – 'child' – to another – 'man' (Mars, 1989). As we shall go on to find out, however, the match between bodily and social change is not necessarily a seamless overlap. For example, initiation to womanhood among Bemba girls happens through a group ritual which, while built around symbols of growth, involves all teenage girls regardless of changes to their body such as the onset of menstruation (La Fontaine, 1966). Across the lifecourse, therefore, the relationship between growing in a bodily sense and growing up in a social sense is complex.

As well as being seen as the biological basis for a lifecourse transition, the body can also reflect or be used to express a social change of identity which the individual has undergone. Thus, in rural Greece, as in many parts of nineteenth-century Europe, the wearing of black clothing signals that a woman has lost her social identity as a wife and taken the social identity of a widow. Similarly, the short-back-and-sides haircut of the new recruit signals an occupational transition from civilian to military employment. From the start, therefore, we are dealing with sets of complex, often circular, interrelationships. Bodily change may be interpreted as a signal for social transition. This, in turn, may lead to changes in the way in which the body is presented. For example, as an individual's body ages, so they may find themselves ascribed a new social status – old-age pensioner, senior citizen, old biddy. If that identity is taken on, individuals may find themselves re-presenting their bodies – for example, they may avoid figure-hugging clothing in sexually inviting colours, feeling comfortable only in fawn polyester.

In summary, when we try to make sense of lifecourse transitions from a social science perspective we are taking on a topic that requires us to think critically about what we understand society to be; about how we understand the relationship between bodily and social change; and about what the relationship between individual and social life might be. Only by addressing these questions can we begin to explain accounts such as Jenny Morris's which testify to a sense of dislocation between something we call the 'personal' and something we call 'society'. While Morris is only too aware of changes that have taken place in her body, she feels no sense of identification with the social identity others assume she has now come to inhabit – 'disabled'. What kinds of theoretical framework, therefore, can we draw upon to make sense of her personal experience of transition?

Accounting for transition

Accounts, the stories, scripts or narratives we tell or are told about ourselves, play an important role in linking the changes our bodies might undergo and the transitions that lead us into new social identities. Sometimes they provide social interpretations of bodily change – for example, retirement ceremonies can be seen as the way in which employers, and ultimately the state, provide an account of the process of biological ageing (Phillipson, 1982). It is an account which results in later life being associated with rest and a release from work, a construction of ageing that came into being in Western societies only at the end of the nineteenth century (Thane, 1983). Some accounts of lifecourse transitions are told retrospectively, in reminiscence, memoir or therapy, a process that can involve creating a shape and a pattern among events which, at the time, were experienced as random and chaotic. Other accounts are told, or perhaps requested, in anticipation: 'What are you going to be when you grow up?' Where such accounts emanate from, how they manifest themselves within lived experience, and how they may be contested are questions that remind us they are narratives situated within the context of social relations.

Chapter 5 explores the changes within the self which we identify as illnesses. They are changes we assume will affect our identity only temporarily. While we are absent from work, or indeed confined to bed, we briefly occupy what is known as a 'sick role' (Parsons, 1951). That role, however, is experienced merely as an interruption to other, more enduring social roles or identities. Here, we are exploring situations where, for example, an individual becomes aware that a self they believed to be changed temporarily through illness is not, in fact, changed but lost – as is the case when their illness is diagnosed as chronic and incurable. Medical knowledge can be seen as one of the most powerful or persuasive accounts of change within the self currently available to us within Western society. Although understood to be 'scientific' in nature, it can also be seen as an interpretation of our selves and our bodies which positions us socially. Whether as 'sick', 'critically ill', 'convalescent' or a 'chronic invalid', these medical categories help to define us socially and have implications in terms of our place within the world and our relationships with those around us.

What we are describing, therefore, are frameworks for understanding and giving coherence to the disruption, disorder or discontinuity that change brings. They can be seen as a way of both asserting the social reality of a break with the past at a point when the individual may be resistant to making such a transition; also as a way of bringing unpredictable social changes, such as an accident or a bereavement, to order. To explore this point in some depth we now take the example of autobiography as an account of lifecourse transition. The opening paragraph of Laurie Lee's autobiographical novel *As I Walked Out One Midsummer Morning* is a description of how the author's social identity underwent a transition at the age of nineteen:

> The stooping figure of my mother, waist-deep in the grass and caught there like a piece of sheep's wool, was the last I saw of my country home as I left to discover the world. She stood old and bent at the top of the bank, silently watching me go, one gnarled red hand raised in farewell and blessing, not questioning why I went. At the bend of the road I looked back again and saw the gold light die behind her: then I turned the corner, passed the village school, and closed that part of my life for ever. (Lee, 1969, p. 11)

Recounted more than thirty years after the event took place, Lee's narrative gives order and form to earlier events and feelings. Using the literary skills of a writer, he seeks to show the reader something of his experience of what a social scientist would call a lifecourse transition. Indeed, as social scientists, we can examine his autobiography analytically and find exemplified many of the features common to all lifecourse transitions. In this particular case the author was not only leaving behind the domestic confines of early twentieth-century village life; at the age of nineteen he was also leaving behind his youth. In making his way alone towards Spain with just a tent, a violin, a change of clothes, treacle biscuits and some cheese, he was also taking on a new social identity or status, that of a man.

What was it, therefore, that happened to Laurie Lee as he 'walked out one midsummer morning'? As social scientists, can we provide an explanation of how this experience differed from the start of a rather adventurous walking holiday? For example, while nineteen-year-old Lee might seem to have 'grown up' in a bodily, biological sense, this does not explain how a change in his social status might be taking place. As already suggested, lifecourse transitions often involve social events which both make and mark change. Initiation rites, weddings and retirement ceremonies provide some of the ways through which human beings come to experience themselves as altered. Without social events of some kind, would we perceive ourselves as altered, as having taken on a changed social identity? The lack of any public ritual at the time of a divorce is something that can make it difficult for individuals to make sense of the experience of coming to the end of a marriage. In Lee's account, however, no formal ritual of transition is described. He is none the less aware of both the expectations of others as well as the changes he is undergoing in relation to others. We can therefore ask what kind of model of the self and of his social sphere is Lee drawing upon?

Family relationships are given particular emphasis in this account, as exemplified in the description of his mother, already cited. Hers is not the goodbye offered to someone setting off on their fortnight's annual holiday. In Harris's view, lifecourse transitions are essentially relational (Harris, 1987). In other words, as individuals, we do not move through a series of fixed points that are external to us: a rigid, pre-ordered series of positions laid in place for us by society. In the case of transitions between social roles, positions or status – youth to adult, wife to widow – our movement is always in relation to others, who themselves are also in transition. Our passage through the lifecourse – our trajectory, as Harris calls it – can be 'reconceptualised as movements over time between positions in social space' (Harris, 1987, p. 20).

Lee's account would seem to be in keeping with this sociological perspective. When he walks out one midsummer morning his physical movement across Wiltshire is experienced in terms of a series of relational shifts. The momentous nature of his departure is represented by his mother, bent in stereotypical farewell, receding into the distance, the gold light, symbolically, dying behind her. He knows that this June morning is 'the right time to be leaving home'; it is a transition already mapped out for him by his three sisters and a brother who have 'gone before me' (Lee, 1969, p. 12). Miles gained are experienced in terms of social space painfully created. He longs for 'hurrying footsteps coming after me and family voices calling me back' (p. 13). His mother's treacle biscuits, eaten on a stone wall, evoke 'the honeyed squalor of home', where his mother and brothers are at tea (p. 13). What prevents him from returning, what propels him forward, is similarly relational in nature – 'I might have turned back if it hadn't been for my brothers, but I couldn't have borne the look on their faces' (p. 13). Seen tramping across the Wiltshire downs, Lee might indeed appear to be setting out on a walking holiday. What his account conveys is the experience of a lifecourse transition. A complex series of changes are transforming the social spaces which both link and separate the individual members of his family.

When Lee chooses to set off alone he is not only effecting changes in his relationship with his family; he is also following a script set in place by older siblings. Thus, while making choices and setting off 'to be independent', Lee none the less appears to be contained within the structures of his family and constrained by an overarching family narrative. As social scientists, we are therefore not just trying to account for one young man's experience. We are also confronting a shared concept: 'adulthood'. In the case of Laurie Lee and his siblings, why was leaving their rural environment an intrinsic aspect of their social transition from youth to adulthood? Though the way is mapped out by older family members, we none the less sense that power is being contested, that adult identity, for Lee, is something born out of opposition or even struggle. Thus he describes the power of 'traditional forces that had sent many generations along this road – by the small tight valley closing in around one, stifling the breath with its mossy mouth, the cottage walls narrowing like the arms of an iron maiden, the local girls whispering, 'Marry, and settle down' (Lee, 1969, p. 12). Social constraints are described in physical terms – the valley, the cottage walls. These, in turn, are felt within the body – the tight mouth of the valley which stifles the breath. Experienced within the body, it is the body which must be removed in order to create social space, in order to achieve a desired change in social identity. The transition from youth to adulthood, in Lee's case, is marked out through a bodily shift from rural to urban space.

Lee is therefore describing a collective experience, but one in which his own actions as an individual are highlighted. His is an account of what social scientists describe as the agency of the actor, of their capacity to make choices and to act on their own behalf, and yet Lee situates his choices and actions within the context of the 'many generations', and indeed his own four siblings who have mapped out his route for him. Harris argues that lifecourse transitions are an area of study deserving of a central place within sociology in that they represent a challenge to the notions of social structure as some kind of fixed entity. Instead, they lead us into a view of social structure as 'merely a moment in a process of societal change of which the choices of subjects are constituents' (Harris, 1987, p. 24). In other words, he questions a model of the lifecourse as a pre-ordained pathway leading from childhood, through youth, into adulthood, middle age and old age, each stage having fixed sets of characteristics which the individual, willy nilly, finds themself taking on. In his view, the lifecourse represents the coming together of two different kinds of time – biographical and historical.

As discussed in Chapter 1, sociology traditionally has divided itself between a focus on structure, which sees social variables such as class or gender as society's building blocks, and a focus on agency, which sees a myriad of micro-level social interactions between, for example, the law-breaker and the police officer, as constitutive of society. Harris argues that if we look at the lifecourse as the coming together of individual biography and collective history, then we have within it the 'different movements of a total social process which has both collective and individual moments' (Harris, 1987, p. 22).

Rites of passage

Social science perspectives that seek to make sense of lifecourse transitions often draw on the notion of a *rite de passage*. This term was first used by social anthropologists to describe rituals which make and mark changes of both an individual kind, as in births, marriages and deaths and also a broader social kind, such as New Year celebrations (Giddens, 1991; James and Prout, 1990; Long, 1989; Schuller, 1989; Stubbs, 1989). The interests of anthropologists are often quite similar to those of an autobiographer such as Lee. Their research methods require close involvement with the everyday lives of the people among whom they are conducting their study. What they produce often gives insight into the experiences of insiders within small-scale social settings, rather than a more abstract overview of a large-scale society. Their work has therefore been important in explaining how the experience of a lifecourse transition comes into being. Thus, they might ask what the symbols that go to make up a ritual of initiation actually mean to the people who are going through a lifecourse transition of this kind. They also ask how initiates are changed as a result of going through the ritual.

Bronislaw Malinowski (1984–1942) used a structural – functionalist approach to show how social customs functioned to meet the needs of the individual – for example, mourning behaviour at a funeral would be seen as a way of alleviating the emotional distress of bereaved individuals. Functionalist explanations were developed by theorists such as A. R. Radcliffe-Brown (1881–1955) and Emile Durkheim

(1858–1917), who saw social institutions and behaviour more in terms of their role in reaffirming the values of society as a whole, and promoting its solidarity. Funeral behaviour would therefore be explained in terms of its function in ensuring the continuity of society in the face of the death of one of its members (Howard, 1993). Within a framework where social equilibrium and the continuity of society were a primary focus, the constant passage of individuals through the cycle of birth, reproduction and death was seen as potentially threatening, a disruption that had to be managed if stability was to be maintained.

In a study of the practice of double burial among the Dayak peoples of south-east Asia, Robert Hertz argued that 'when a man dies, society loses in him much more than a unit; it is stricken in the very principle of its life, in the faith it has in itself' (Hertz, 1960, p. 78). Social behaviour at the time of a death, a birth or a marriage – life-course transitions – was therefore understood as a way of managing otherwise disordering change within an enduring social system. In 1908 Arnold Van Gennep provided an approach to rituals of transition which, ultimately, became a framework for understanding social changes of all kinds. Initially grounded in a view of society as a fixed entity which endures despite the passage of its individual members, Van Gennep's model of the *rite de passage* has been developed as a broader way of understanding processes of change and conflict within society. In later work by social anthropologists, society ceased to be conceived of as an external entity which somehow caused certain behaviours to occur in order for it to survive. Instead, society came to be seen as the product of the behaviour engaged in by those who participate in a rite de passage (Bloch and Parry, 1983).

What Van Gennep argued is that lifecourse transitions involve shifts within or between fixed points within social systems – for example, childhood, marriage, death. In moving between different social statuses, individuals are, briefly, ambiguous in terms of their social identity. For example, a young person entering adulthood is neither a child nor a man or woman. Thus, people who are newborn, pubescent, about to be married, about to leave work or about to die are moving across social boundaries and cannot easily be categorised within the framework of an existing belief system. However, in contemporary Western societies, some individuals find themselves experiencing transitions that are unmarked in terms of public ritual – for example, divorced, disabled or chronically sick people. In that they fail to move between socially legitimated positions, and indeed are not oriented towards re-entry into an established social role, such individuals can find themselves in a permanently marginal position in relation to their fellow members of society. Van Gennep argues that movement between social roles is accomplished, traditionally, through a three-stage ritual or rite. He uses the terms *separation, liminality* and *reintegration* to describe these stages. In order to change status, to make a lifecourse transition, the individual must be separated from their previous position within social structure. That they are moving into a new social category – wife, adult, widow – is signalled by their passage through a differently structured or anti-structural boundary zone which separates them from both their previous and future positions within social structure. This is the liminal period, a word deriving from the latin *limen*, meaning threshhold. The time of change and ambiguity, according to this model, is safely sandwiched between times of stability and permanence. As noted, however, Van Gennep's initial ideas have been used by anthropologists and other social scientists to develop a broader explanation of the ways in which enduring aspects of society relate to its more fluid elements. For example, just as the new social identity of the adult individual or the married individual is created out of their experiences during the liminal period, so, it is argued, the ordered use of time and space within the working week emerges out of the differently ordered experience of the weekend, the holiday or the carnival. In the sharp contrast between what happens during the liminal period and the time and space that precedes and follows it, individuals find their sense of who they are both transformed and clarified. Importantly, in this view, it is the agency or culturally specific choices and behaviour of individuals which produces a particular kind of social order.

The boundary zone, whether it be a time of initiation, marriage, childbirth or death, is therefore critical as an aspect of the system through which groups of individuals are distinguished from one another. It gives shape to the entire social structure. At the same time, it is threatening or dangerous in that it represents the confusion of categories. Passage through the liminal period involves exposure to danger in that customary rules are upturned. However, that which is dangerous is also that which is powerful, and it is the intensity of the experience, often involving ordeals of pain or humiliation, which ensures that a change has taken place.

Other examples of societies' boundary zones are the no-man's-land between battle lines, the limbo between Heaven and Hell, the betwixt and the between period which comes after a death and before a funeral.

Liminality also characterises the airport departure lounge – the boundary between earthbound and airborne travel; the doctor's waiting room – the boundary between lay and medical space; and the church porch – the boundary between secular and sacred space. In each example, uncertainty prevails in some form, and normal rules of activity or behaviour may be suspended. Liminal periods are the times and spaces that allow us to engage in a process that Victor Turner calls 'describing the continuous in discontinuous terms' (Turner, 1974, p. 297). That is, they allow us to know and understand our social and material environment as a result of the distinctions we make between its salient features. Without boundaries we would not be able to distinguish one aspect of our environment from another. However, individuals who are undergoing social exclusion – divorced, disabled or chronically sick people, for example – may experience a permanent liminality in that they are not moving between established boundaries. Turner used the term 'liminoid' to describe such social groups (Turner, 1974).

What we often find at boundary times and spaces are ambiguous beings who epitomise the confusion of the categories we normally use to organise ourselves and our worlds. Examples are drag queens and pantomime horses, beings who appear in the times between periods of daily work – such as Christmas time, New Year or carnival time. They are neither men nor women nor animals. As beings who occupy the boundary they confuse or play with the way in which we label the world around us. In being both male and female, or human and animal, at one and the same time, they remind us of the distinctions we are accustomed to making between genders and species. Sometimes they help us to remain clear about the way we normally see the world; sometimes they become disturbing reminders that the world may not be as we assume it to be.

To what extent does this kind of model help us to understand experiences such as Laurie Lee's departure from his childhood home? When he sets out from the fixed point of his village, he leaves his family behind him and moves into a period of nomadic wandering, a time of uncertainty and insecurity. He is betwixt and between youth and manhood, carrying forward the sustaining food and the nurturing memories of home, yet soon to become reliant upon his own means of independent subsistence, his violin. Indeed, the customary food of his childhood, the treacle biscuits, changes its meaning when eaten on a roadside stone wall. Rather than being just a reliable source of pleasure and nutrition, it becomes a symbol of a domestic world he has left behind, something which, once consumed, will not be replaced. When individuals enter one of the liminal spaces of later life – the residential or nursing home – they often have similar experiences, as the following example indicates:

> The passage of deteriorating individuals through Highfield House is submerged in this unchanging, depersonalised environment. Only the small bedside rugs, the trinket boxes, the remnants of former dinner services or table linen, and the mantlepiece clocks serve as personal reminders – or iconic representations – of entire, lost domestic contexts. (Hockey, 1990, p. 99)

Just as Lee's experience of his mother's food is transformed when framed within the liminal space of a lifecourse transition, so these older people relate differently to domestic objects which once formed part of an enduring whole but now stand, abstracted, as items of personal memorabilia rather than of family use or ornament.

The theme of passage into a period of ambiguity or indefinability as a way of producing changed perceptions, and therefore personal transformation, is characteristic of the way Van Gennep understood the concept of rites of passage. He defines them as 'rites which accompany every change of place, state, social position and age' (Turner, 1969). Laurie Lee, for example, describes 'tasting the extravagant quality of being free on a weekday'. Four years as an office junior had, he said, 'kept me pretty closely tied' (Lee, 1969, p. 14). The extravagant quality that time now acquires for Lee can be seen as a product of its ambiguous status. Lee has left paid employment but is still seeking to gain a living, through independent busking. His time is therefore neither clearly defined as work time nor as leisure time, the two key opposed temporal categories through which life is organised in twentieth-century Western societies. As we shall see in further examples, changed perceptions of time are a frequent dimension of lifecourse transitions.

Building on Van Gennep's concept of liminality as the key to change of both an individual and social kind, we can move on to look at other examples. Contrast, often referred to as opposition, and ambiguity are the central characteristics that Van Gennep and other social anthropologists such as Turner have associated with liminality (Turner, 1969). In the example of traditional Christian marriage, passage through a time of uncertainty which contrasts markedly with both single and married life is evident in the experiences of the bride and bridegroom. Customarily, they are kept in isolation from one another to mark the first stage of their wedding ritual. This corresponds to what Van

Gennep would see as the first stage of a rite of passage, separation. Divided from one another they are then introduced into an ambiguous time and space where alcohol plays a primary role in disorienting and dislocating the familiar order of their lives. The greater licence granted to young men in their everyday public lives often calls for more extreme forms of dislocation, and some bridegrooms eventually find themselves trouserless and chained to a lamp-post at some distance from home. However, young women too will engage in explicit sexual banter, in some cases being paraded in the streets by workmates with lewd slogans pinned to their clothing. Sally Westwood provides an account of such a ritual among young women in a hosiery factory in the early 1980s. Prior to a wedding, a 'working day' would be given over to putting the bride-to-be in fancy dress, made during working hours from the factory's materials, and a long lunch hour of heavy drinking. This upturning of customary rules and roles culminated in a noisy group of women careering through the streets and tying up the bride-to-be in public space outside the factory. Management took no steps to curtail this ritual (Westwood, 1984). On the basis of this kind of evidence, we can argue that the differentiation normally made between being single and being married, often a boundary that parallels that between youth and adulthood, is held in place by a liminal period. Here, time and space is used very differently, chaos appears to rule, and rules themselves are upturned. The young woman on her hen night is not therefore just having a wild night on the town with 'the girls'. She is leaving behind the rule-bound 'freedom' of her youth and making a lifecourse transition into the role of wife, a social category where a different system of order will pertain.

Marriage is an institution characterised by the union of two separate people. We can see this in the use of the image of marriage to symbolise the union of the Christian with God, the nun becoming the metaphorical 'bride' of Christ. Yet marriage is entered into via a spatial and temporal boundary where bride and groom are kept apart. As a central, liminal period, it has characteristics that contrast markedly with the time before, when bride and groom first 'got together', and the time to follow, when man and wife will become 'one flesh'. The first and third stages of the ritual stand in opposition to the middle stage. Yet within the chaos of the stag and hen nights, we find elements that presage the priorities and values of the married life for which bride and groom are being prepared. The transition from sexual inactivity, traditionally required of women prior to marriage, to sexual activity with one partner within the privacy of home and family, is experienced via an overstated public performance of sex-related behaviour. Similarly, animals customarily used to highlight the stereotypical differences between masculinity and femininity, the aristocratic deer and the backyard chicken, are drawn upon, in quintessentially male and female forms, the stag and the hen, to frame the time and space of transition. Having grown 'close' during their engagement, bride and groom, hen and stag, are rigorously set apart, before finally being 'joined together in holy matrimony'. The required marital sex, conducted within the framework of stereotypical masculinity and femininity, is therefore both alluded to and parodied within the liminal period. While sexual mores of this kind are no longer common among many social groups within contemporary Western society, allusions to pre-marital virginity for women persist in practices such as the wearing of white bridal gowns. Although many people are not practising Christians, within the context of a nominally Christian culture the myth of sexual innocence followed by sexual fidelity arguably can be seen as a condensed symbolic form through which the more generalised exclusivity associated with highly privatised social relationships is made visible in contemporary society.

It would seem that by developing a model of a rite of passage Van Gennep has provided social scientists with a way of explaining the experience of 'getting married'. Drawing on this model, we can show how participation in a traditional Christian wedding can produce a sense of changing, and being changed, from a single to a married person. As noted, however, aspects of this ritual may none the less fail to concur with contemporary beliefs and practices. For example, couples without Christian beliefs who are expecting their first child may nevertheless choose to marry in traditional style in a church. In this sacred space, the death ritual of non-believers may also be staged, an event within which both the mourners and the minister may feel unable to fully acknowledge features of the dead person's life that are at odds with core social values – for example, the grief of a previous spouse; stigmatising illnesses such as AIDS; mental health problems; and suicide. In the material that follows we examine rites of passage in more traditional societies where, it might appear, holistic forms of social consensus persist. By looking outside the West, social anthropologists in particular have traced patterns of belief and practice which suggest a more coherent social milieu. However, it is important to recognise that many such societies are also characterised by inequalities based on gender (Jeffery, 1979); and power and control may be the outcome of interpersonal struggles rather than the unfolding of traditional patterns of authority (Strathern, 1971). Rites of passage can therefore be as much about legitimating inequalities, or symbolically reconciling long-term political tensions, as they are about providing for the expression of individual aspirations and emotions.

From this perspective, we now look in more detail at some examples of lifecourse transitions from this body of material. They reflect three separate points in the lifecycle – birth, marriage and death. Questions will be raised in connection with three themes that are central to this chapter: What kinds of connection are made between social and biological change during a rite of passage? To what extent can rites of passage be seen to create lifecourse transitions that are relational? And how is the relationship between individual and social change articulated through a rite of passage? The first example to be examined is childbirth among the Zulu of South Africa, as described in Harriet Sibisi's ethnography (Ardener, 1993).

Childbirth, initiation and death

Sibisi's account of childbirth among Zulu women exemplifies the notion of a lifecourse transition as a time of danger, for pregnancy among the Zulu was associated with the threatening boundary zone between life and death. In becoming mothers, therefore, women passed through a liminal time and space within which the biological changes associated with pregnancy, childbirth and lactation were imbued with particular social meanings. Biological and social change could therefore be said to concur. For many Western women, the social transition to parenthood and the physiological changes associated with reproduction are similarly concurrent, though a more detailed comparison shows that the exact relationship between social and bodily change is different in different societies. Thus pregnant Zulu women often smeared the soles of their feet with red ochre to protect them during their dangerous passage. They were required to withdraw completely from society into a house of confinement at the time of childbirth, there to be attended only by married women. During the ten days following the birth they were allowed out only if covered by a blanket. Following this period it was required that they smear exposed parts of their bodies – arms, legs and face – with red ochre. During lactation, as in pregnancy, the soles of their feet were likely to be smeared to protect them.

The lifecourse transition Zulu women went through at the time of the birth of their children took a particular social form by virtue of the implications of this transition for the male members of the society. As wives and mothers, women were seen to possess negative mystical forces which intensified during the liminal period of a rite of passage. In other words, pregnancy, childbirth and lactation among women was a social change which carried profound threats to men's cattle, crops and virility. Zulu society traced descent through the male but not the female line, and men's power was strongly associated with their virility. However men's dominance endured only if women were fertile – a relationship of dependency that was a source of potential power for women. The rite of passage experienced by women in this setting was therefore one that rendered them invisible, either literally when they were in the house of confinement, or metaphorically when blanketed and smeared with ochre. Social practices such as these produced a society where men's power was uncontested, and women's power was made illegitimate.

Sibisi's example is one that concurs with the concerns of an anthropology which sought to understand how social stability was maintained in the face of the passage of its members. Childbirth is an occasion when lifecourse changes throw up forms of power that threaten to destabilise a balanced, gendered asymmetry. What Sibisi shows is how that threat is defused and stability maintained.

If we move on to examine female initiation among the Bemba of north-eastern Zambia, a focus in the work of both Audrey Richards (1956) and Jean La Fontaine (1966), we find similar issues of gender-based power foregrounded within a lifecourse transition. Initiation into marriageable adulthood for adolescent Bemba girls came about through a ritual known as *chisungu*. Turner describes it as 'one of the best examples of the metaphorical destruction of structure that I know' (1974, p. 295). By this he is referring to its extended and elaborate liminal phase during which the underlying structures of girlhood were systematically and symbolically destroyed. This example illustrates the often complex relationship between biological growth and social transition. The Bemba would say that 'We do the rite to grow the girl' (La Fontaine, 1966, p. 121). In other words, although it is a ritual that took place during adolescence, it might or might not coincide with the onset of menstruation, the biological change seen by Westerners as indicating the end of childhood. *Chisungu* was a group ritual, and not all the girls 'made to grow' would have begun to mature physically. Richards described *chisungu* as both a ceremony and a ritual, in the sense that while ceremonies mark changes that are already under way, ritual creates change. This ceremony/ritual therefore not only marked whatever biological growth the girls might already have displayed, it also created their social transition from girlhood to womanhood through a complex series of tests – crawling backwards and jumping over fires, for example. It was the successful performance of these new behaviours by the girls that produced 'growth' – the required outcome of the ritual.

The 'growth' of the girls was, however, just one aspect of lifecourse transition among the Bemba. Theirs was a society where descent was traced through the female but not the male line, yet where men sought to create for themselves a dominant position. *Chisungu* ritual preceded the marriage of young girls to men to whom they were already betrothed. Its symbolism presaged the complex gendered inter-dependencies that were the hallmark of Bemba girls' future lives. Thus the young bridegroom who symbolically entered the *chisungu* ritual did so in the vulnerable position of an outsider who was seeking member-ship of a female dominated extended family, or lineage. Only the girl's ritual performance of submissiveness would entice him in. It was a performance that belied her family-based power as a woman, yet she too was vulnerable in that the female-dominated group required bride-grooms in order that they might reproduce their line. Similarly, while the new bridegroom initially occupied a low status position as an outsider, his future daughters would eventually draw in a further generation of male outsiders who, as his sons-in-law, would become his followers. The girls' lifecourse transition was therefore one that served to reposition her female kin, her father and her bridegroom as well as to create the conditions for the production of her future offspring. Lasting for about a month, this ritual had, in fact, relational implications which endured across generations and family lines of descent.

Bemba girls therefore made the transition to adulthood and marriageability as one movement within a whole range of others. Their individual biography can be seen to be intimately linked with collective social life. What this example also shows, in considerable detail, is the nature of the relationship between the individual's world view and wider cultural values and beliefs. Thus Bemba girls were repositioned within social space in such a way that their culturally specific world view underwent changes. Rituals of initiation are often described as a time when secret knowledge is imparted to novices. What Richards and La Fontaine highlighted was the fact that the knowledge to which Bemba girls were exposed was neither secret nor new. Rather than a body of knowledge, what the girls learnt was to think about and experience the world from an adult standpoint. That which they 'knew' previously was re-learnt and understood differently. Gardening, for example, which had previously been performed in a leisurely manner, now had to be approached with a new sense of urgency and responsibility; its meaning for the emergent woman had changed. Her world view, as an individual, derived from her exposure to, and appropriation of, culturally specific bodies of knowledge.

Chisungu shows the characteristics of Van Gennep's rite of passage in that it involved the separation of the girls from their previous positions within social structure, a process achieved through both their seclusion from the everyday world, and through the destruction of symbols of their previous social status. During this liminal period they were made subservient to older women, a position within which they were receptive to the acquisition of new knowledge and skills. Returned to Bemba society at the end of the ritual, they were reintegrated as women rather than girls. Not only were they regarded by their fellows as different people; they were also, within themselves, reoriented towards their social and material world.

Finally we consider Hertz's account of funeral ritual among the Dayak people of Borneo (Hertz, 1960). Again, we ask how social and biological changes are linked within this ritual, what the relational dimensions of death ritual might be, and whether it encompasses individual as well as collective life. What appears to differentiate this form of funerary ritual from Christian funerals in the West was its shape. At death, the body of the deceased was ritually located on a platform, often high up in a tree: its first 'burial'. This was associated with the soul's departure from the body and the separation of bereaved people from their customary roles and duties. While the flesh disintegrated, the soul and the survivors remained isolated, occupying an ambiguous or liminal position in relation to those among whom they formerly lived. Only when the body achieved its final skeletal state was the body interred: its second 'burial'. This ritual transformed the wandering soul into an ancestor. It also repositioned the survivors within society in their new roles – as widow, orphan or new family head. Funerary ritual comprising two 'burials' and a linking period of bodily, spiritual and social ambiguity, clearly conforms closely to the classic *rite de passage* model, subsequently formulated by Van Gennep.

For the Dayak peoples, therefore, the lifecourse transition of a death ritual was a social process built around a continuum of biological changes. This contrasts with the contemporary Western concern with death as a biological event that takes place at a fixed moment in time – a boundary which divides without connecting. Indeed, we are accustomed, as Westerners, to ethical debates as to the precise moment that death can be said to have occurred. Legal and medical opinions vary as to whether it is the loss of brain function or the cessation of the heartbeat and independent breathing that constitutes death. In the tragic case of Tony Bland, the young man who suffered irreversible brain damage in 1988 as a result of being crushed in the crowd at Hillsborough football stadium, medical technology allowed his lungs to continue to inflate and his heart to beat. The ethical dilemma concerned the act of switching off his life support machines. If Tony Bland was defined as 'living', then that act was one which 'killed' him. If he was defined as 'dead' then medical technology was merely manufacturing the symptoms of life in a corpse. What the months of legal and medical wrangling indicate is that this young man represented an ambiguity in that he could not easily be categorised as either alive or dead.

The absence of a liminal period between life and death within contemporary Western society has become an implicit focus within work addressed to death, dying and bereavement from the 1960s onwards (Kubler-Ross, 1970; Parkes, 1972). Unlike the extended periods of mourning Victorian women underwent, the transition from wife to widow is given little public ritual expression nowadays, other than the thirty minutes allotted for a funeral. As a result, individuals can experience difficulty in making sense of what has occurred, finding themselves unable to reintegrate the dead into their lives, albeit in a new form (Walter, 1996). In a similar vein, the transition from childhood to adulthood for Westerners, though marked by what might appear to be the liminal space of adolescence, is none the less unclear (James and Prout, 1990). For example, in the UK, the age of consent to heterosexual intercourse is sixteen; the age of consent to marriage is eighteen; the age at which a motorbike licence can be granted is seventeen; and the age at which alcohol can be purchased and a vote cast at elections is eighteen.

Among the Dayak, the twin concepts of life and death, while being distinguished from one another, were, however, connected by a liminal period. Thus the social transition from wandering soul to ancestor and from bereaved relative to repositioned member of society took place in close association with the corpse's organic processes of decomposition – a period which could last from between seven months to six years. While the cost of the second burial often meant it was postponed until resources could be accumulated, this social event still remained closely tied to biological changes in that the body had first to attain a skeletal condition. As in the case of *chisungu* ritual among the Bemba, the social process of a lifecourse transition was linked with biological changes, but in a complex fashion.

The parallel transitions of the body, the soul and the survivors not only reveal a particular relationship between social and biological change, they also illustrate the relational nature of lifecourse transitions. The death of one of the society's members resulted in a series of transitions – the world of the ancestors admitted a new member, and the living were eventually reintegrated into society in new positions. However, as Hertz noted, the bodies of children aged under seven were often enclosed in trees, the place from which their spirits were believed to have come, rather than making the transition to the social world of the ancestors. As Hertz said, 'since society has not yet given anything of itself to the child, it is not affected by its disappearance and remains indifferent' (1960, p. 84). Older people who had ceased to participate in social life were similarly exempt from extended funerary ritual in societies such as native Australian peoples. Their eventual death carried few relational implications, as others had already taken over their roles.

How does Hertz's anthropological account relate to Harris's concern with time and transition as both individual and collective experiences? Hertz was writing during an era when human emotion was seen as something to be studied only in terms of individual experience. Like Durkheim however, Hertz was interested in the social nature of apparently individualistic phenomena. Thus, Durkheim sought to show that the suicide rate was a 'social fact' in that aspects of people's social lives, such as their marital status or their religious practices, had a causal effect upon the rate of suicide within a given population (Durkheim, 1952). Hertz began his account of the practice of double burial with an acknowledgement that, at the time, it was felt that 'we all believe we know what death is because it is a familiar event and one that arouses intense emotion. It seems both ridiculous and sacrilegious to wish to apply reason to a subject where only the heart is competent' (Hertz 1960, p. 27). What he went on to argue was that the application of the social scientist's 'reason' facilitates an understanding of how 'personal feelings' become subject to the requirements of the 'social consciousness'. Death, he argued, 'is the object of a collective representation' (p. 28). In the work of Hertz, as well as Durkheim, we therefore find social scientists offering accounts of how the individual and the social relate to one another. In both cases, society is seen as an overarching entity that shapes individual experience. Thus Hertz says 'whatever [mourners'] personal feelings may be, they have to show sorrow for a certain period' (1960, p. 27). This view of the susceptibility of individual emotion to collective behaviours or representations is echoed by Durkheim, who argues that 'Men do not weep for the dead because they fear them; they fear them because they weep for them' (Huntington and Metcalf, 1979, p. 33). In other words, participation in collective practices such as ritual weeping produces emotion within the individual – in this case, fear that the dead might become malevolent.

The notion that emotional experience is something learned through social participation is, however, at odds with the commonsense Western view that emotion is a 'natural' phenomenon that in some way rises up unpredictably within the body (Hockey, 1993). If we take this 'commonsense' view, social institutions such as religion will be seen as strategies that have developed in order to organise, control or civilise our more animal-like or instinctual natures. Social scientists, from Durkheim onwards, have taken issue with this view, although the alternative explanations they have provided are not necessarily consistent with one another. Here we have examined an example of the view that individual experience is profoundly shaped by society. It is a view of society as something greater than the sum of its individual members and can be contrasted, broadly, with the view of social reality as the product of a myriad individual interactions, theoretical views which were discussed at greater length in Chapter 1.

Postmodern or post-traditional?

Each of these three ethnographic examples is drawn from a society outside 'the West'. While the notion that these are 'primitive' or 'less evolved' societies has been shown to be both inaccurate and racist (Lévi-Strauss, 1966), they can none the less be described as more traditional societies. In other words, their forms of social organisation and patterns of behaviour are less fluid and heterogenous than those to be found within contemporary Western society. In comparison, contemporary Western society has been described as postmodern in that the major large-scale institutions of modern Western states – for example, the Church, corporate industry, health services – have become fragmented and fluid in both their structure and function (see Docherty, 1993). The same may be said for their belief systems or ideologies. Some commentators are less persuaded of this view, arguing that large scale social structures remain firmly in place, particularly where less wealthy or less powerful members of society are concerned (see Doyal, 1995).

Giddens argues, more convincingly, that contemporary Western society can be described as post-traditional rather than postmodern (Giddens, 1991). This perspective echoes Durkheim's notion of the shift from societies that functioned through mechanical solidarity, with all individuals making similar contributions to forms of social and economic organisation, to societies that functioned through organic solidarity, with individuals contributing interdependently in more specialised and differentiated ways to society as a whole (Durkheim, 1984). Giddens highlights the breakdown of taken-for-granted patterns of thought and behaviour. In their place, he suggests, has come a degree of diversity and choice that is foreign outside the West. As noted throughout this volume, the notion that individuals can stand outside something called 'society' and make entirely subjective choices is highly problematic. Giddens, however, counters the charge that choice is available only to the wealthy or powerful by providing evidence of innovative lifestyles being developed among the members of social groups where regular paid work and fixed patterns of heterosexual, patriarchal family life are uncommon. In social contexts where there is an absence of any taken-for-granted passage through life, choices are being made about living arrangements and economic resources. These choices may not receive the approval of more powerful groups within society, being condemned on both moral and legal grounds. They may be highly limited. Indeed, they may not be deemed desirable by those who make them. They can, none the less, be contrasted with fixed patterns of social and economic organisation that are followed unquestioningly across generations within traditional societies.

If, as social scientists, we continue to seek understanding of life-course transitions, what are the implications of a perspective that argues that contemporary societies are no longer patterned by tradition, and indeed for many individuals transitions such as marriage, apprenticeship or retirement are now uncommon? Traditional Christian weddings have already been cited as events consistent with Van Gennep's model of a rite of passage. Indeed, Diana Leonard's study of weddings in Swansea in 1968 yielded material showing a passage through a three-stage ritual, marked by separation, liminality and reintegration. Choice lay in the area of *who* to marry, rather than *whether* to marry. As Leonard says 'One does not choose not to get married, one fails to get married' (1980, p. 9). What none the less must be recognised is that such a pattern is now followed as a matter of choice. As Giddens argues, even those who engage in traditional behaviours, do so in the knowledge that this is a choice rather than an inevitability. For example, Christian rites of passage such as baptism, confirmation, marriage, the churching of women, and even the funeral, are often engaged in as a matter of choice. Individuals cannot remain unaware, on some level, that alternatives are open to them. Registry office weddings and humanist funerals, for example, are viable options for many contemporary Westerners. They can be compared with rituals such as *chisungu* that are powerful by virtue of the fact that their liminal periods involve the exclusion of alternative pathways or ways of seeing. They present the initiand with injunctions. The world is, without question, the way it is represented.

This is not to say, however, that post-traditional societies are without rituals that operate in this way. Evangelical Christianity, for example, offers rituals which take effect precisely through a strategy of excluding alternatives. 'I am the Way, the Truth and the Light' is a statement that does not admit of other avenues to religious experience. Those who attend evangelical rallies may feel a compulsion to participate. To go forward for baptism comes to be seen as the one and only viable form of behaviour. Choice is redundant. Nevertheless, participation in religious rituals of this kind takes place within a broader social forum where religious affiliation and practice is now very much a matter of choice. Indeed, religious freedom is seen to be one of the hallmarks of democracy, and the representation of conflict in Northern Ireland as the use of violence towards individuals because of their different religious affiliation is viewed very critically by many English people.

If choice characterises lifecourse transitions in ways that are alien outside the West, to what extent does the model of a *rite de passage* help us understand how social identity is not only formed but also transformed. In Giddens' view, a post-traditional world is one where social change has accelerated to an extent that profoundly affects the nature of individual lifecourse transition (Giddens, 1991). He contrasts it with a traditional society where ritual enabled the reorganisation of personal identity, and where 'things stayed more or less the same from generation to generation on the level of the collectivity, the changed identity was clearly staked out' (1991, p. 31). In a post-traditional society, he argues, 'the altered self has to be explored and constructed as part of a reflexive process of connecting personal and social change' (p. 31). Thus he cites therapy and self-help personal growth manuals as being more central to contemporary lifecourse transitions than collective ritual.

The exercise of choice is indeed evident in studies of Western life-course transitions. While Leonard's study of weddings in Swansea in the late 1960s suggested an undiminished commitment to marriage among young people, K. Beuret and L. Makings' mid-1980s research found that within the context of high unemployment among young working-class men, young women employed as hairdressers were approaching the traditional lifecourse transitions of courtship and marriage in a far more flexible way. For example, the authors found them unwilling to abandon female friendships during the courtship period, interested in delaying marriage to boyfriends, and even questioning the advantages of marriage at all. Young women are cited as making observations such as:

> When I left school I couldn't wait to get married. I used to stick pictures of wedding dresses in my bedroom even. But now I'm thinking twice.

and:

> I've got used to being independent now. I do love John but I prefer seeing him rather than living with him. I work hard at this job and I want to start my own business soon. Marriage could put paid to all that. One day but not now. (Beuret and Makings, 1987, p. 71)

An independent income, the pleasures of female friendship and the self esteem accrued through a varied lifestyle were attractions women set alongside love, sex and marriage when anticipating their futures. Material gathered in this study exemplifies Giddens' argument that the self has now become a reflexive project, an entity to be selfconsciously constructed rather than unquestioningly lived out. Furthermore, Beuret and Makings' informants were not middle-class therapy-group participants, but young working-class women. Their views on marriage suggest that choice is not something that is merely the prerogative of wealthier, middle-class individuals.

Unemployment has been a central focus in many studies of lifecourse transitions among young people. C. Griffin reviews a range of such studies, putting forward the view that male unemployment is often overemphasised in terms of its tendency to lead to 'broken transitions', while the role of sexuality, courtship, and indeed employment, among young women is under-researched (Griffin, 1987).

Conclusion

This chapter has examined lifecourse transition as both a theoretical issue and a substantive topic. We have traced the development of social science perspectives from early sociological and anthropological views, which tended to use a model of society that highlighted both its permanence and its overarching cohesiveness. Individual transition was therefore understood in terms of a potentially disruptive movement from one fixed point to the next, rites of passage having the function of protecting both the individual and their fellows from disorder and confusion. Society itself was conceived of as an entity external to the individual, but which exercised considerable control over their life. As we have seen, developments within social theory have now highlighted the actions of individuals and groups as the source of society itself. In other words, rituals associated with lifecourse transitions not only serve to produce new social individuals, but also through their symbols regenerate the belief system of the social group as a whole.

In tracing the development of social theory across the twentieth century we have also asked about the effects of profound social and economic change upon patterns of everyday life. Leonard's (1980) and Beuret and Makings' (1987) work on weddings encompasses a fairly brief twenty-year period. However, the changes in young people's employment patterns during this period are of so far-reaching a nature as to have significant effects upon the ways in which the lifecourse transition of marriage is undertaken by young women. In Giddens' view, the formal rite of passage undergone by the participants in Leonard's study of weddings is not defunct but profoundly altered in that it is now one of the range of options an individual may select, and not an unquestioned requirement (Giddens, 1991).

While the rites of passage described in non-Western societies – childbirth, initiation and death – have bodily change as their focus, it would seem that within many contemporary Western societies, economic rather than biological change is central to lifecourse transition. Thus graduation, once the prerogative of those granted a university degree, is now staged for those gaining other qualifications such as Higher National Diplomas. Gowns, ritual headgear, worthy speakers, parents and official photographers, the elements of a traditional graduation ceremony, are now brought together when other kinds of qualification are conferred. Central to these occasions is the belief that individuals now possess enhanced economic potential.

In summary, while some traditional rites of passage may have changed in nature, by virtue of becoming optional, others have disappeared or become less common. Research that highlights the loss of traditional transitions often relates this development to changes in patterns of work. Thus unemployment is seen to account not only for a different approach to weddings, but also a changed experience of retirement, a transition that has traditionally marked the onset of later life. T. Schuller argues that retirement 'is increasingly a process which extends over time, rather than a clear-cut event, and this process involves a much higher level of ambiguity than previously' (1989, p. 44). Material such as this illustrates Harris's argument that individual biographies can no longer be separated from broader historical developments. As such, the study of lifecourse transitions, in his view, is of broad relevance as a way of making sense of the relationship between the individual and society.

4

Sexuality

What is sexuality?

At first sight, the question with which we begin this chapter seems unnecessary. At a commonsense level we all know, or think we know, what sexuality is, and it pervades life in our culture. Virtually everything is sexualised, from battleships to lavatory paper. Sexuality is used to sell commodities, and indeed we ourselves are commodities, snapped up or 'left on the shelf' according to our sexual desirability. Nevertheless, when we reflect more deeply we quickly see just how complex the notion of 'sexuality' is. It is different from, but related to, those of 'sex' and 'gender', and each of these terms is conceptually complex in its own right. J. Weekes (1986) notes that the term 'sex' refers to an act, to a category of person, to a practice and to a gender.

There are no simple, agreed definitions and there are differing viewpoints, theoretical perspectives and research traditions. Knowledge and understanding are inseparable from personal and political values and power relations. In this chapter we shall explore some of the ways in which people have attempted to understand sexuality and the issues these raise. Indeed, on a broader front, if we wish to examine the relationship between biology, culture and the self, sexuality is a useful area to explore as tensions between differing discourses and levels of understanding are very clear.

Weekes draws our attention to one central paradox in our thinking about sexuality:

[It] is an assumption which is deeply embedded in our culture: that our sexuality is the most spontaneously natural thing about us. It is the basis of our most passionate feelings and commitments. Through it, we experience ourselves as real people; it gives us our identities, our sense of self, as men and women, as heterosexual and homosexual, 'normal' or 'abnormal', 'natural' or 'unnatural'. Sex has become, as the French philosopher Michel Foucault famously put it, 'the truth of our being'. But what is this 'truth'? And on what basis can we call something 'natural' or 'unnatural'? Who has the right to lay down the laws of sex? Sex may be 'spontaneous' and 'natural'. But it has not stopped an endless barrage of advice on how best to do it. (Weekes, 1986, p. 13)

If sexuality is something deeply rooted in our 'nature' how is it that we need to learn how to do it and develop a variety of religious, moral and even legal rules and regulations about who it is appropriate to do it with, when, where and how? This question highlights a tension between our concepts of 'nature' and 'culture', which is apparent in much that is said or written about sexuality.

Nature or culture?

The assumption that sexuality is fundamentally a biological pheno-menon is widespread and powerful. The existence of observable differ-ences in the external sex organs of men and women gives credence to the immense social significance ascribed to sex difference. This extends far beyond our reproductive function into every aspect of our lives. There are some parallels between this and the significance ascribed to observable differences in skin colour. What might be seen as a functional physical difference is invested with social meaning which, in both cases, works as a powerful oppressive ideology by over-simplifying a complex phenomenon. One way in which difference is simplified is by categorising it into dichotomies or binary opposites, such as black and white, or male and female. This leads us to disregard the vast range of human complexions and ways of being male and female.

Further oppressive simplification is accomplished by a form of 'reductive' reasoning that has dominated Western scientific thinking and research throughout its history. This form of reasoning can be a valuable tool and basically involves the notion that complex pheno-mena can be reduced or broken down into simpler or more basic elements. In the history of science this has led to a search for more and more fundamental explanations, such as seeing the structure of all matter in the universe as made up of fundamental particles. It is a way of thinking that can be very powerful and has proved fruitful in the development of science. However, reductive thinking can become an ideology itself – 'reductionism' – when it is elevated to the model of all scientific reason and seen as mirroring the construction of the world. This can lead to whole structures being seen as no more than the sum of parts or elements, and to disregarding the importance of the intricate ways in which these interact. Former Prime Minister Margaret Thatcher's view that 'there is no such thing as society', is a case in point. Such thinking can be dangerous and can result in highly complex phenomena such as 'race' and sexuality being reduced to simplistic biological categories and linked directly to psychological and social attributes. As a result characteristics such as 'emotionality', 'irrationality' and 'low intelligence' are picked out. They are defined as in some way immature or inferior and linked to the possession of dark skin or female genitalia. In this way, reductionism is used to justify discrimination and oppression.

In this context, let us answer the question as to whether sexuality is a matter of biology or culture, nature or nurture by rejecting the assumption. The question as posed is unanswerable. In this form it suggests a false dichotomy (an either/or) which only serves to illustrate how the ideology of sexism works by oversimplification. Sexuality is determined on a number of biological, psychological and cultural levels, each complex in itself and existing in complex interaction with other levels. J. Reinisch and R. Beasley identify nine categories necessary to describe human sex, gender and reproductive capacity (Reinisch and Beasley, 1991). These are: chromosomal sex; gonadal sex; hormonal sex; sex of internal organs; sex of external organs; sex assigned at birth; gender identity/role; and sexual orientation identity. They link these categories with the development of sexuality from conception to adulthood. Each combines, in a whole range of ways, with characteristics in each of the other categories to determine the sexuality of any one person. Moreover, we must not discount the importance of choice or self-determination. Sexuality is also a form of chosen self-expression sometimes linked with and defining a form of personality and a whole life-style.

We can see, then, that the inclination to think of sexuality as something 'natural' or biologically given is one of the ways in which existing power differentials between women and men are perpetuated. However, the present authors, like Weekes, lean towards a definition that emphasises the cultural and historical construction of 'sexuality', including its construction through theoretical models in sociology and psychology which define, for example, 'normality' and 'perversity'. Seen in this way, 'sexuality' brings together:

> a host of different biological and mental possibilities – gender identity, bodily differences, reproductive capacities, needs, desires and fantasies – which need not be linked together, and in other cultures have not been. All the constituent elements of sexuality have their source either in the body or the mind…But the capacities of the body and the psyche are given meaning only in social relations. (Weekes, 1986, p. 15)

So, sexuality must be seen as something produced socially, in complex ways and in struggles between those who have power to define and regulate, and those who resist. We have begun to see how our 'commonsense' constructions as well as our more systematic knowledge and research traditions are involved in such struggles. In our view, therefore, it is important to see sexuality in terms of a range of characteristics, behaviours and identities that can be partially understood in the light of a variety of theories and research. These, in turn, are discourses and must be seen as representing particular social and political viewpoints. With this in mind, it is to research into sexuality that we must now turn, both to see how our knowledge and understanding are enhanced by theory and research and to ask some critical questions about the ways in which the knowledge produced reflects and perpetuates relationships of power and discrimination.

Research and 'common sense'

There has been an enormous amount of research and writing about sex and sexuality, even if we exclude broader categories of gender research. All this research and writing must, of course, be approached in a reflective and critical way. We must ask: What are the assumptions of the writers and researchers; what questions are they asking, and why? What is the context – cultural/historical, disciplinary/theoretical? What is the political or theoretical viewpoint of the work? Who is reporting; is the source a research report or a discussion of work done by others? What methods and data are involved; in what way does the work seek to describe or explain; how generalisable are the claims and so on? Nevertheless, we look to research for reliable knowledge and rightly see it as having transformed our everyday thinking, freeing us from some of the more repressive traditional and religious beliefs and prescriptions about sex. We have every intention of continuing to recommend critical investigation, but at the same time caution against seeing research as belonging to an entirely different order of thinking than 'common sense'. Frequently, with hindsight, we can identify ways in which, as well as liberating our thinking, research can perpetuate traditional, and often oppressive, views.

Davidson and Layder (1994, ch. 1), for example, demonstrate some of the striking ways in which Western scientific research, first developing in the nineteenth century, reproduces the basic dichotomies and prescriptions that existed in traditional Christian thinking. Scientists, looking at the animal world and seeing sex purely in the context of reproductive activity, argued that species' survival was best served by male dominance, aggression and promiscuity. Extrapolating from this 'evidence' to human society led to the justification of accepted social norms and gender roles, including, of course, men's dominance, aggression and promiscuity, as being 'natural' and ensuring reproductive success. Socially-disapproved activities and relationships, such as promiscuity in women and homosexuality, were similarly seen as harmful, 'unnatural' or 'perverse'. Nineteenth-century sex scientists, or 'sexologists', such as Richard von Krafft-Ebbing catalogued these sexual 'perversities' and defined much non-reproductive sexual activity as 'pathological'. Freud and other psychoanalysts also tended to judge non-reproductive sex negatively, but sometimes saw it, in more developmental terms, as 'immature'.

Whatever the dichotomy implied – moral versus immoral (Christian tradition); natural versus unnatural or beneficial versus harmful to species survival (biology); normal or healthy versus pathological (sexology and medical science); or, mature versus infantile or immature (psychoanalysis) – existing social norms were reinforced. The active sexuality, dominance and aggressiveness expected of men in relation to the passivity, and even masochism, of women was justified, as was the privileging of heterosexuality over other forms of sexual expression.

The exchange between scientific research and 'commonsense' traditional thinking is very much a two-way process. Research findings reflect commonsense judgements in ways that contradict the view of science as 'objective' and free from social values, but equally research findings permeate everyday thinking and affect common sense. It is interesting to note too that in modern Western societies it is under the cloak of science that we feel most free to discuss the details of sexuality, an area of our lives that has been clearly marked as belonging to the private sphere. At other times and in other cultures sexuality has been more in the public sphere, and information and instruction have often been derived not from science but from religious texts such as the fourth-century Hindu text the *Kama Sutra* and ancient Chinese Taoist writings.

Let us now, cautiously and without losing our critical and reflective attitude, explore some of the research and theory relating to sexuality. It is necessary to order and structure our thinking in some way, but this poses some problems as there are a number of different ways of categorising theories and research. We have chosen to organise our thoughts, initially by considering work in two broad traditions, previously introduced, which seek to explore and describe sexuality and sexual activity in relatively 'value neutral' and atheoretical ways. First we shall focus on positivist–empiricist work which can be defined as that which seeks primarily to describe and record 'facts', and identify patterns and correlations or systematic links between variables. It may employ survey methods, interviews, observation and experiments of various kinds. This is a very familiar form of research and we shall include here the ground-breaking work of Alfred Kinsey and that of W. H. Masters and V. E. Johnson. Second, we shall consider briefly interpretative/ethnographic research, defined as that which seeks in some way to describe and understand the subjective experience of people without judging it. It uses self-descriptions such as life stories and narratives, documentary material, case studies and participant observation of cultures and communities.

While acknowledging the value of all this work, we question assumptions implying that it can be value-neutral and atheoretical (see also Chapter 1 of this volume, 'Mapping the Social World'). In the second half of this chapter we shall move on to work that is more explicitly theorised, which consciously goes beyond attempting to describe and categorise and embarks upon the even trickier task of going beneath the surface of observable phenomena and direct experience, to offer explanations of the behaviour and experience described. This approach will be exemplified by work in the psychoanalytic tradition, with the focus on Freud's enormously influential theories in which sexuality is deemed to be both a central motivating force in human life and fundamental to the formation of identity.

All this describing, categorising and explaining encompasses a range of theories and methods, some of which can be seen as being complementary to each other, and some as incompatible or contradictory. None the less, the differing theories and methods all make some claim to being 'scientific' in their approach to sexuality, to be seeking 'truth' –

reliable knowledge free from value judgements and political bias. All the theories and methods fall, in general terms, under what we refer to in Chapter 1 as the project of the Enlightenment and can be viewed as 'modern'. Towards the end of this chapter we shall look at some of the work that is critical of this whole project, is more self-conscious in relation to its value assumptions and political implications, and considers 'scientific' theories and research as discourses that gain power through claiming, as 'science', a monopoly on 'truth'. In this context of 'postmodernism', the stories we tell about ourselves, the narratives we both construct and are constructed by have become a central focus and we shall briefly introduce the study of sexual stories.

Describing and categorising behaviour and experience

To begin our exploration of work in the positivist–empiricist tradition the survey research of Alfred Kinsey and the Kinsey Institute will be reviewed. This American organisation did much to establish and make 'respectable' research in the area of sexuality. Reinisch and Beasley (1991) provide a short summary of its history. They note that in 1938 the Association of Women Students at Indiana University in the USA petitioned the administration for a course in human sexuality for students who were engaged, married or considering marriage. At that time, accurate sexual information was almost impossible to obtain. It was illegal to import or send through the US mail materials with explicit sexual passages, or even contraceptive information. The university asked Alfred Kinsey, a Harvard-trained professor of zoology known for his biology text books and research on gall wasps, to co-ordinate the course. Kinsey found it difficult to find reliable 'scientific' data on human sexual behaviour so he began to collect his own, based on confidential interviews, initially with his students and later with the residents of Bloomington, Indiana, and other towns and cities in America. He asked questions such as: 'Were you a virgin when you got married? How often do you have intercourse? How many sexual partners have you had? Have you ever had an extramarital affair? When did you begin to masturbate and how often do you do so'?

Kinsey's research was controversial and pioneering. By 1941 it had gained financial support from the National Research Council, funded by the Rockefeller Foundation, and in 1947 the Institute for Sex Research was established as a 'not-for-profit' private corporation affiliated to the university. Kinsey's vision was that the Institute would supply accurate, research-based, information with which people could make informed decisions about sexual behaviour.

> In 1948 Kinsey's first book, *Sexual Behaviour in the Human Male*, was published; it included data collected from individual interviews with more than 5,000 males of all ages. For the first time, Americans would be able to find out precisely what went on behind bedroom doors that were not their own. They learned, among other things, that more than 90% of the males questioned said they had masturbated and more than a third said they had at least one sexual experience with another male before puberty. (Reinisch and Beasley, 1991, p. xvi)

Importantly, the book also showed sexual behaviour often continuing until people were into their seventies and eighties. Despite its dry, academic style and tables of data it became an instant best-seller.

> In 1953 the institute released *Sexual Behaviour in the Human Female*, and the public learned that half of the nearly 6,000 women interviewed said they had not been virgins when they married and 25% reported they had engaged in extra-marital sex. This volume, also a best seller, caused much clamour in the press, among the clergy and in Congress. Although most Americans in the early 1950s were willing to accept the fact that men were sexually active beings, few were ready to believe that women engaged in sex for anything other than procreation. (Reinisch and Beasley, 1991, p. xvii)

This volume was published at a time when 'McCarthyism', the 'witch-hunt' of Communists inspired by Senator Joseph McCarthy, was rife in America. The Institute came under attack for doing 'the devil's work' and even for paving the way for a Communist takeover of the United States. It lost funding but managed to survive, and it still survives into the late 1990s as a primary source of sex information in America.

Even this short account serves to indicate the significance of the context of research, its assumptions and methodology. Davidson and Layder (1994) discuss Kinsey's research in some depth, considering sampling techniques and interviewing methods and styles. They also consider its assumptions – for example, that of equating the male average with 'normal'. Kinsey reported that three-quarters of males reached orgasm within two minutes, whereas females, 'who are so adversely conditioned to sexual situations', may require ten to fifteen minutes of careful stimulation and many never climax in their whole lives. He concluded, therefore, that it is demanding the male to be quite abnormal in his ability to prolong sexual activity without ejaculation if he is required to match his female partner (Davidson and Layder, 1994, p.15).

Following Kinsey, survey research into sexual experience and behaviour has remained popular in America and Britain. As well as more serious studies, popular magazines survey readers on a regular basis, maintaining the continuum between common sense and science noted above. We can learn much from all of this, but we must be sensitive to its limitations, and in particular to its tendency to reproduce cultural bias and prejudice. *The Hite Report*, a substantial popular survey first published in 1976, for example, was based on questionnaire responses from 3000 American women (Hite, 1989). It contains verbatim accounts of women's masturbation, their feelings at orgasm, and their evaluations of their sexuality. The research was, however, criticised by some feminist writers for its heterosexual bias, and *The Hite Report on Male Sexuality* took this criticism into account to some extent (Hite, 1990).

Staying within the positivist–empiricist tradition we now move to a consideration of differing methods, of structured observations and physiological studies. The detailed study of sexuality in America pioneered by Kinsey was, as we have seen, largely survey research. However, Kinsey, somewhat impatient of the necessarily second-hand nature of data gathered at interviews, also initiated the use of more direct observational techniques. This paved the way for the structured observations and physiological studies of Masters and Johnson, begun in the 1960s. These, nevertheless, attracted considerable publicity when they were first published (Masters and Johnson, 1966). Although technically-comparable physiological research into the digestive system had been undertaken a century previously, the Masters and Johnson studies were still socially controversial, based as they were on direct observation of sexual activity in structured laboratory settings. Masters and Johnson described 'the sexual response' in terms of four stages based on their observations of 10 000 'sexual cycles', or orgasms. Three-quarters of these were those of women, but they still studied a large number of men's cycles. They observed orgasms achieved in a variety of ways and their four-stage description of the human orgasm applied to both men and women. It was independent of the nature of the sexual activity by which it was achieved and consisted of an 'excitement phase', a 'plateau phase', an 'orgasmic phase' and a 'resolution phase'. The details of what happens to the sexual organs of men and women is different because of their anatomical structure but, according to this research, the physiological mechanism of arousal is the same. This emphasis on similarity is in sharp contrast to much research on sexuality, which seeks to describe and measure differences between men and women. The Masters and Johnson research also focused attention (contrary to that of Sigmund Freud, as we shall see below) on the importance of the clitoris in mature female sexual arousal, whatever the form of sexual activity. The vagina is relatively lacking in nerve endings. Fortunately, in our view, it also supported the somewhat radical notion that female sexual pleasure was quite 'normal'.

This research has been very influential, particularly in the development of 'new sex therapies', which have moved away from an earlier psychoanalytic approach to sexual difficulties towards a combination of behavioural, educational and 'permission-giving' work. There is no doubt that many individuals and couples have been helped to a more satisfying experience of their sexuality as a result of such therapies. Nevertheless, both the research and the therapies assume a basic biological sex drive or appetite directed towards the release of tension through orgasm, which is therefore held to be a measure of good health and an essential component of happiness. So good sex has been defined, in modern sexology, as orgasmic sex, and sex without orgasm has become 'dysfunctional'. There is thus an inbuilt bias towards behaviourally-described, functional performance and, at least implicitly, towards heterosexual encounters culminating in penetration and orgasm.

Survey research and the Masters and Johnson studies exemplify a strong tradition, in Anglo-American research, of gathering large amounts of data. The kinds of generalisation that they make are in terms of averages and norms and, if they seek explanations, these are in terms of suggested causal relationships based on statistical correlations. Comparisons between populations such as 'men' and 'women' are often made, and it is always important to note that, for example, emphasising average differences, which might be statistically significant, tends to divert attention from considerable overlap in characteristics between populations. Moreover, as we have noted, it is often claimed, as it was by Kinsey, that such research is atheoretical, seeking only 'facts' uncontaminated by values or cultural bias. We have already questioned such claims, and we might add that the very notion that it is possible to investigate sexual or any other behaviour without considering the meanings people attach to it, is itself a theoretical assumption, though a common one in the positivist–empiricist tradition. As Davidson and Layder point out, because Kinsey ignored these meanings, he overlooked the problems inherent in classifying sexual behaviours and it is impossible to count the frequency with which something occurs until it has been classified. For example:

> When a prostitute performs the same sex act with a client and with a dearly loved partner, do they count as the same, or should they be classified under different headings? If a wife has non-orgasmic sex with her husband out of a sense of obligation, is this an 'outlet' for her sexual urges? . . . Can rape be counted as an 'outlet' for a man's sexual drive? (Davidson and Layder, 1994, pp. 113–14)

They rightly ask, if these and other sexual acts are counted as the same because (heterosexual) penetration occurs, then what do figures about the frequency of sexual activity contribute to our understanding of human sexual life? We can learn, and have learnt, a great deal which is of value from research in the positivist–empiricist tradition, but it is important not to be 'seduced' by facts and figures into forgetting questions relating to the meaning of sexuality.

We must turn to interpretative/ethnographic work for explorations of meaning. Work in the 'human science' or interpretative tradition, as we saw in Chapter 1 (see the section entitled 'Analysing and Constructing the Social World') seeks to understand social worlds by empathic engagement with people, and by exploring and describing the subjective meanings of social actions. Such meanings are embedded in cultures, or to use Raymond Williams' elegant phrase, 'structures of feeling' (Williams, 1965, p. 64). 'Ethnographic' studies try to describe the quality and texture of a culture, a way of life or 'life-style' from the point of view of the participants. They seek to provide what Geertz (1993) has called a 'thick description'. Robert Stoller provides us with a good example, with his study of the S & M (sadomasochistic) scene in West Hollywood (Stoller, 1991).

Stoller, a practising psychoanalyst, spent several months meeting and interviewing 'sadomasochists'. Early in his book he warns of the dangers of theorising based on too little information, and reminds his psychoanalytic colleagues of the way that technical jargon can obfuscate. Reflecting on a typical psychoanalytic quote, 'Narcissism is the investment of the self-representation with libidinal cathexis, while in masochism a fusion of aggressive and libidinal energies is directed against the self-representation', he comments:

> For I do not know what narcissism is . . . I do not know what libido is or what cathexis is and certainly not what libidinal cathexis is . . . Therefore, I

feel comfortable warning colleagues of some of the mistakes I made: We must be careful, especially those of us who pride ourselves on our empathy, not to think we understand experiences that are well beyond our own; we must be especially careful when our convictions are buttressed by consensual validation. What 'Freud says' may not be good enough. (Stoller, 1991, pp. 4–6)

Stoller audio-taped conversations and used transcriptions as a way of presenting information in an open-minded way. His explorations revealed such a wide range of behaviours that he argues they cannot be viewed as a unitary phenomenon. Over a hundred different kinds of activity were distinguished, and very few included actual pain. Although they could all be classified as 'sadomasochism' from the outside, participants distinguished between S & M; B & D (bondage and discipline) and S & D (submission and dominance), and he concludes that there is no 'sadomasochistic perversion' as such. Whilst Stoller's is essentially an ethnographic study that provides much 'thick description', he does theorise explicitly to some extent. He considers links with childhood trauma and argues that the theatricality of the practices allows people to play out fantasies of harm, humiliation and revenge without actually hurting anyone. Games such as 'master–slave' and 'parent–child' offer an opportunity for past suffering, pain and humiliation to be re-enacted in a dramatic form which allows control over them:

> The imitation of humiliation is carefully constructed *never* to produce true humiliation. The imitation of trauma . . . is not traumatic. Constant high attention to one's partner's experience is more caring and safer than the blundering, ignorant, noncommunicating obtuseness that governs so many 'normal' people's erotic motions . . . We should distinguish those who harm from those who, in trying to undo the effects of harm inflicted on them early in life, play at harm. I believe it is immoral for psychoanalysts to hide their moralising in jargon-soaked theory. (Stoller, 1991, p. 21)

Although ethnographic research has the intention of describing a way of life from the point of view of the participants, it is concerned with the translation of meanings and, as such, cannot avoid a theoretical view. For example, we can see from the above quotation that Stoller represents sadomasochism as 'therapy', a very particular interpretation. Moreover, while empathic in that an 'insider' experience is described and not judged, ethical issues are certainly raised by some of the methods. Covert participation, for example, requires researchers to conceal their identities and deceive the people being researched.

Humphreys (1975) acted as a 'watchqueen', or lookout, for men engaging in casual homosexual behaviour in public toilets: 'tearoom trade'. His study involved both concealment of his own identity as a researcher and the covert noting of car licence-plate numbers which he used for follow-up interviews. Critics have pointed out that confidentiality was at risk by the very fact that such information had been collected and could have got into the wrong hands. Moreover, informed consent was not obtained for the interviews, as both the nature of the research, and the fact the Humphreys had already, covertly, observed behaviour in the toilets, were concealed.

It is clear that all research, whether positivist–empiricist or ethnographic, involves theoretical viewpoints, value positions and ethical issues (see Davidson and Layder, 1994, for a fuller discussion). More recent research in both these traditions tends to be more sensitive to these issues, recognising the relationship between data collection and theory building, while not always being framed with a particular theory or hypothesis to test. It may be prompted by an attitude, such as Stoller's, of curiosity and open-mindedness and can add greatly to our understanding. A further example of such work is provided by Davidson's own research into prostitution (Davidson and Layder, 1994, ch. 9). Nevertheless, one general issue raised by ethnographic research is that of the focus, in common with much anthropology, on 'exotic' subjects such as homosexuality, 'perversion' and prostitution. Stoller caught himself thinking of studying 'specimens in their natural habitat' and had to 'turn from the naive pejorative of *specimens* to the necessary awareness that these are people' (Stoller, 1991, pp. v–vi). This issue is less evident, at least in the area of sexuality, in work in the positivist–empiricists tradition. Perhaps 'normal' sexuality was 'exotic' enough for earlier researchers, and we must remind ourselves of the general tendency, of which much sociology is guilty, to concentrate on categorisations of people, such as 'women', 'the working class', 'ethnic minorities' and 'black people', who are defined by those with power as 'problematic'.

Searching for explanations: the psychoanalytic tradition

As indicated above, work of a quite different order, with a much stronger emphasis on explaining behaviour, feelings and experiences, and in developing a deeper theoretical understanding, can be found in the psychoanalytic tradition rooted in the work of Sigmund Freud. Freud's own ideas and methods were developed over a long period of time, from the 1890s to 1939. Moreover, varying forms of psycho-analytic theory have developed since Freud's time. In addition to a strand of theory often identified as 'Freudian' (including the work of Jacques Lacan), a second important strand associated with the later work of Melanie Klein and of Donald Winnicott, and termed 'object-relations' theory, developed in the 1930s. Social theorists, many feminists amongst them, have drawn on Freud's work and on post-Freudian theory to produce varying interpretations and 'readings'. These include Juliet Mitchell (1975), Nancy Chodorow (1978 and 1994), and those of French feminists such as Luce Irigaray, Julia Kristeva and Helen Cixous (see, for example, Marks and Courtivron, 1981). Freud's approach and fundamental ideas, then, have had a profound influence. They have permeated our everyday understanding as well as having an impact over a wide range of studies and theoretical perspectives. It will not therefore be possible here to do more than sketch some central notions, and our focus will be on Freud's own ideas, particularly those linking sexuality and identity. We shall also indicate how Freud's method involved looking below the surface of experience to develop theoretical concepts to explain it in terms of hidden or 'unconscious' structures and processes.

The central organising concept of psychoanalytic theory is therefore the 'unconscious', and this runs through all the variations. The notion of the 'unconscious' provides a significant conceptual tool for exploring the idea that powerful desires and irrational forces, largely inaccessible to consciousness, can make sense of aspects of experience and behaviour not amenable to explanation in terms of ordinary theories of socialisation. Through it some understanding of the persistence of relations of domination and oppression may be gleaned, and the concept of the unconscious is often brought together with that of ideology in attempts to understand the structured relations of oppression in modern societies.

The formation of individual identities takes place in specific cultural and historical contexts, and we have seen the importance of recognising variations, not only in the ways in which identities are experienced and lived in differing cultures, but also in the ways in which concepts of personhood vary. Nevertheless, human beings are embodied, creatures of flesh and blood, and the biology/culture tension is always present in attempts to understand identity. Moreover, all human beings (apart from the exceptional intervention of modern reproductive technology) are the result of sexual contact between men and women, they are born of women, and all known societies construct a socially significant binary opposition between men and women, and masculinity and femininity. Psychoanalytic theories provide differing ways of conceptualising the psychological and social significance of these seemingly universal dimensions of human experience and their implications for the power differentials related to gender and sexuality.

Freud himself was a physician specialising in neurological disorders and seeking causal explanations as a way of discovering 'cures' for his patients' distressing 'symptoms'. He became interested in some of his patients whose problems appeared to be physical but had no identifiable physical causes. While experimenting with hypnosis, he found that symptoms sometimes disappeared when patients remembered early, traumatic experiences. This led him to abandon hypnosis and concentrate on helping his patients to relax and talk freely about their thoughts, without censoring them. This became the famous 'talking cure' still central to the psychoanalytic method of therapy and of investigation. Freud found that improvements occurred when traumatic experiences were remembered and the emotion associated with them discharged. Painful memories, however, seemed powerfully blocked, and they took a lot of talking and listening to bring to the surface.

The blocking or 'forgetting' of painful experiences led Freud to develop his theory of 'repression'. He came to the view that painful memories could be pushed into and locked away in the 'unconscious' part of the mind, to all intents and purposes 'forgotten'. However, it is not only particularly traumatic experiences that are coped with in this way. Powerful desires and losses linked to early attachments that we all experience as a normal part of infancy, form the common basis of the unconscious and repression is a normal and necessary process in development. Material in the unconscious is, according to Freud, unavailable to the conscious mind under ordinary circumstances. The unconscious nevertheless exerts a powerful influence upon us and is the source of our psychic energy and the seat of motivation. Unconscious material has energy attached to it, and this energy has to find an outlet, which may be in some symbolic form. Physical symptoms, dream images and obsessive behaviour are just some of the symbolic forms in which unconscious material may be expressed.

We can see that, in searching for a way of working with and understanding his patients' problems, Freud developed a method of clinical practice that was also a tool for researching the workings of the mind. This led to a theoretical model of the structure and workings of the mind based on a distinction between 'conscious' and 'unconscious' processes. His ideas were based on in-depth 'case studies' of a relatively small number of people in varying forms of mental distress. He considered 'abnormal' to be exaggerated forms of 'normal' behaviour and experience, and generalised from the former to the latter. Freud's interest in exploring conscious and unconscious meanings and in searching for underlying structures and processes to explain surface observations is deeply rooted in European philosophical traditions, and we find similar concerns in Marxist and structuralist theories and research discussed elsewhere in this book. The question of how structures and processes work to produce and reproduce social and psychological experience is fundamental to these approaches.

Sexuality is pivotal in Freud's own theorising, but he held a broad and complex view of this derived from the bodily preoccupations of young children. It relates to the drives or desires, satisfactions and frustrations linked to bodily functions, and to the mother's central role in the infant's life. Our own reading of Freud owes much to Minsky's account (1996). In his 'Three Essays on Sexuality', Freud talks of drives linked to the pleasure in basic bodily functions (Freud, 1977). The focus of pleasure shifts, during the process of development, and each shift entails powerful experiences of loss. The shifts are from the oral satisfactions of feeding at the mother's breast and the loss of the breast at weaning, through anal satisfactions and the losses associated with bowel function and control, to the pleasures of exploring the penis and the clitoris. So Freud describes development in terms of a process of moving through overlapping stages. It is at the third or 'phallic' stage that the child discovers sexual difference and gender. The child's own active and pleasurable exploration of its genitals is associated with the pleasure of its mother's physical care, and merge into a passionate desire for total possession of, or reunion with, its mother. Both male and female children share this desire. Its frustration is intensely painful but necessary in order for them to develop separate identities. Separation, however, involves different tasks for male and female children, and its achievement results in the mature, heterosexual, genital sexuality sanctioned by culture.

In a later paper, 'On Narcissism', Freud connects sexual desire explicitly with the construction of personal identity (Freud, 1984). 'Narcissism' represents a state of transition between an infant's auto-eroticism, or self-love (a source of identity based on the pleasure of its own bodily sensations), and a relationship with a separate person. In the narcissistic phase the infant projects its bodily experience on to another, usually its mother, whom it then loves as its 'self'. This 'self' is still fused with the mother because she is not yet seen as a separate person. We are more familiar with this notion in the context of romantic love, where we fall in love with ourselves projected on to a lover, who is not really experienced as a separate person but as our 'other half', or a mirror-image that reflects us and with whom we are fused. This kind of love renders us very vulnerable if the loved person rejects us or dies. We are familiar with many tragic stories of lost love, classically Romeo and Juliet, in which the remaining partner is unable to survive alone. Freud argued that we always retain some potential for narcissistic love. However, we can see just how crucial is the task of separation from the mother, for the infant's formation of an identity that is independently viable. Separation requires the involvement of a third person, a potentially destructive rival, usually in the form of the father, and the external world of law and culture that he represents. Its accomplishment involves a resolution of what Freud calls the Oedipal crisis after the Greek tragedy in which Oedipus (unknowingly) slays his father and marries his mother. Resolution of the crisis results in both a gendered identity and the formation of the unconscious.

In Freud's view, therefore, the small boy enters into his masculine identity through the terror of castration, linked to his perception of sexual difference (his mother/females do not have a penis), and his fears that his murderous feelings towards his powerful rival, his father, will be punished by the loss of his penis (both his primary source of pleasure and his narcissistic identity). The crisis is resolved when the boy accepts symbolic castration by his father, in that he submits to the painful reality that he must lose his mother to his more powerful father and, at the same time, give up his primary identification with her. This entails the repression of his mother and all that she represents – his potential femininity – into his unconscious. The boy must substitute an identification with his father and what he represents in the form of the outside world of culture. In contrast, the small girl perceives that, in common with her mother, she has no penis to lose. Nevertheless, her mother desires one, in the form of a relationship with her father. The girl angrily rejects her mother for not giving her a penis, gives up her clitoral activity (her clitoris cannot compete with her father's penis for her mother's love) and seeks consolation from her father from whom, she fantasises, she might obtain a penis. This wish for a penis or 'penis-envy', as Freud calls it is therefore linked to the girl's sense of a lack of what her mother desires, of not being good enough for her mother. For the full achievement of her femininity it must be transformed into the wish for a baby from her father. Disappointed in this fantasy too (if she is to conform to the demands of patriarchal culture), she must re-identify with her mother, as a woman. She must repress her masculinity or active sexuality, in order to attract a man in the future and fulfil her feminine identity through having her own baby.

This very condensed account by no means does justice to Freud's ideas, but we have perhaps said enough to convey something of their power and also to indicate how controversial they are. Some of the controversy surrounds the way in which a claim is seemingly made that these structures and processes are universal. They perhaps best describe those of Western patriarchal societies in their representation of feminine and masculine identities, and in the privileging of heterosexuality as the only fully mature sexuality. This is something that has been debated widely among feminists and people critical of our anti-homosexual or 'homophobic' culture. More specifically, recent research and writing has highlighted the exclusion of gay men and lesbians from a number of leading psychoanalytic training organisations (see, for example, O'Conner and Ryan, 1993; and Ellis, 1994). According to Ellis, these organisations are reluctant to own an explicit policy of exclusion, although some might claim theoretical justification. For example, Klein's theory is influential and, taking the view that homosexuality is 'immature', she expressed the view that heterosexuality is a major criterion for the outcome of a successful analysis. There is certainly clear evidence of exclusion, and some prominent analysts are quite open in expressing their views. For example, Charles Socarides is well known for his belief that homosexuality is a severe psychopathological condition, and that the explicit task of the analyst is 'to spoil the perverse gratification'. Professor Socarides was invited by the Association of Psychoanalytic Psychotherapy (part of the British National Health Service) to give its prestigious Annual Lecture in 1995. The invitation was, however, withdrawn following vociferous protest (see British Psychotherapists (1995) letter, with multiple signatories).

All this being said, we must nevertheless acknowledge how significant Freud's ideas remain. Freud himself was aware of some of the tensions and contradictions in his work. He did, after all, maintain that:

> All individuals, as a result of their bisexual disposition and cross inheritance, combine in themselves both masculine and feminine characteristics, so that pure masculinity and femininity remain theoretical constructions of uncertain content. (Freud, 1977, p. 342)

As O'Conner and Ryan note, Freud recognised social pressure as a source of unhappiness but did not himself believe it was the analyst's task to induce conformity (O'Conner and Ryan 1993, p. 74). Although he struggled with the demands of patriarchal culture, he also retreated to the view that homosexuality is both perverse and pathological, as well as expressing views on women that are sometimes distinctly misogynous. All in all, many people have found theoretical tools in Freud's work and in post-Freudian writings which help in understanding the psychologically and socially damaging effects of patriarchal society. The notion of the unconscious is one that prompts us both to look beneath the obvious and to recognise powerful irrational forces, such as sexual 'instincts' and desires, at work in human relationships. Too strong an allegiance to the Enlightenment's view of rationality and progress can lead to a dangerous disregarding of powerful psychological and social processes that 'defy reason'.

Beyond 'scientific' description and explanation: discourses and narratives

Although Freudian and other psychoanalytic writings point beyond the over-emphasis on rationality of the Enlightenment, in that they recognise the power of irrational forces, they still hold on to the Enlightenment project of the search for truth. Psychoanalytic theory purports to be scientific, seeking to understand the true nature of reality through systematic observation and reason. We have seen that, like Marxist and structuralist approaches, it postulates the existence of an underlying psychic structure, a deeper reality, the foundations of which give rise to and explain the surface features of experience. We have also seen that this whole project of the Enlightenment has been questioned by an intellectual movement or movements known, sometimes interchangeably, as postmodernism and poststructuralism. Postmodernism questions the attempt of scientific disciplines to establish a secure foundation for knowledge, resting on privileged concepts that are themselves uncontaminated by ideology. It is argued that, although the knowledge or insight provided by a science may claim to offer emancipation, from domination by some form of irrational belief system or power structure, it will instead institute new forms of domination. We have seen above how theories of sexuality and research into sexuality may be liberating in some ways, but often serve to reinforce traditional views by adding 'scientific' authority, or themselves construct norms of 'good sex', in terms of which many can fail.

Michel Foucault has been influential in providing ways of understanding this process. A brief discussion of his writing on sexuality will illustrate the links he makes between disciplines of 'knowledge' and 'disciplinary power'. Foucault argues that the historical changes that brought about Western industrial societies allowed certain discourses or 'knowledges' (such as medical and psychological discourses) of the person to develop. According to Foucault, it is these discourses that have 'produced' a particular form of individual, similar to the 'self-contained individual' we identified in Chapter 2, and which manage the control of society and its members without recourse to force. Government is by 'disciplinary power', which operates through schools, clinics and other institutions which define and regulate 'normality'.

Foucault links the emergence of the concept of 'population' in the eighteenth century to a growth in numbers of people and consequent problems of housing, public health and so on. The idea that the inhabitants of a country constituted a 'population' brought with it notions of management and control not previously applied to people. With it the body in general, and sexuality in particular, became a major site of power relations. Birth and death rates, life expectancy, age of marriage, fertility, legitimate and illegitimate births and the like became the subject of analysis and regulation:

> At the heart of this economic and political problem of population was sex... Of course it had long been asserted that a country had to be populated if it hoped to be rich and powerful; but this was the first time that a society had affirmed, in a constant way, that its future and fortune were tied... to the manner in which each individual used his sex. Things went from ritual lamenting over the unfruitful debauchery of the rich, bachelors, and libertines to a discourse in which the sexual conduct of the population was taken both as an object of analysis and as a target of intervention. (Foucault, 1981, pp. 25–6)

As sexuality became a focus of the state's interest, agents of authority in the Church and state had the power to investigate and extort confessions about sexual practices and, Foucault argues, it was only at this point that the notions of 'sexual perversion', 'unnatural practices' and 'sexual immorality' became possible. The concept of 'normality' developed with the power to define permissible and non-permissible practices, and people were encouraged to internalise the process of control by scrutinising their own behaviour and questioning their own 'normality'. The power to encourage this self-scrutiny passed into the hands of the medical profession in general, and psychiatry in particular. Psychoanalytic discourse, as we have seen, places sexuality at the centre of self-understanding, and we are encouraged to uncover the true nature of our sexuality in order to resolve our personality and relationship problems. Foucault locates psychoanalytic discourse in a Western tradition of confession dating at least from the Middle Ages:

> the confession became one of the West's most highly valued techniques for producing truth . . . It plays a part in justice, medicine, education . . . in the most ordinary affairs of everyday life, and in the most solemn rites; one confesses one's crimes, one's sins, ones thoughts and desires, one's illnesses and troubles; one goes about telling, with the greatest precision, whatever is most difficult to tell. One confesses in public and in private, to one's parents, one's educators, one's doctor, to those one loves, one admits to oneself, in pleasure and in pain, things it would be impossible to tell anyone else. (Foucault, 1981, p. 59)

Psychoanalysis demands that patients disclose all to the therapist and agree with their analysis. The claim that interpretations are validated by a patient's recognition of their truth is belied by the psychoanalytic concept of 'resistance'. Our tendency to 'resist' painful or unpalatable insights is in itself defined as part of the 'illness'. Those who persistently disagree with interpretations can thus be seen as persisting in their neuroses. We can place in this context the exclusion from psychoanalytic training of gay and lesbian people who refuse to define their sexuality as problematic. So the connection Foucault makes between psychoanalytic techniques and confession helps to make the more general point about it being one of a range of discourses about sexuality which, while claiming to be emancipatory and therapeutic, serve to construct it in particular ways and fix it in a context of social control and discipline. Personal life is pathologised or related to psychological prescriptions of 'normality', and thus becomes a site of intervention for 'experts'. Foucault's specific account has been criticised for being historically simplistic (see, for example, Wilton, 1995, p. 40). Nevertheless, his approach is significant and, importantly, he draws attention to how it is not just particular behaviour that is constructed historically, as a 'perversion' for example, but whole identities. So homosexuality is not defined in terms of practices but as 'a kind of interior androgyny, a hermaphroditism of the soul' (Foucault, 1981, p. 43). To be 'homosexual' is to be a particular kind of person whose identity is defined by their sexuality.

From Foucault's perspective, the proliferation of 'sexology' literature from the nineteenth century is more about producing classifications and categorisations in terms of which people can be regulated and controlled, than about increasing knowledge and understanding. In this way he reverses the 'repressive hypothesis', the notion that our present-day interest in sexuality is a liberation from earlier repression. Instead, he argues, it is related to the development of widespread techniques of surveillance and normalisation that have become the predominant methods of social control in Western industrial societies.

Foucault's work, then, has been important in showing how sexuality, far from being something natural or given, is socially constructed, produced in discourses or 'knowledges'. Even more importantly, he has linked the production of such 'discourses' of sexuality to the production of sexuality as a site of social control through disciplinary power. His work has been drawn upon widely. The myriad studies exploring the ways in which sexualities are constructed, particularly those concerned with issues of power, testify to its influence (for example, Weekes, 1985; Caplan, 1987; Kitzinger, 1987; and Richardson, 1996). It has also, inevitably, attracted criticism, not least by feminists who have also valued much within it (notably, McNay 1992). Foucault's work may be claimed to be postmodernist in offering a critique of the disciplinary discourses of social science and showing how, once formed as 'knowledges', they assert a privileged position in relation to 'truth'. They thus oppress by silencing less powerful alternative voices and viewpoints. However, Foucault can be accused simultaneously of proposing an alternative discourse accounting for the construction of power relations in historical processes. Although he was careful to avoid any explicit claim to truth, speaking instead of 'regimes of truth' where one regime is no more correct than another, it is difficult to avoid the conclusion that his own viewpoint is still, in some respects, that of a privileged, knowing 'outsider'. Foucault can, in some ways, be seen as being caught in the trap in which the postmodernist assault on 'truth' leaves us. While raising important questions about the links between knowledge and power, which take us beyond previous formulations of ideological control, we are left in a potentially dangerous position of having no basis for argument. If all truth is relative, might becomes right, capable of being challenged only by greater might. We shall explore this further in the final chapter.

For the moment we shall explore the interest in narratives aroused by the doubts raised about the scientific quest for firmly-based knowledge. In similar vein to Foucault, Jean-François Lyotard has described the search for overarching theories, of the 'reality' underlying our experiences and our commonsense accounts, as inherently oppressive. He sees them as containing the seeds of terror and totalitarianism in seeking to impose a consensus in the name of truth:

> The nineteenth and twentieth centuries have given us as much terror as we can take. We have paid a high enough price for the nostalgia of the whole and the one...Let us wage a war on totality. (Lyotard, 1984, pp. 81–2)

Lyotard does not use the term 'discourses', but likens theories to stories or narratives in terms of which we make sense of our lives. He calls all overarching theories and belief systems, including those of social science, 'grand or meta-narratives' and describes the 'postmodern condition' as one that abandons the search for these. Instead, he sees creativity and imagination as containing liberating potential, and argues that, in science as well as in everyday life, it is small-scale theories and accounts that should claim our attention, 'the little narrative remains the quintessential form of imaginative invention' (Lyotard, 1984, p. 60).

All this can be linked to an increasing interest among social researchers in stories of all kinds, from the great myths and mythological traditions to the everyday stories we tell about ourselves. Those interested in stories are often conscious of the problems in claiming any one story as historical truth or reality. However, this sometimes leads to a disconnection from the material nature of human relationships and the effects of power, which insults the powerless. Life is reduced to stories and texts. It is as though there is nothing beyond the symbolic realm of language and culture. We have to remind ourselves of the reality of torture, that bullets kill, and that stories alone cannot feed the starving or house the homeless.

This tendency to reduce social life to the symbolic can be linked to the way in which, in Western philosophy, mind and matter are conceptualised as two distinct kinds of stuff that cannot interact. Ideas and the material world are consigned to separate spheres, and this repeatedly leads to the opposing views that either reality is purely symbolic or that matter is real and ideas can describe but not effect change in the world. While perhaps not resolving this philosophical puzzle, Foucault's work does hold on to the material nature of power, and his use of the term 'discourses' embraces a view of 'lived experience' that includes ideas, feelings, behaviour and the pattern of our social relationships and power struggles.

Coming from a somewhat different perspective, but with similar intent, a recent study by Ken Plummer focuses on the plethora of sexual stories in our culture. In a passage reminiscent of Foucault's discussion of confessions, Plummer comments:

> Sex, then, has become the Big Story. From Donahue and Oprah getting folk to tell of their child sexual abuse to Dr. Ruth's televised advice programmes listening to the stories of 'rape survivors'; from the letters of men and women to a Nancy Friday telling of their changing sexual fantasies to the collected writings of lesbians and gay men 'coming out'...a grand message keeps being shouted: *tell about your sex.*
> Tell about your sexual behaviour, your sexual identity, your dreams, your desires, your pains and your fantasies... Tell about your sexual dysfunction, your sexual diseases, your orgasm problems... Let us know what you get up to in bed – or what you don't get up to. (Plummer, 1995, p. 4)

Plummer is interested in the stories themselves, but he is particularly interested in the social activity of storytelling, its function and effects. It is, he states, 'time to go beyond the text'. He argues that social life can be approached metaphorically as a text but it is not in reality a text. Plummer adopts what he describes as the now 'revitalising' but century-old 'symbolic interactionist' position. This views the social world as a 'vast flow of ever-changing symbolic interactions in which we are set actively adrift in a never-ending stream of practical activities' (p. 20). Human beings are social world-makers, though not under conditions of their own choosing. They are born and raised in particular circumstances and relationships which have real effects on their lives, limiting and opening up possibilities. Plummer locates his sociology of storytelling in this process. He is interested in the nature of stories, their form and content; the social process of producing and consuming stories; the social role of stories, including the ways in which they contribute to maintaining and changing social relationships; and in the social and historical conditions that enable particular stories to be told and received. For Plummer, like Foucault, power is a central concern, and he sees stories as part of the political process:

> Power is not so much an all or nothing phenomenon, which people have or don't have, and which resides either here or there. Rather, it is best viewed as a flow, a process, a pulsate – oscillating and undulating throughout the social world and working to pattern the degree of control people experience and have over their lives... Power is a process that weaves its way through embodied, passionate social life and everything in its wake. *Sexual stories*

live in this flow of power. The power to tell a story, or indeed not to tell a story, under conditions of one's own choosing, is part of the political process. (Plummer, 1995, p. 26)

Plummer chooses one genre of story for his study, which he describes as 'the personal experience narrative'. He considers three forms of this genre: 'breaking the silence' stories, about rape or abuse; lesbian and gay 'coming out' stories; and 'recovery' stories about therapeutic transformations. These are all stories of the twentieth century, stories 'whose time has come'. They are stories of sexual suffering, silence and secrecy, the need for action, transcendence, redemption and transformation. Plummer asks what is it that allows a story to be told at a particular point in history and in a particular cultural place. Rape stories, for example, could rarely be told, and hardly ever heard and believed, as recently as the 1970s. Today, in the late 1990s, at least some stories are told and heard, they are politically more feasible and, as they are told, some lives are empowered. Moreover, the telling and hearing contributes to the creation of more spaces for women to come together and talk, and for their collective voices to contribute to the transformation of police and court practices.

Plummer then explores the texts of these stories but also goes beyond the texts. He sees the texts themselves as being constructed in social activity in which different people play different and socially important roles. There are the story-tellers themselves, those who elicit and encourage stories, and the consumers, readers and audiences who receive them. Stories are produced and consumed in social worlds; they require 'interpretative communities', in which they make sense, and 'in being told and received' they contribute to producing, reproducing and changing social relationships and communities.

Conclusion

In this chapter we have explored some of the ways in which social research has contributed to our understanding of sexuality. In so doing, we have raised many questions and considered different ways of describing and explaining experience. We have seen that there is no consensus about the nature of sexuality, and our opening question remains unanswerable. One important task of this chapter has been to examine some aspects of the relationship between the contexts in which research is produced, the methods of research and the kinds of knowledge produced, and we have seen how our experience of our-selves as sexual beings is influenced by attempts to define and understand sexuality. We have looked at the complex interrelationship between scientific knowledge and common sense, and between knowledge and power. We have also traced and followed the shift, apparent in recent social research, from a modernist to a postmodernist position. The modernist 'scientific' concern to discover the 'truth' about sex (to define it, to describe and categorise behaviour and experience, and perhaps to explain it) has given way, to some extent, to a more postmodernist position in which the concern is not the 'reality' behind experience, but rather the lived experience of social relationships themselves, in which realities are constructed and lived in discourses and stories, and through which power is maintained and challenged. So in focusing on sexuality we have illustrated differing research traditions in social science and some persisting themes and problems relating to the very possibility of knowledge of the social world and the ways in which knowledge and power are inextricably linked.

5

Health and Illness

Bodily changes

This chapter introduces the maps or models that social scientists, rather than doctors, have used when exploring ideas and experiences to do with health and illness. It highlights the variety of ways that human beings have interpreted changes in their bodies and asks how one interpretation can become particularly powerful while others are taken less seriously. In particular, we shall focus on the power of Western medical models of illness and Western health-care practitioners, and examine the different ways in which social scientists have sought to explain this. As we shall see, this power may not correspond directly with the capacity of Western medicine to provide individuals with good health.

During socialisation we come to recognise ourselves as particular individuals, learning, if not necessarily consciously reflecting on, aspects of self-identity such as gender or social class. However, as Chapter 3 argued, our culturally and socially-specific self-identity is one that is not fixed, but changes over time. We live with the paradox of knowing ourselves as distinctive entities, yet recognising that we are also beings that undergo change. For example, the human body transforms itself dramatically during the lifecourse in its movement from babyhood to later life. Major changes in our size, body shape, skin texture, and amount and colour of hair are biological processes which each individual will undergo. How they will understand and experience such changes, however, depends on their position within a given society. For example, change in the colour of a person's hair is a simple biological process, but socially it carries different meanings for women and men in

111

many Western societies. Conservatism and loss of sexual vitality may be assumed to be the personal traits of grey-haired women, while wisdom and charm may be the expected personal traits of grey-haired men.

This raises the question of how we come to make interpretations of change within the self. As already suggested, there may appear to be a tension between our idea of ourselves as specific people and our sense of ourselves as 'self'-transforming. Furthermore, some changes may be welcomed and others feared. In the example of greying hair, an observable bodily change can be seen to carry a range of social meanings, some of them positive – as Western men we are seen to gain authority – and some of them negative – as Western women we are seen to lose our sex appeal. Bodily change can also bring a changed social identity – again, one that is either welcomed or feared. While the breaking of the voice and the appearance of facial hair among male Western adolescents is believed to bring about a temporarily confused sense of self, it is none the less a positively-perceived change, social approval being given to those who show signs of 'growing up' into 'manhood'. In other words, while observable changes may threaten our sense of who we are, the altered, emergent self can, in some cases, represent a desired and an expected development.

This chapter focuses on the physical and mental changes we may come to think of as illnesses, changes which may bring with them an unwelcome altered sense of self. It asks how we come to see certain changes as illnesses and others as natural processes. For example, the events of women's reproductive lives – menstruation, childbirth and the menopause – are seen in some societies as illnesses and in others as the epitome of naturalness. Among many Western women, some forms of menstruation are thought of as a natural monthly change in bodily state. However, other forms are categorised as illnesses and given medical names such as dysmenorrhea and amenorrhea. For some women, all forms of menstruation are described in a lay, or common-sense, language of illness, 'I've come unwell'. In other words the changes we describe as illnesses may not always be easily distinguishable from other changes.

We also need to ask not only why some changes are seen as illnesses and others are not, but also how we come to find the concept of illness persuasive as a means of explaining certain changes. Furthermore, we have to ask why one set of ideas about illness – Western medical models – has been believed so extensively, not only within the West but also throughout the world. Answering this question requires us to consider the role of religious beliefs, alternative medicine, and the indigenous healing systems of more traditional societies. Only then can we begin to understand how particular sets of beliefs about what is going on in our minds or bodies can lead to certain kinds of behaviour. For example, once we have come to believe we are ill we may agree to parts of our inner body being removed, we may swallow chemicals at regular intervals, we may stay in bed for several days, or we may spend an hour each week talking about ourselves to someone we believe to have special expertise. Given how painful or disruptive we may find some of these behaviours, what, and in particular, who persuades us to engage in them?

A comparison between different societies, both contemporarily and historically, shows that different people in different times and places have understood and experienced mental and physical changes in different ways. Indeed, among some social groups there has traditionally been no distinction made between illness and other unwelcome occurrences. G. Lewis describes the Gnau of New Guinea who use the word 'wola' to refer not only to depression but also the concepts of 'ill', 'bad', 'evil', 'wretched', 'harmful', 'forbidden' and 'potentially dangerous' (Lewis, 1986). Similarly, during the medieval period in the West the concepts of disease, sin, deviance and crime were not distinguished clearly from one another, a lack of clarity which, it has been argued, reflected the absence of rigid boundaries between the institutions of religion, medicine and the law (Turner, 1987). If we compare contemporary biomedical models with those that occurred at other times during the medieval period in Western history, depression was seen as an illness resulting from an excess of black bile, one of the body's four 'humours' (Turner, 1987); among contemporary Chinese villagers, illnesses are understood in terms of a balance of yin and yang (Martin, 1987); and contemporary UK lay health beliefs attribute colds and chills to the penetration of the body by rain, winds or draughts (Helman, 1990).

If we try to make comparisons of this kind in relation to a single illness we are, however, confronted with the problem that we cannot be sure that, for example, depression, melancholia and 'wola' (Lewis, 1986) are, in fact, descriptions of the same thing. While we may think we are talking about similar biological changes and discovering them to be interpreted in a variety of ways, how can we really be sure that the 'change' is the same one in each case? What we have to remember is that our distinction between the biological and the social realms of the self and society is itself problematic. As the discussion of personal identity in Chapter 2 argued, we can only know ourselves and our environment through the maps or metaphors our society makes available to us. It is therefore difficult for us to talk about a biological or material reality that prefigures our social responses to it, in that it is only through socially-specific sets of ideas or images that we are able to perceive and make sense of that material world. As human beings we have no external position from which to observe the material/physical world and the social world as two separate entities. While this chapter will not be arguing that what we think of as illness is just a figment of our shared social imagination, it is important to recognise the difficulties associated with trying to separate out an objective material reality – a tumour, a gene or a virus, for example – from the kinds of social maps or frameworks through which we understand it.

If we compare contemporary Western ideas about the human body and mind with those held by people in other times and other places, we may feel drawn towards a commonsense view that says, for example, that medieval beliefs about humours – as with the previously-mentioned black bile – were a kind of proto-knowledge which in part matches what we now 'know' to be true. We might believe that, with the development of medical knowledge, we now have a much more accurate or 'true' understanding of our minds and bodies. What this chapter will help us to think about, and perhaps to question, are some of the reasons why we 'know' this to be the case and why we often base our decision-making and our actions upon it. However, it will not only ask questions about why we believe that medical models really do describe us and our bodies, but also why, sometimes, we question them. More complex still, we need to ask why we sometimes find ourselves believing both medical and other, contradictory models or maps of the human mind/body at the same time. For example, the Manus of the Admiralty Islands in the South Pacific are described as having a 'hierarchy of resort' to a plurality of healing systems (Stacey, 1988). While Western medical models are seen as providing a useful description of an illness, the Manus go to their own system of ideas for an explanation of its cause, usually the power of a ghost ancestor or the sorcery of living people. Similarly, in the West, biomedical practitioners and homeopathic doctors sometimes work alongside one another, the patient choosing to follow treatments grounded in very different models of the mind/body and of illness (Scambler, 1991).

Mapping the mind and body

Medicalised models of illness behaviour describe a process whereby we decide to visit the doctor when we feel 'ill', return home with our illness transformed into a 'disease' as a result of the doctor's 'diagnosis', follow the course of treatment prescribed by the doctor, and eventually feel 'well' again. Our 'disease' is 'cured'. An encounter that takes place within the public sphere of the health centre or GP's consulting room therefore shapes our private experiences of our bodies. The functionalist sociologist, Talcott Parsons, describes this process in terms which echo a medical model (Parsons, 1951). He defines illness as an event that makes it difficult for the individual to participate appropriately in society. Illness, in his view, is potentially disordering, as social norms can no longer be upheld by the individual. However, the institution of medicine provides a way of giving a more orderly shape to the event of illness and providing the individual with a recognised, if different, role in society. Visiting the doctor is therefore the duty of the individual no longer well enough to conform to their normal social roles. Once the disease had been diagnosed and treatment prescribed, the individual is legitimately released from social participation, and is required to take up the 'sick role'. This new role involves relinquishing responsibility for their condition to the doctor, and following the doctor's instructions with a view to regaining health as soon as possible. In her account of women in America in the nineteenth century, C. Smith-Rosenberg argues that the sick role, in the form of hysteria, provided a way in which women could respond to the discontinuities between the role into which they were socialised as children – to be gentle and refined – and the requirements of adult womanhood – to be a source of strength for her family and to bear pain and illness with fortitude (Smith-Rosenberg, 1984).

It remains to be explained, however, how we come to know that we are 'ill' in the first place, how we decide that we should tell the doctor about our illness, how the doctor constructs our diagnosis and therefore our disease, and how we choose whether or not to follow the treatment recommended. It also presupposes that the diagnosis of a disease always has its roots in the patient's experience of illness. However, the development of medical technology has allowed diseases to be diagnosed before they have produced any symptoms that the patient can detect. Genetic screening has even made it possible to predict the future onset of a disease which is not yet present within the body. Finally, the 'sick role' model put forward by Parsons rests on the assumption that patients and doctors share the same agendas or priorities with respect to health and illness. It takes no account of situations where patients perceive their experience of symptom relief as a cure, even though the disease diagnosed by the doctor is still present; and doctors believe that a cure has taken place even though the patient is left with symptoms or side-effects they find distressing (Helman, 1990).

In order to explore these issues we can begin with some fundamental questions about the way in which mental and physical changes come to be identified as illness or disease, whether by the individual, another lay person, or someone recognised as having health-related expertise. As noted at the beginning of this chapter, the changes we identify as mental or physical cannot be placed neatly within the realm of biology and then examined in terms of the maps or models through which different societies or social groups have tried to explain them. As human beings we can only ever discuss what we call our physical or biological selves, via the maps available to us at any one time. Foucault has argued that biology itself, together with other 'sciences of man' such as sociology, anthropology, psychology and medicine, came into being within Western societies at the end of the eighteenth century (Armstrong, 1987). Yet, as Armstrong argues, 'sociologists . . . have accepted the body as a given, as the point at which and from which they start their analyses' (1987, p. 65). They therefore overlook the fact that a biological map of the body is itself culturally specific, emanating from a particular point in history.

Cross-cultural comparison reveals that while Westerners assume a biomedical model of the body to be 'true', in reality there exists a range of models of the body. For example, it has been perceived in terms of its structure, with that structure varying from place to place and time to time. Health has been seen as the balance of different elements or forces within the body. In ancient China, India, and then in Greece, these elements were liquids or humours: blood, phlegm, yellow and black bile; and their influence pervaded both the body and the personality. A humoural model of the body held sway throughout the Roman Empire, and from their spreading to North Africa, Spain and Latin America. Lay health beliefs in Latin America, Islamic societies and Indian Ayurvedic medicine all reflect a humoural model of the body. The concept of balance also informs a Chinese perspective, where health was conceived of in terms of contrasting cosmic principles: the dark, moist, female yin; and the hot, fiery, male yang. This kind of model contrasts markedly with two of the dominant Western models of the body: the plumbing or hydraulic model; and the machine model. According to the first, the body's internal structure consists of chambers and tubes, all eventually connected to the body's outer surface, and health is the outcome of a free flow of substances through the system, while disease is the outcome of blockages. The machine model is built around notions of power and energy which drive the body but need refuelling, and replaceable body parts that can wear out. A more specialised machine model, the computer, is often used to make sense of the brain, which can then be 'programmed' or 'rewired' (Helman, 1990).

If we were to examine each of these maps or models in turn we would be able to trace the connections between its internal characteristics and the wider social context within which it is believed to hold true. Thus the machine model that informs a Western biomedical view of the body can be seen as one aspect of the mechanistic or scientific world view that emerged during the seventeenth century. Whereas the natural world had previously been understood in Aristotelian terms that highlighted the integration of all living organisms, scientific models such organisms as sets of mechanical parts. The body therefore came to be separated from the mind, the 'corporeal' divided from the 'incorporeal' (Doyal, 1979). It also came to be separated from its surrounding environment, a separation which, paradoxically, reveals the intimate relationship between models of the body and their wider social context. Within a world view characterised by fragmentation, one would expect precisely this kind of separation to occur.

From within Western society, J. Okely provides an example of the links between a model of the body and its wider social context in her ethnography of the culture of Traveller Gypsies (Okely, 1983). In their case, the body is seen as an entity that is strictly divided into its inner and outer surfaces, a model in keeping with the social relations of traveller life. While contact with non-gypsies is threatening to the purity of gypsy identity, it is none the less economically essential. 'Calling' for scrap, begging or selling to non-gypsies inevitably pollutes the body of the Traveller. This problem is managed through a model of the body that disallows any contact between its external polluted surface and its inner pure surface. The rigid separation of dish-washing from clothes washing is the kind of practice through which Travellers keep the two parts of the body in isolation from one another.

Knowledge and power

The emergence in the late eighteenth-century of a Western biological map of the human body, and its development in the specialisms of anatomy and medicine, therefore needs to be understood in terms of its social context. In particular, it has been linked with changes in systems of social control at that time. Foucault highlights a shift away from control grounded in the visible power of the king, manifested in hangings and other forms of public punishment (Foucault, 1973). In its place came control grounded in the surveillance of the visible individual by faceless representatives of state power, such as doctors and prison governors. In this new social context, the human body came to be perceived and experienced through the disciplinary 'gaze' of the doctor. Thus, Foucault argues, the patient comes to believe in the 'truth' of an anatomical map of their body and a medical model of the changes it undergoes as a result of surveillance by the medical practitioner. This gaze is exemplified in the stethoscope applied to the chest of the passive patient, yielding sounds which the patient neither hears nor can interpret. As the object of medical surveillance, the patient comes to 'know' their body and their disease through their encounter with the medical practitioner. In parallel with the gaze of the general practitioner can be set the ear of the psychiatrist. Not only the body but also the mind of the patient is offered for surveillance. In each case, that which is apprehended is accessible only to the medical expert, in whose terms the self of the patient comes into being. In comparison, person-centred counselling represents an attempt to shift the balance of power away from the therapist and towards the 'client' (Mearns and Thorne, 1988). The power inherent within medicine and the medical profession is therefore constituted through the knowledge that is yielded in the course of medical practice, or surveillance. That knowledge, in its turn, persuades through the power to which it gives rise. In other words, in Foucault's view, knowledge and power are mutually constitutive.

Foucault's argument therefore gives us one way of understanding how the diagnosis of disease offered by the medical practitioner comes to be found persuasive by the patient. He is suggesting that actions such as the medical examination are not just the way in which the practitioner finds out what is happening to us; as actions they provide, and confirm, a particular model of the body itself. They are powerful in that it becomes difficult for us to think about bodies through frameworks other than those represented by medical practice.

A focus on the kind of actions that take place during medical encounters has been useful in explaining how medical models come to be believed. Helman discusses them as forms of ritual in that they serve more than just practical or technical purposes; they have the effect of securing the patient's consent to a specific set of values, norms and beliefs about the body and about health care (Helman, 1990, pp. 192–213). This effect is achieved through the use of symbols – that is, objects or forms that carry a whole range of meanings, many of them not immediately obvious to the patient. Symbolic aspects of the medical encounter are the doctor's white coat, the bleeper, the objects in the surgery such as framed qualifying certificates, medical books and instruments, and a large desk. Entry to hospital is also marked by events that have symbolic as well as practical dimensions, such as the replacement of personal clothing with nightwear and slippers. Helman draws out the meanings or associations of the doctor's white coat, pointing out that when we encounter someone wearing the coat we make assumptions about them. Thus we believe that the wearer of the white coat encountered in a hospital or surgery has had medical training, is a professional, has the power to examine our body and ask about intimate details of our lives, is reliable, clean and respects confidences, and has a high social status. Were we to encounter someone similarly dressed in the supermarket we would, however, make very different assumptions. Symbols therefore do not operate in isolation but become meaningful when we encounter them in ritual times and spaces such as the surgery or the hospital. Moreover, in recognising the power of medical practitioners and their diagnostic capacities, we simultaneously recognise ourselves as altered in terms of our social identity. Personal or private social identities – bank manager, cellist, union leader, market gardener – are set to one side once admission to the public space of the hospital marks entry to the more dominant identity of 'patient'.

Thus we can see medical encounters as highly structured events that can help to secure our consent to particular ways of mapping changes that are happening within our minds or our bodies. It has been argued that, in reflecting broader and more pervasive aspects of society, the symbolic forms that go to make up such encounters implicitly draw on wider structures of power, such as social class, gender and ethnicity, thereby subtly reinforcing our belief in medical models. Furthermore, in participating in medical practice, we, as patients, are affirmed in our acceptance of society's dominant values and beliefs. By looking outside the medical encounter itself we can see how broader sets of social values come to be tied up within it. For example, the scientific claims made for Western biomedical models can be seen as an aspect of the value attached more broadly to science with the West, one that, Doyal argues, plays an important part in legitimating the dominant order within such societies (Doyal, 1979). Furthermore, the organisation of health-care provision, exemplified in the hierarchical relationship between doctor and patient, reflects a taken-for-granted social hierarchy where professionals of all kinds are drawn from higher social classes, and their status and expertise reinforced by their position within society. The power of a particular model of the mind and body is therefore intimately bound up with other forms of social power, one sustaining the other in a reciprocal relationship.

Thus far we have addressed questions about beliefs and explored the processes through which changes in the mind and body come to be interpreted as 'illness' or 'disease'. In so doing it has become evident that our maps, models or metaphors are generated and put into practice within the context of social relations. Furthermore, the structure of social relations and the distribution of power and inequality within society, are, in part, constructed, contested and sustained through health-related beliefs and practices. Therefore, if we move outside the medical encounter between doctor and patient, we find it to be connected with more extensive networks of social relations. These stretch out into the patient's family, their community, and indeed into society more broadly, in both the present and the past. In the next section we shall examine the wider framework of social relations within which health-related ideas and practices of all kinds have informed individual experience, beginning with an historical perspective.

Social relations and the historical development of biomedicine

As already noted, models of the human mind and body have varied enormously across cultures and throughout history. If we look back into Western history prior to the scientific revolution of the seventeenth century, we find not only very different ways of understanding the mind and body and the changes they might undergo, but also a very different social context for health-related beliefs and practices. Human growth, development and decline at that time took place almost entirely within the private sphere of the family, or in small, localised communities where individual illnesses, once made evident, were interpreted socially as 'sickness', rather than diagnosed medically as 'disease'. This setting can be compared with the post-seventeenth-century social world, described by Foucault, where the individual and their body became open for the first time to the public gaze of impersonal representatives of the state, such as medical practitioners (Foucault, 1973).

In 1500, 94 per cent of the population of Britain lived in localised rural settings, and in 1700 the figure was still 84 per cent (Stacey, 1988). Health care was provided predominantly within the home, by women. In this respect we can see a continuity with the present where, it is argued, women take unpaid domestic responsibility for 'health promotion, health maintenance, health restoration and caring for the disabled' (Stacey, 1988, p. 206).

Prior to the seventeenth century, orally-transmitted and written systems of belief and practice often remained entirely within the private sphere, being passed down through generations of women, to be modified in turn by each woman's practical experience, so that it was within the private setting of the home that health and illness were interpreted and managed. Women drew on a variety of healing systems, from plants and minerals through to ritual healing involving prayers, charms or spells. While individuals would go outside the home when domestic remedies failed, healers were to be found within the local community, their health-related role being non-specialised, their practice going hand-in-hand with other occupations such as housework, carpentry or weaving. While health care represented an aspect of women's domestic work, community healers might be both women and men. Indeed, in that healing in all its forms drew on a range of maps or metaphors of illness, so distinctions between practitioners were often blurred. Housewives, folk healers, apothecaries, barber-surgeons and physicians all played similiar roles, none of them at a significant remove from the patient's domestic sphere, and few of them operating in public or specialised locations (Stacey, 1988).

The issues of power and control, which medical sociology has high-lighted as key aspects of the provision of health-related expertise, were here associated not with a professionalised body of medical practitioners, but with the Church. Thus the medieval Church claimed for itself healing powers that were often pagan or magical in character. It also recognised with disapproval the powers of individual healers, whether to bless or to curse. Healers therefore often took pains to couch their practice in Christian terms, prescribing, for example, the recitation of prayers (Stacey, 1988). Problematic within the terms of a Christian medieval model of health and illness was the practice of healing for economic rather than charitable purposes; the notion of illness as requiring a cure rather than to be borne as submission to God's will; and the grounding of much medical practice in the secular models of Greek science and Hippocratic medicine. Bryan Turner argues that the development of medical ethics and an emphasis on the doctor's moral responsibility for their patient can be understood partly as way of reconciling the differences between the institutions of religion and medicine (Turner, 1987).

The power relationship between practitioner and patient during this period has been described as being more egalitarian than that which predominates within contemporary British society. This has been attributed to the lack of highly specialised medical knowledge, patients themselves therefore being informed about the nature of their condition and the efficacy of particular forms of healing (Porter, 1987). Their situation can again be contrasted with that described by Foucault, where the silent patient submits to the gaze of the doctor via the stethoscope, the nature of both their illness and its cure lying firmly within the hands of the doctor. When we consider the place of healing within social relations across time we are tracing a movement out of the private, domestic or community sphere and into a professionally-bounded, public space. Contemporary Western medicine appears to lie largely in male, middle- and upper-class hands, when once it lay predominantly in a female, working-class domain. To argue that the power to heal has been wrested directly by one group from another is, however, misleading. An accurate understanding of this process in Britain requires that we look more broadly at the nature of social change between the sixteenth and twentieth centuries. Again, we have an example of the importance of locating health-related beliefs and practices within the specific cultural and social climate of their day (Porter, 1987). Among the wealthy members of American society, for example, doctors have less freedom to determine the terms of their relationship with patients, since the cost of treatment is borne by the patient via insurance.

M. Stacey argues that the development of a 'market' for healing was crucial in terms of the subsequent gendered division of healing labour and the eventual dominance of Western biomedical beliefs and practices (Stacey, 1988). Even during the medieval period, men were dominant among that small proportion of the population who lived in urban settings and who had control of the Church, Parliament, the judiciary, the military, the universities and the schools. As the relationship between the rural domestic and urban public worlds began to shift during the seventeenth and eighteenth centuries, so the relative prominence of male-dominated social spaces and institutions within towns and cities grew. Healing therefore came to find a place within a market that was predominantly under male control. Those who, in time, would form the medical 'fringe', the community-based folk healers, were not only 'wise women' but also 'cunning men'. It was therefore not only along gendered lines that the location of health care began to shift. To understand this process we need to set it within the context of urbanisation, the growth of the market and gender relations, a complex interrelationship that appears to have led to the dispossession of those previously sought after for their expertise in healing.

However, although the growth of the market appears to be critical to the eventual professionalisation of biomedicine and its focus on the body, during the seventeenth and eighteenth centuries it represented merely a forum within which a pre-existing range of approaches to healing vied with one another for economic survival. If we look to this period for insight into the reasons why biomedicine came to be dominant, we find little evidence that it was either more efficacious or more popular (Porter, 1987). Stacey draws on the earlier work of Porter (1983), arguing that 'it would be a forlorn task to try to draw hard-and-fast lines between "proper" practitioners and quacks using criteria such as integrity, scientific method, or therapeutic efficiency' (Stacey, 1988, p. 51). While our discussion yields insight into the reasons why healing passed more exclusively into male hands once it developed into an economic activity, it remains to be shown why one form of healing took precedence over others.

From the beginning of the eighteenth century onwards, medical practitioners ceased to compete on equal terms with other healers in the market place; instead, we find the beginning of a professional medical monopoly. As a result of lay concerns from clergy, local dignitaries and royalty, hospitals were set up as special spaces within which care could be provided for poor and sick people. Those who would otherwise make visible their infirmities in public space were drawn into the institutional space of the hospital. It was this domain that provided medical practitioners with the scope to develop both a specialised body of knowledge and a high-status profession. Those who were traditionally excluded from infirmaries – such as children, pregnant women, infectious cases, epileptics, or consumptive or dying patients – also came to be seen to be in need of such services, and the practice of home visiting was established. The expansion and effectiveness of this project, in terms of the growth of professional medicine, lay initially in the existing relationships between practitioners and their wealthy patients. Physicians and surgeons played a key supervisory role within hospitals but gave their services without charge, routine medical work being carried out by their students. This role had a number of effects. It enhanced their reputations with wealthy patients who, as a result, were willing to donate to hospital funds. It also provided doctors with revenue in the form of their students' fees. With a growing income in the form of donations and fees, hospitals became established as crucial centres within which teaching and research could be carried out (Stacey, 1988). It would seem, therefore, that at this stage the conditions had been established for the rise of professional medicine in the West. The appropriation of one particular view of the mind and body, the mechanistic model, by a powerful professional group, appears to provide an explanation for the persuasiveness of a medical model.

When we move into the nineteenth century, however, we find other dimensions to the growth of biomedicine. During this period, professionalised biomedical practice increasingly took place within the hospital. Furthermore, as the relationship between urban and rural worlds continued to change, with cities expanding with great rapidity, so health and illness became increasingly intertwined with political issues. While the shift away from community-based health care had resulted in the loss of non-gendered healing and the growth of male-dominated health care, the very rapid growth of cities also produced class-based tensions which, in part, were managed in terms of health and illness. Thus, while wealthy people continued to pay for the services of doctors in their own homes, where they enjoyed an egalitarian or even superior position in relation to the medical practitioner, the voluntary hospital or the workhouse became the site for the health care of poorer people. In this setting, not only did people's bodies become 'sites' within which the practice of medicine could be developed, but patients themselves became accessible to forms of moral regulation that were seen to contribute to the well-being of the population as a whole. Indeed, health care in these settings represented an attempt to manage the contradictions of a political commitment to a free market economy with minimal state interference where concerns were, none the less, being felt about the health and moral welfare of the population. Stacey cites discipline, religious observance and hierarchy as the means through which the institutionalised poor were regulated (Stacey, 1988). In addition, medical theories which sought to explain the epidemics that swept nineteenth-century urban environments were often couched in implicit class contagion terms. Thus the concept of miasma, a 'noxious emanation' – as an explanation for the spread of disease – was associated with the slum areas that housed working-class people. In these settings, both adequate sewerage and burial facilities were lacking. The notion of miasma can be seen as just one of the ways in which the proximity of working-class and middle-class people within the city was problematised. Strategies for remedying this problem included the development of public health legislation, segregating areas of housing according to class, by-laws concerning the use of public space, and the regulation of leisure activities, which resulted in the growth of class-differentiated forms of sport.

In sum, nineteenth-century urban life was a context within which illness among working-class people was seen to be problematic in that it represented a threat to the nation's expansion, both economically and imperially. Social evolutionary views about the need to maintain both the purity and the strength of British 'stock' similarly reflected concerns about the position of Britain internationally. Epidemics were understood not only in terms of 'miasmas' emanating from working-class urban slums, but also as intrusions from potentially threatening, foreign parts of the world (Doyal, 1979).

In tracing the transition from the mixed economy of the eighteenth century health-care market place to the dominance of a unified medical profession, Stacey cites one factor as being critical (Stacey, 1988). Within the context of the emergent London medical schools, the previous conglomerate of surgeons, physicians and apothecaries began to join forces, with the result that by the middle of the century pressure to restrict entry to the profession led to the 1858 Medical Act. This Act created a definitive boundary between biomedical practitioners and other healers. It also firmly excluded women from qualified medical practice, their niche within the system, as nurses, stemming from the belief that, as women, they were suited by nature to the task of caring. The rational, intellectual task of curing was seen as being appropriate for men, a perspective closely underwritten by biological accounts of sex differences. While women struggled throughout the second half of the nineteenth century to gain access to medical training, by 1901 only 212 were qualified out of a total of 36 000 registered medical practitioners (Stacey, 1988, p. 90).

Social relations and illness behaviour

An outline of the historical transition from a community-based mapping of illness to a professional, medicalised model of disease provides the necessary background for thinking about the wider structures of social relations within which that process is embedded in the twentieth century. Thus, the growing power of medical models to provide a persuasive system for interpreting change within the self has been linked intimately with the gender-, class- and ethnicity-based structures of power particular to Western society. We have part of the answer to our question about how one model of change within the mind or body can come to be seen as 'true' and therefore used as a basis for health-related decision-making and action. However, this does not explain why the medical profession deal with only a small proportion of what we define as our illnesses. D. Hannay's study showed that many symptoms of illness do not get reported to doctors, a finding that gave rise to the concept of the 'clinical iceberg' (Hannay, 1980). Earlier, we asked why so persuasive an account of illness is sometimes questioned or ignored. We also noted that individuals might draw on medical models in conjunction with other approaches, as was the case with homeopathy and biomedicine. In this section we examine the wider context of social relations within which biomedical models are located, and ask about the ways in which individuals appear to conceive of and manage change within their minds and bodies.

In addition to a professional sector of health care, Scambler also identifies popular and folk sectors (Scambler, 1991). The popular sector encompasses self-care, including self-medication, and also self-help groups that exist without the support of professional health-care workers. The folk sector includes alternative or non-orthodox healers. While the 1858 Medical Act created a clear boundary between medically qualified and other healers, those who have practised without an orthodox medical training from medieval times onwards continue to represent the site within which the majority of health care takes place. These are women caring for their families, and alternative therapists such as homeopaths and acupuncturists. We need to find explanations as to why those who practice according to an apparently more persuasive medical model are not dealing with the majority of illnesses.

In the previous section we saw how the growth of the market and the development of the hospital provided the conditions within which professionalised biomedicine could develop. In addition, it was noted that biomedicine's structural links with men and masculinity, and with the middle and upper classes were critical to its success. Its efficacy in curing disease, nowadays often taken as self-evident proof of its validity as a model of the mind and body, was not, however, central to its initial growth. Other factors are cited as being more central. Doyal , for example, takes the view that one source of the power of medical models lies in their scientific foundation (Doyal, 1979). She argues that the nineteenth century saw an undermining of hitherto persuasive religious frameworks as a legitimation of forms of social organisation such as gender. Science, the underpinning of industrial, and therefore economic, expansion, held sway as a way of understanding the world. As Weber noted, it was a social world characterised increasingly by rationality rather than tradition (Weber, 1978). Within this social context the models of medical science took on a central role in legitimating the changes in social relations resulting from the emergence of a middle class of industrialists. They did not, however, have a significant effect upon the nation's health. The improvements in health that did become evident from 1870 onwards are widely acknowledged to be the result of the development of public-health legislation and improved material conditions among working-class people, rather than the growth of the medical profession (Doyal, 1979). Indeed, specialised medical health care was available only to a tiny minority of the population during this period.

Within Western society during the second half of the twentieth century, medical remedies such as antibiotics or surgery have been producing dramatic changes in the state of individuals diagnosed as suffering from a disease. While critics such as Ivan Illich have warned that these are short-term benefits that may result in the longer-term dependency of populations upon medical support, the capacity of medical science to provide cures is now firmly established (Illich, 1975). The question therefore remains as to how the curative power of biomedicine relates to the much wider framework of beliefs and strategies through which individuals manage changes to their minds and bodies.

In addressing this question, the issue of social relations is central. Helman describes an ill person as being at the centre of therapeutic networks made up of family members, friends and neighbours, who provide advice as to how illness should be managed (Helman, 1990). These networks connect the individual to the three health care sectors identified by Scambler: the professional, the popular and the folk (1991). As described by Helman, therapeutic networks radiate out from the close friends and family of the ill person through neighbours, friends of friends, to healers of one kind and another, and to self-help groups. They can provide a channel through which the individual is brought into consultation with a healer. For example, A. de Swaan argues that the expansion of orthodox medicine is reliant upon the presence of lay proto-professionals (de Swaan, 1990). That is, individuals who have a formal education or an occupation that is allied to medicine in some way often draw upon popularised medical frameworks in order to transform the troubles of their friends and family into problems meriting a medical encounter of some kind. These people might, for example, be dentists, chemists or even receptionists in a health-care setting. The ill person themself is, however, more than just the passive object of the actions of others. In each society there are recognised verbal and behavioural modes for revealing the presence of mental or physical changes (Zola, 1966). Thus, an appropriate disclosure may be essential before the resources of the network are mobilised. Conversely, individuals who signal no subjective experience of change may, none the less, find their behaviour circumscribed as a result of the ways in which others make sense of it – for example, 'There's no way you should be at work with that chesty cough' said by a manager to employee can effectively recategorise the individual as being 'sick'. In addition, therapeutic networks serve not only to channel individuals towards healers, but also to provide an interpretive context within which the recommendations of healers will be made sense of, complied with or ignored. It is therefore often within the therapeutic network that the decision to replace one form of healing with another will be made, whether it be orthodox or alternative. Similarly, it is within the therapeutic network that the healer's diagnosis of an individual's illness will be brought into play as legitimation for the individual's failure to adhere to their normal social roles. Illness is therefore not only a product of a particular interpretive process, whether provided by an orthodox healer or a lay person, but also the product of a complex, interactive social process.

The medical model can be understood as an umbrella term that encompasses what Helman describes as a 'repertoire of interpretive models – biochemical, immunological, viral, genetic, environmental, psychodynamic, family interactionist and so on' (1990, p. 90). It is therefore inappropriate to think of medical 'advice' as something that is given in a consistent form by the members of a single profession. The range of definitions of what constitutes health and illness is, as has been shown, far wider. Thus the interpretation of mental or physical change is a social process that takes place as an aspect of social relations. What is striking is that very similar changes, such as backache, may or may not be interpreted as illnesses. Fox (in Helman, 1990, p. 92) describes the way in which wealthy members of society in a town in upper New York State usually reported backache to their doctor. Poorer people regarded it as 'an inevitable and innocuous part of life and thus as inappropriate for referral to a doctor'.

Arthur Kleinman uses the notion of explanatory models to describe the interpretive process. By this he is referring to a map or metaphor – such as the body as a system of plumbing – which helps the individual to understand how it should work and how it might go wrong (Helman, 1990). While Kleinman argues that consultations between doctors and patients can be seen as transactions between lay and medical explanatory models, it can be argued that the discussion of illness at any point in the therapeutic network often has the nature of a transaction between competing models. For example, while a child may explain abdominal discomfort as impending sickness and diarrhoea that will require time off school, the child's mother may interpret such discomfort as the result of a hurriedly-eaten breakfast and no bar to attendance. As this example indicates, an explanatory model may be made to 'stick', to the extent that its proponent stands in a powerful position in relation to someone espousing other models. As members of more powerful social categories, the explanatory models of doctors and mothers may carry more weight than those of patients and children.

In exploring the social production of illness, we come to see a biomedical model not only as one among a range of belief systems; we also understand it to be a socially-mediated rather than a purely professional framework of ideas. While Kleinman argues that the explanatory models of doctors are based on 'single causal trains of scientific logic', while those of patients are characterised by 'vagueness, multiplicity of meanings, frequent changes, and lack of sharp boundaries between ideas and experience', the clarity of this distinction is open to criticism (Helman, 1990, p. 95). It was certainly the case that Helman, in his study of medical folklore in a north London suburb, found that scientific medicine had little impact on folk beliefs (Helman, 1984). However, the frameworks in use among patients were often shared by their doctors. Thus he describes a folk model where 'the metaphor of "germs" as invisible forces "out there" which cause suffering to the innocent, seems to have become a pervasive social metaphor' (1984, p. 15). In transactions or negotiations that took place between doctor and patient, the doctor often used the same 'germ' map or metaphor as the patient. While the doctor's primary motivation for this collusion might have been to secure the patient's compliance, it may also, in Helman's view, serve to reinforce the folk model. Furthermore the 'scientific logic' that Kleinman attributes to medical explanatory models was not always in evidence in Helman's study. He found that many doctors did not, or could not, differentiate between viruses and bacteria. Hence the ubiquitous 'germ theory' of illness. Their diagnoses were often couched in terms such as 'You've picked up a germ', 'It's just a tummy bug – there's one going around', or 'You've got a germ in the water' (1984, p. 15). Kleinman's clear distinction between lay and medical explanatory models is therefore perhaps over-simple. When it comes to a decision about consulting the doctor, de Swaan, as already noted, highlights the informal influence of proto-professionals, individuals whose educational background has given them some access to medical models (de Swaan, 1990). However, as Helman's study demonstrates, medical models may not represent the form in which doctors present their diagnoses. Instead, they may select from a range of more popular models of the body and its workings in order to find a map or an image to which they believe the patient might respond more readily.

W. Stainton Rogers goes further, in arguing that individuals and their health beliefs are in no way wedded to one another. Rather, she argues, individuals of all kinds, both healers and others, draw on a range of possible explanatory models depending upon their evaluation of different social contexts. Thus their choice of a particular explanatory model depends upon their assessment of its usefulness for them as an individuals and its value in interpersonal or collective functions (Stainton Rogers, 1991).

She interviewed seventy individuals, both lay and professional, about their health beliefs and identified, in the resulting material, eight alternative accounts of health and illness: the 'body as a machine' account; the 'body under siege' from external forces such as germs or viruses account; the 'inequality of access' to medicine account, which understands illness as the product of inadequate medical provision; the 'cultural critique' of medicine account, which might represent illness as a side-effect of medical treatment; the 'health promotion' account, which stresses individual responsibility for health; the 'robust individualism' account, which highlights the individual's right to a satisfying life; the 'God's power' account; and the 'willpower' account, which stresses 'mind over matter'. Making sense of the way in which the individual might draw on any of these simultaneously present (or 'sympatric') accounts when they feel ill, Stainton Rogers argues that 'a notion of account sympatricity is thus one which portrays people as story makers who weave a narrative in and out of different "texts"' (1991, p. 228).

When theoretical perspectives such as those developed by Stainton Rogers are examined, questions emerge concerning their fit with the notion that health and illness are understood in Western society predominantly through biomedical models. This chapter has explored the historical emergence and contemporary practice of biomedicine in an attempt to show how a particular view of mental or physical change within the self comes to be believed. Furthermore, in its persuasiveness, this model also represents a basis for decision-making and action. Yet, as is evident from the material presented here, biomedicine continues to co-exist alongside beliefs and practices grounded in entirely different interpretations of health and illness. It is also under-used in the sense that much illness goes untreated. Stacey cites a range of studies which show that there is little difference between individuals who consult a doctor over symptoms and those who do not (Last, 1963; Wadsworth *et al.*, 1971; Hannay, 1979, all cited in Stacey, 1988). Hannay's study of a population in Glasgow showed that 86 per cent of respondents had symptoms which, in his view, were an appropriate cause for a medical consultation. However, only about a third of those with symptoms had consulted a doctor, while another 10 per cent had sought advice from a lay person. Hannay uses the image of an iceberg to describe the presence of a body of symptoms hidden within the population as a whole, one that is much larger than that which surfaces for the attention of doctors (Stacey, 1988, pp. 197–8).

In the following, final section of this chapter we review a range of theoretical perspectives which address the role of a biomedical model within the contemporary world, in order to evaluate their usefulness in making sense of the health-related experiences of both individuals and populations.

Theories of medicine

Authors such as Lesley Doyal and Viccente Navarro, who write from Marxist perspectives, often highlight the part played by biomedicine in legitimating or reinforcing the structures of a capitalist society (Doyal, 1979; Navarro, 1976). As already indicated, Doyal argues that nineteenth-century industrial expansion has its roots in scientific frameworks which, through an associated medical model, were also used to legitimate the social inequalities associated with industrialisation. The exclusion not only of women, but also children and older people from the workforce was, for example, underwritten by medicalised concerns for their health and welfare. Biologistic models of women's 'natures' which represented them as vulnerable, reproductive beings were central to a model of femininity that assured women's dependency at a time of growing feminist activity. Confined within the home, however, middle-class women came to play an important symbolic role in lending a sense of respectability to their newly wealthy husbands and families (Jordanova, 1989). Debarred from medical practice themselves, they none the less constituted ideal private patients for the members of an expanding medical profession.

Contemporary medical practice has been described by Marxist authors as the benevolent face of a capitalist system which, in fact, engenders illness through poverty and occupational hazards. As Doyal notes, the association between capitalism and illness is not straighfor-ward (1979). Thus industrialisation under capitalism has increased life expectancy and improved the quality of life for certain social groups. This has, however, been carried out at the expense of populations in other parts of the world whose health has suffered as a result of colonialism and the loss of their own resources. Furthermore, associa-tions can be made between capitalism and new forms of illness stem-ming from occupational and environmental hazards such as pollution. While there is strong evidence of links between early mortality rates and membership of a lower social class (Townsend and Davidson, 1982), recent research has suggested a relationship between the unequal dis-tribution of wealth within a population and levels of ill-health (Wilk-inson, 1994). Poverty alone seems not to be the key to illness.

The individualistic nature of a biomedical approach to illness has also been argued to play a part in upholding a capitalist system, in that the social and economic causes of illness become reduced to a personal matter to be dealt with in the encounter between doctor and patient. The lifestyle of the individual is therefore scrutinised, and smoking and lack of exercise, for example, rather than poverty and pollution, are identified as causes of illness for which the individual is enjoined to take responsibility. Health problems are thus located within the private sphere of the individual, and public solutions are less likely to be called for.

The development of medical technology and an associated pharma-ceutical industry are in themselves important aspects of capitalist expansion in that they represent important economic developments. However, their role is not only economic but also ideological, in the view of Marxist authors such as Doyal (1979). Not only does orthodox medicine legitimate the scientific frameworks that underpin capitalist industrialisation, it also validates the hierarchical relations of capitalist production through its own internal professional hierarchies, and through the unequal relationship that pertains between doctor and patient.

To some extent, this view of orthodox medicine is echoed in the work of authors writing from feminist perspectives. Indeed, Doyal offers a critique of medicine from both a feminist and a Marxist perspective. Ann Oakley has explored women's experiences as patients, particularly in association with their reproductive lives. Drawing on her observations of encounters between maternity patients and doctors, she argues that women are constructed as powerless and stupid within the frameworks of professional medicine (Oakley, 1984). One of the ways in which this takes place is through doctors' use of language. In keeping with the findings of Helman and Stainton Rogers, explanatory models of health and illness are drawn upon flexibly by both doctor and patient in the maternity consultation. By moving between commonsense and technical explanatory models, doctors are able to retain a largely unquestioned position of dominance. Tracing nineteenth-century notions of women as being at the mercy of their wombs, Oakley goes on to show how a male-dominated profession took control of childbirth, previously the domain of the female midwife. In promoting the view of women as predominantly reproductive beings, she argues that a medical model created a double bind which confirmed women's inferiority in relation to men. Menstruation, childbirth and the menopause were constructed as illnesses meriting medical attention. As such, they rendered women 'ill' throughout their lives. On the other hand, those women who eschewed traditional feminine roles of care and service to the family for more intellectual professional occupations also put themselves at risk of illness by riding roughshod over their own biological 'natures'.

In this and other feminist critiques of orthodox medicine, the notion of medicine as a system of social control is evident (Ehrenreich and English, 1979; Roberts, 1981; Doyal and Elston, 1986; and Graham, 1987). Like the Marxist argument that medical knowledge and practice serves the ends of the state, feminist critiques such as Oakley's argue that medicine serves the interests of patriarchy – that is, the dominance of men within both public and private spheres. Parsons similarly saw medicine as having a part to play within society, over and above the treatment of illness. As a way of managing the threat to society posed by illness, medicine was therefore functional in maintaining society's equilibrium (Hillier, 1991).

Concurring with the notion that medical knowledge and practice carry additional layers of meaning and fulfil purposes other than the cure of disease, the view has also been argued that biomedicine represents a framework for managing an ever-widening range of human experience. Thus the concept of the medicalisation of life is a way of explaining the demand for a medical management of social problems such as hyperactivity, obesity, violence, alcoholism and child abuse. Hillier cites Paul Halmos's view that medicalisation has replaced the criminalisation of many aspects of human life, such as suicide or homosexuality, in that suicide is often seen as a mental health problem, and homosexuality has been represented in some quarters as an outcome of a genetic mutation (Hillier, 1991). As such, in Halmos's view, it represents a preferred alternative. Others, such as Irving Zola, argue that this is a wholly negative development (Zola, 1975). While it is questionable whether medical practitioners do have the power to expand their frameworks of knowledge indefinitely, particularly in the light of competing legal and religious perspectives, de Swaan's work on the management of 'normality' does argue strongly for the power of a medical regime to inform many aspects of our lives (de Swaan, 1990). For example, he draws attention to the requirement that we eat certain foods, exercise and resist pollution in the name of our health. This he interprets as evidence of a medical regime, one that is not necessarily congruent with the views and practices of the medical profession itself: 'Everyone lives under medical supervision', he argues, 'at least in today's advanced and affluent societies' (de Swaan, 1990, p. 57). Referring to individuals who would not describe themselves as ill, he says:

> The rest of the population is not so much healthy as not-yet-sick and live under a light medical regime: in more and more aspects of their daily life they mind their health, with regard to food and cleanliness, physical exercise, and their environment. Sometimes they do so at the urging of doctors, but frequently they talk one another into it in the name of (often imaginary) medical opinions. (1990, p.57)

In this, de Swaan is therefore not following the 'medicalisation of life' critique, which argues that the medical profession itself is imperialistically expanding its sphere of expertise. In other words, medicine serves the professional interests of doctors, rather than the political ends of the state or patriarchy. What de Swaan argues is that medical frameworks have come to be seen as a way of managing social contradictions. These include the allocation of scarce resources, such as housing or institutional care, personnel selection, environmental or occupational hazards, abortion, ageing, absences from work, sex criminals and violent delinquents, all of them areas of social conflict that come to be seen as manageable once they are redefined as medical problems. He explains this development as the outcome of a multiplicity of interactions between individuals and organisations seeking conflict resolution, and doctors. As members of a professional body, however, medical managers and educators have resisted a deliberate expansion of the discipline's areas of expertise in this way, since they forsee problems of legitimation should this occur. If policy were to be formulated for medical arbitration in areas of social conflict, conflicts internal to the professional itself, concerning both knowledge and practice, would be held up to unwelcome scrutiny. Looked at from this perspective, we can see the boundaries between medicine, religion and the law as not only being situated differently at different points in history, but also shifting in line with the wider political agendas of the day. For example, while medical opinion is brought to bear in making decisions about the prolongation of life in Britain in the late 1990s, in America this issue is seen to fall more obviously within a legal domain.

Each of these theoretical perspectives: Marxist, functionalist, feminist, social control, medicalisation or conflict management, take as their focus either the practice of orthodox medicine or the conceptual frameworks associated with it. While authors such as de Swaan locate the power and persuasiveness of medical frameworks within individual or organisational encounters, the overall aim, in each case, is to provide an account of the place of orthodox medicine within society as a whole. They are largely macro-level explanations. We need to ask how useful they are in helping us to address the questions raised at the beginning of this chapter, concerning the reasons why we believe, question or make use of particular ways of explaining changes that are occurring within our minds or bodies. Helman and Stainton Rogers exemplify an approach which suggests that as members of a particular society we have a range of interpretive frameworks available to us. Furthermore, as we move between social contexts, different accounts will be selected and articulated depending upon our appraisal of what suits our ends in those contexts. These are micro-level explanations of how we manage change, and we still need to ask how they might relate to macro-level theories.

One perspective, already discussed, is the Foucauldian view that forms of power which serve the ends of the state are, none the less, in operation only at the micro-level. In other words, rather than the visible exercise of centralised power in events such as public hangings, a more effective form of discipline is exercised through an invisible micro-politics of power inherent within the practices of agents of state power such as doctors, magistrates and social workers. Such practices serve to construct the self and the body. As forms of surveillance, they provide the frameworks through which normality and health are defined and identified. Though persuasive as an account of the workings of power, Foucault's work has been found to be lacking when it comes to explaining resistance and individual autonomy. A system of power that is so all-pervasive would seem impossible to resist. However, David Armstrong has argued that it is precisely its pervasiveness which leads some people to resist it. Thus, he argues, 'an upraised hand to avert the gaze of surveillance marks the beginning of a self-existence for the nascent individual' (Armstrong, 1987, pp. 68–9).

In asking how we come to make interpretations of the changes that occur within our minds and bodies, we have already noted the problematic nature of a separation between a fixed, material reality and the range of interpretations we might make of it. Implicit within our question as to how we come to be persuaded by an account of the body is an assumption that, beyond or beneath our interpretation, there lies something that is not the concern of the social sciences, but rather a matter for the natural scientist, the anatomist, the biologist, the doctor.

In exploring a postmodernist approach to health, Fox provides ways of thinking about this problematic separation (Fox, 1993). He suggests that the social scientists' commitment to unravelling the nature of power is compromised, in that they too seek to exercise power and control. In other words, the 'critiques' of medicine offered by medical sociology can be seen to play their own part within the structures of power they seek to deconstruct. Thus, not only are the claims of medicine logocentric – that is, they claim to have access to an authentic 'truth' – but so too do the studies carried out by medical sociologists. For example, the work of each of the theorists outlined in this section of the chapter could be described as an attempt to explain how the world of health and healing is in reality. As such, these accounts could therefore be said to help sustain the logocentric position from which medical science itself offers its view of the body.

Developing Foucault's notion that the body comes to be seen and experienced as being 'diseased' or 'healthy' as a product of the gaze of the doctor, Fox points out that he is not arguing that ill-health and good health are a mere overlay upon a material reality. Instead, he suggests, the bodily symptom – a rash or a swelling – becomes a sign in that it is 'read' by the doctor. It is something that is inscribed on the body but can be read only by the medical expert. As Fox argues, 'One principle of the Foucauldian approach is to concern oneself always with the effects of power at the sites of its action' (Fox, 1993, p. 31). Another example would therefore be stigma, something that is often seen as spoiled identity. The implication of this view is that there is a pure identity which becomes encased in undesirable stigma. From a postmodern perspective, stigma is seen as the identity. And indeed, this would appear to correspond with the subjective experience of stigma as something integral to the self.

'Health' in this view is therefore something inscribed on the body. For example, the 'fitness' of those who exercise is not a matter of muscle tone or heart rate. Rather, it entails 'a discipline of the self and a necessary self-reflexivity about being a particular kind of person who "does fitness"' (Fox, 1993, p. 34). Similarly, with reference to his ethnography of surgery, Fox describes the competing discourses of surgeon and anaesthetist:

> Surgeons constituted their patient within a framework of her/his disease, while the anaesthetist was concerned with the patient's 'fitness', that is, her/his capacity to undergo the rigours of surgery and recover'. (1993, p. 43)

In that these discourses arose from and fed back in to the 'treatment' offered by each specialist, working in tandem, we begin to develop a sense of a notion of 'health' that is inscribed upon the body.

From this perspective we can reconsider our questions about the persuasiveness of particular systems of health care and their associated models of the body. Studies such as Stainton Rogers' revealed the fluidity of explanatory models of health (1991). Material from Fox's ethnography of surgery similarly shows individuals moving between accounts. If we examine the shifts between accounts or discourses we can begin to think about health and illness not just as sets of biological changes, variously interpreted at different times and in different places, but rather, to quote Fox, as 'highly contested, fragmented and fluctuating struggles for the body' (1993, p. 43).

Conclusion

This chapter has challenged medical and popular views of the body as a given, whether in sickness or in health. To this end it has reviewed the diversity of ways in which human beings, at different times and in different places, have understood changes within their bodies. We examined the maps or models that individuals draw upon to understand these changes, and asked why one or more maps are selected and others are excluded; and why some categories or groups of people are seen to be more expert than others when it comes to responding to these changes. Central to this chapter are questions of power, and we have shown how different social scientists have provided accounts of how power associated with health and illness is constituted and exercised. When it comes to health and illness, we find that they are not isolated or discrete areas of human life but instead, in terms of how they are both interpreted and treated, reveal much about wider values, priorities and systems of control. Similarly, when we examine the ways in which social scientists have addressed this particular area, we discover much more about their more general conceptions of the individual, society and the relationship of these with one another.

6

Doing and Being at Work

Structures of work

In Chapter 1 we saw that the early social scientists were concerned to explain the range of social and economic changes that occurred with the development of industrialisation and the transformation of production. At the end of the twentieth century it is taken for granted that work is a major social activity and that it is supported by a range of organisational structures. In this chapter we shall pursue the main themes of this book by focusing on the social construction of work and the conflicting, contradictory and complex meanings of this seemingly ordinary activity. In doing so we shall draw on the concepts of major social theorists, including Marx, Weber and Durkheim, who all saw work as being central to social life.

Following our concerns in earlier chapters with identity, the self and social roles, we shall now address the question of how the self develops within the social organisations and institutions in which work takes place, and the ways in which personal identities are both formed by and shape organisations and institutions. Of particular importance to life in Western societies is the value attached to the concept of 'doing' rather than 'being', and the role of work is central to this notion. However, the practice and meaning of work is constructed through a range of social factors and is by no means an activity as clearly differentiated from other areas of people's identities as the distinction between doing and being might suggest. Aspects of what we have called social structure, including class and gender, are factors in the construction and meaning of work.

Previous chapters have shown how the development of self and self-identity, and the transitions through which this self moves are part of the social world. We have also questioned the perceived dichotomy between the personal and the social world, between the 'private' and the 'public'. In Western societies the private world of the self is regarded as separate from and often in conflict with the social world, even though the self is constructed primarily through interaction with others. Part of this social world consists of the organisations and institutions of society – schools, families, marriages, universities, hospitals, churches, political organisations, government and other bureaucracies, business, manufacturing and commercial organisations.

What characterises institutions and organisations is their relatively formal structure and purpose (although they may serve other, less formal and unintended, functions) and their tendency to persist over time, independently of particular individuals, although not necessarily unchanged. They are also characterised, in Western societies at least, by the fact that within them people engage in routines of active and public work. In everyday language, organisations and institutions are social arrangements for accomplishing a range of social tasks, including work of various kinds.

It is not immediately apparent from its commonsense meaning that individuals engage in 'work' within social institutions such as marriage and family, and we shall elaborate on this later. At one level, institutions such as marriage and family are private, but at another level they are public, as indicated by the structure of legal and policy regulations and moral prescriptions surrounding them; for example, we commonly hear criticism directed at a separating or divorcing couple for 'not working hard enough at their marriage'. Criticism of parents for the misdoings of their children similarly implies they have failed in their 'job' of being parents. The public nature of such institutions is what, in part, makes them an aspect of 'work' for individuals. Until recently, social science has tended to concentrate on formal structures and emphasised the centrality of public 'doing', rather than private 'being'. In this chapter we shall show that the 'private' is also part of the 'public' organisational world (Giddens, 1991; Hearn *et al.* (eds), 1989; Martin, 1990).

Institutions and organisations of all kinds are major providers of social scripts that guide and in some cases direct the development of our selves, which was discussed in Chapter 2. Once we begin to look at social institutions and organisations in this light we begin to address issues of power and control and the way in which, while giving direction, they also limit the freedom of the individual to develop an autonomous self (see, for example, Deetz, 1992; and Townley, 1994). The institutions and organisations in which we are involved constitute 'scripts' which construct and reinforce our social selves.

The concept of 'work' implies, among other things, notions of order, regulation, purpose and structured activity. This structured activity can be seen as part of the process through which individuals, social institutions and whole societies reproduce themselves. Much of this continuity of social practices is ensured by the constant appraisal work people do within the structures provided by social institutions and organisations (Giddens, 1984, pp. 199ff). We discussed this at some length in the section entitled 'We Are All Social Theorists' in Chapter 1. Part of such reflexivity consists of rationalisations for action, accounting for what we do, and these are embodied in institutional and organisational practices: for example, nurses and careworkers write up reports for the next shift; and teachers of all kinds assess and write reports on their pupils and students.

If social structures constrain us and 'work', involving social relationships, is needed to maintain these structures, then we need to ask how this work is involved in creating and structuring social identities. As indicated earlier, if people 'work', not only at their jobs, but also at their marriages and their families, at school, and at social life in general, then the commonsense definition of work as employment, or having a job, is inadequate. From the examples given we can see that the term 'work' implies instrumental or purposeful activity by individuals. (see, for example, Sayers, 1988). Once we assume instrumental activity by individuals in any setting we begin to raise questions concerning the how and why of such activity, and return to issues of power and control involved in institutional and organisational scripts.

Work, meaning and identity

Some of the perspectives from which social scientists have studied 'work' indicate that 'working', or 'going to work' may have important functions in defining a person's status and sense of identity. Sue Sharpe, for example, showed how important paid work outside the home was for mothers, despite problems in reconciling such work with child care and domestic responsibilities:

This job's sort of changed my attitude. I mean you're teaching people to solve their own problems and to get the most out of life and teaching them skills, and it does build up your confidence tremendously. (Sharpe, 1984, p. 83)

Another of Sharpe's respondents was less concerned about earning than that 'somebody wants me for what *I* can *do*' (p. 78; see also Martin and Roberts, 1984; Sayers, 1988; and Cockburn, 1983).

Some classic studies of male workers demonstrate that the meaning of work is not confined to the workplace. Many of these studies deal with working situations much changed in the late 1990s. *Coal is Our Life* first published in the 1950s (Dennis *et al.*, 1969) shows how the dangerous, difficult work of mining coal created a male culture of mutual dependence, which continued outside working hours into leisure and other activities. The men lived in a mining community and defined themselves almost exclusively in terms of their work. Although expressing the wish that their sons would take up different work, 'boys in Ashton are destined to be Ashton miners and girls to be the wives of these miners' (Dennis *et al.*, 1969, p. 234). Mining families expressed wider aspirations for their families, but life in the community prevented children from perceiving themselves in other than conventional ways.

Studies of unemployment, paradoxically, tell us much about the way in which paid work gives meaning to people's lives. Unemployed men suffer loss of self-esteem and status, often seeing themselves as failures, unable to provide for their families. Losing a job also means losing a network of social relationships, and consequently loss of a sense of identification with others (see, for example, Kelvin and Jarrett, 1985; Fagin and Little, 1984).

Socially, not having work is upsetting, especially if you've been a fairly tough sort of bloke. You do lose something of your self-respect in the company of people who are working. You go into a pub, people look at you critically. (Seabrook, 1982, p. 126)

While most studies of unemployment have concentrated on unemployed males, women's psychological well-being is also threatened by unemployment (see, for example, Coyle, 1984).

Marienthal, the classic study of an unemployed Austrian community in the 1930s, shows how people's pride and participation in the community declined (Jahoda *et al.*, 1971). Although unemployed people had more time, they participated less in leisure and cultural activities such as reading. Men in particular ceased to be punctual for meals and so on, 'for punctuality loses meaning when there is nothing in the world that definitely has to be done' (p. 76). Women's sense of time was less disrupted because they still had a domestic routine to follow, but many wanted to return to work because they missed the social contact of the factory. Despite economic stringencies, researchers found 'irrational' patterns of spending – for example, on a cream cake, or a picture book for a child. Although there was a general food shortage, some people grew flowers, rather than vegetables, explaining that 'One can't just live on food, one needs also something for the soul' (p. 55), indicating that work provides not only subsistence but also the means to meet other psychological and spiritual needs (see, for example, Sayers, 1988; and Collinson and Hearn, 1994).

In the tellingly titled *Living the Fishing* Paul Thompson has shown how the paid work that supports a family may shape its members' lives: 'The fishing family, like the families of peasants and small farmers, or small business owners and shopkeepers, may be held together by more than ties of emotion. Where family boat-ownership continues, the family constitutes not merely a home, but also the basis for an economic venture' (Thompson, 1983, pp. 176–7). It can be argued that studies of occupations such as fishing and mining deal only with work in relatively isolated communities that no longer exist, if indeed they ever did (see, for example, Critcher, 1979; Cohen, 1980; and Bell and Newby, 1971). Pahl's study of the Isle of Sheppey, however, shows the continuing embeddedness of work in community and locale in a period of economic recession (Pahl, 1984). In examining 'divisions of labour' he explains the complexity of and connections between formal paid work and more casual work, including exchange of labour between neighbours and friends, and men and women, and indicates how people's selves and identities are bound up with work in a variety of forms. Here, work is less clearly differentiated from other aspects of life. The distinction between the public and the private is more blurred, although work is still concerned with economic life, with getting a living, and there are parallels here with many non-Western societies. This complex pattern of work embedded in family relationships, is to be found within some ethnic minorities in Britain (see Westwood and Bhachu (eds), 1988). These studies also show that economic and social structures, including 'race' and gender, constrain people's freedom to work, or not to work. Within these constraints individuals create their own informal structures of work and a meaningful economic life (see also Dex, 1988; and Casey, 1995).

Social production

The centrality of work and its attendant problems was the initial springboard for the development of sociology. As we saw in Chapter 1, the 'founding fathers' of the discipline addressed the profound changes in the social organisation of work occurring in late-eighteenth and early-nineteenth-century European societies. For Durkheim, changes in the division of labour appeared to create a new type of 'organic' social cohesion. Marx was much more critical of the capitalist organisation of work, which he thought would be superseded. Weber too, was pessimistic about the transformation of work by the late nineteenth century, but taking a very different methodological approach from Marx, he emphasised the complex relationship between economic activity and cultural beliefs (Eldridge (ed.), 1971; Lee and Newby, 1983). The work of these theorists has influenced much of what social scientists have to say about work and social identity.

In formulating his influential analysis of how societies function and change, Marx addressed a range of related issues including a view of what constitutes our essential human nature, arguing that 'man' as a 'species-being' (all human beings, as a group) is essentially a producer and needs to produce in order to live. It is through this process that human beings construct both themselves and an objective world (Fischer, 1973, pp. 31–6; and Grint, 1991, pp. 91ff). He also argued that human societies are formed and structured on the basis of this irreducible fact: that purposeful economic activity forms the foundation of social activity, social institutions and social relationships, and that we have no choice other than to participate. He recognised the enormous potential of human beings to produce, not only the basic necessities of life, but also music, art, and other aspects of society – what we often refer to as culture in its widest sense (Billington *et al.*, 1991).

Marx's theory concerning the nature of humankind and society also emphasises that power and conflict between different economic interests are embedded in all social relationships and institutions. The 'relations of production' is the term Marx uses to indicate the fundamental importance of work and economic activity as a central and instrumental aspect of social life and relationships. The emphasis he places on the economic foundations of society and the exploitative relationships between people resulting from this is much disputed, but Marx's fundamental insight that human beings are by definition workers and creators of social life is valuable.

Like Marx, Weber emphasised the historical development of certain kinds of economic activity. Both theorists were concerned with the development of the particular type of economic and social system we refer to as capitalism. While not rejecting Marx's emphasis on the essentially productive nature of humankind, we can argue, as Weber does, that the centrality of work to social life in modern societies stems from the origins and development of capitalism in the West.

Social action and rational work

While sharing some similar concerns with Marx, Weber argued that economic interests and activities were not the sole motor of social change and activity. All 'social action' – action directed towards other people, and which has meaning to the 'actor' – falls logically into one of four types, Weber argued (1978, pp. 7ff): (i) rational, goal-oriented action (*Zweckrational*) is where the individual calculates the outcome and deliberately sets out to achieve it – for example, my goal is to save £x each week and therefore I decide to walk to work each day instead of using my car; (ii) rational value-oriented action (*Wertrational*), is carried out to achieve or realise a particular ideal – for example, I walk to work each day, regardless of bad weather or the time this takes, because my goal is to avoid polluting the atmosphere; (iii) traditional action is based on custom or habit, and, according to Weber, is not rational but more or less automatic, or sometimes unconscious – for example, I walk to work because this is normal for people of my generation; and (iv) affective action is based on an emotional response and is also not considered by Weber to be rational – for example, I walk to work because I am afraid to drive.

Weber's analytical scheme of social action bears out the point made earlier, that people act in an instrumental way: we have goals and we 'work' at social life. The concept of social action assumes that even though constrained by circumstances, individuals have choice and free will. The notion of rationality will help us to explore further the idea of work as a chosen and instrumental activity.

To Weber, the process of rationalisation is what characterises modern societies and he saw capitalism itself as a particular form of rationalisation. By rationalisation, he meant:

the process by which explicit, abstract, intellectually calculable rules and procedures are increasingly substituted for sentiment, tradition and rule of thumb in all spheres of activity. (Wrong (ed.), 1970, p. 26)

Science dominates over religious beliefs, machine technology dominates over craft skills, and the result is what Weber called 'disenchantment'. Emotion, intuition and custom no longer provide the impetus for social life. Increasingly, 'formal' or 'technical' rationality supercedes 'substantive' or 'practical' rationality that is ultimately based on values or beliefs.

In any real social situation, Weber assumed all four types of social action would be involved (in themselves they are logical, pure types, for analytical purposes only; see Weber, 1978, pp. 29–30). However, the process of rationalisation means that life becomes increasingly dominated by instrumental rationality. Typically, people engage in the type of social action he called *zweckrational* – essentially activity motivated by achieving a calculable end – at the expense of action based on the goal of value achievement. An example here might be students studying to gain a paper qualification rather than an educational experience, or people becoming more instrumental about paid work, undertaking it for the wage or salary it produces, rather than for the satisfaction of engaging in the work itself as the 'Affluent worker studies showed, for example (Goldthorpe *et al.*, 1968–9).

Organising social action

Although Weber's approach emphasises individuals acting socially, rather than the organisational and institutional structures within which they operate, his concern with rationalisation and with mechanisms of power and dominance led him to look at types of organisation. Social action creates organisations and structures that ultimately constrain individuals. He was pessimistic about the results of increasing rationalisation, emphasising its effectiveness as a system of dominance; a system in which some people had power over others. Modern societies are characterised by rational-legal domination and types of organisation – where people act according to clearly laid out rules that have their basis in codified written law – compared to earlier societies, where power and organisation were based on tradition and custom. Bureaucracies such as a hospital, a university or the Department of Health and Social Security are obvious examples: organisations with a hierarchy of posts in which people fulfil clearly-specified functions. Officers are selected and appointed according to their technical competence for the post, rather than by favouritism or patronage. This model of bureaucracy is an 'ideal type' – that is, it contains all the essential features, although it may not be found in reality.

A great deal of work by sociologists and others criticises Weber's ideal type of bureaucracy, showing that an organisation based solely on formal rationality is dysfunctional, and only the existence of other informal systems of action enables the whole to function. For example, officials bend the rules to take account of individual circumstances, or break confidentiality in order to relieve their work stresses (Lee and Newby, 1983, pp. 198ff). Weber gave priority to rational activity in his analysis, and did not consider non-rational action to be goal-directed. David Lee and Howard Newby note that Weber locates non-rational action (traditional and affective) on the 'borderlines' of social action and as such is therefore not really the subject matter of social science (Lee and Newby, p.176). However, the implication of his pessimism concerning the erosion of value-achieving action, together with his point that both traditional and affective action occur *alongside* rational action in any social situation, is surely that rational action is never entirely the dominant mode.

Rosalind Bologh shows that Weber equated the rationality of modern life with freedom of the individual:

> Traditional and emotional modes of action, the only alternatives to rational action according to Weber's schema, are not free because they are not the outcome of conscious deliberation and choice. (Bologh, 1990, p. 122)

Bologh's feminist critique is that there are *other* types of social action, concerned with aesthetics and feelings. They are normally associated with women in the 'private' and domestic sphere, but can also be considered to be rational and equally essential to social life in the public sphere (see also Seidler, 1994; and Coleman, 1991; and Putnam and Mumby, 1993). Bologh's argument is that our work as social beings does not consist entirely of instrumental and value rationality, and that the type of instrumental activity that often characterises organisations and the ('masculine') public sphere inadequately conceptualises the way organisations actually function, and how individuals operate in them.

This raises questions about the dichotomous relationship usually formulated; the association of the formal, public organisation with rational instrumental action, and the private, domestic sphere with feeling, emotions and non-rational action. It is often assumed that the two 'spheres' are separate, and that work in its commonsense meaning belongs in the public sphere. Belief in a public versus private, rational versus non-rational dichotomy influences the way individuals think of themselves in relation to work, and the way social scientists have examined the topic.

The notion of work as public, separated off from the rest of life, has its roots in the development of industrial organisation and culture, and was clearly articulated and idealised in nineteenth-century Europe and America. With industrialisation, work and economic and political activity became increasingly differentiated from home, family and private life (see Davidoff and Hall, 1987). Nineteenth-and early-twentieth-century European liberalism made a similar distinction between civil society and domestic society. The two spheres of public and private were also perceived as separate in a gendered sense: women belonged to the private sphere and men to the public. However, the two worlds were considered mutually necessary, and family and domestic comfort highly valued as a refuge from the harsh world of industry, commerce and politics. There were many exceptions to this ideal of 'separation of spheres', and many challenges, not least from feminists, who argued that the moral, aesthetic and personal values associated with private life and embodied in women's roles were also requirements for public life, if its moral and practical values were to be enhanced. This is essentially the point that Bologh is making a century later. The idea that work – concerned with 'doing' – and domestic life – concerned with 'being' – are and should be separate, continues to influence profoundly our perceptions and definitions of 'work' (see, for example, Gamarnikow *et al.* (eds), 1983). It is apparent also that commonsense definitions of work have an in-built 'masculinity', a point we shall elaborate upon later in this chapter.

Meanings of work

Social scientists' thinking about work in part reflects, but also goes beyond, commonsense definitions. The sociology of work has concentrated on structural relationships between workers and managers, and a range of issues concerning the formal and informal organisation of work and the labour process (Grint, 1991). More recently the subjective and experiential aspects of work have been examined (see, for example, Rose, 1989; Collinson, 1992; Fineman (ed.), 1993; Watson, 1994; du Gay, 1996; and Casey, 1995). Pahl has commented on the confusion of meaning surrounding the concept of work and how it has changed historically in Western societies, pointing out that social scientists have paid too much attention to work narrowly conceived of as productive employment (Pahl, 1984, pp. 18–19). He reminds us that, prior to the development of industrial capitalism in the West, much work was not so rigidly gendered either; it consisted of tasks necessary for subsistence and survival, and these were carried out by whoever was available – including, quite often, children and elderly people.

You will notice that we have extended the notion of work from our initial definition of 'instrumental activity', indicating that it is often a gendered activity – that it is a role. We have also repeated, in more concrete fashion, Marx's point that work is production and necessary for survival, but in addition have suggested, as indeed Marx did, that work is concerned with the 'reproduction' of social life. Anthony Giddens has considerably extended this latter meaning of work, arguing that for individuals living in 'the late modern age' the development of the self is now a project to be worked at, rather than a fixed, socially ascribed role (Giddens, 1991 and 1992). So the concept of social reproduction means not simply the reproduction and construction of patterns and regularities of social life and institutions, but also the construction of our own self-identity, which can no longer be taken for granted. The 'project of the self' may include productive work in its narrow definition, but also other types of 'work', as we shall see later.

However, to define work as production gives clear boundaries to the concept, and these are narrowed further if we assume that work is synonymous with paid employment. Much of the psychology and sociology of work has made this assumption. Similarly, writing by social scientists on work in organisations has privileged the formal (public) organisational practices (those that Weber called rational–legal) rather than the less structured and informal activities that are also part of organisations and the practices of people at work (Fineman (ed.), 1993). Such approaches often assume that organisations are entities or systems with their own needs, goals and aims, leading to a reified view, with organisations being in some way independent of human actions and practices (see also Silverman, 1970; and Eldridge and Crombie, 1974). It can be argued that this view of organisations as having needs and imperatives fits remarkably well with the perceptions of managers and leaders and ignores other social actors (and their needs) in the organisation (see Rose, 1975, p. 245).

Neither approaches to organisations which define them as formal systems or structures in terms of goals identified by managers and leaders, nor radically opposed phenomenological approaches such as Silverman's, which emphasise organisations as socially constructed by their participants, deal adequately with who has power and how it might operate. This point is made by M. Rose, taking a relatively straightforward structural approach, stressing what he calls 'the importance of objective social constraints on human freedom' (Rose, 1975, p. 249; see also Collinson, 1992). However defined, power is an integral part of organisations, whether it is viewed as a property of formal organisational structure, part of the interactions of individuals who work within the organisation, or part of the knowledge and practices of organisations and other aspects of social life – what Foucault calls discourses (Macdonell, 1986).

Meaningful work

Following on from Marx, some studies have shown the activities and experiences of paid work in industrial societies to be unpleasant, exploitative and alienating. They meet the necessary purpose of earning a living, but do not fulfil other emotional, aesthetic, creative and spiritual aspirations we might have (see Chinoy, 1955; Sayers, 1988, pp. 722–41; Rose, 1989). A spot-welder at a Ford assembly plant described his job like this:

> I stand in one spot, about two-or three-feet area, all night. The only time a person stops is when the line stops ... I don't understand how come more guys don't flip. Because you're nothing more than a machine ... They give better care to that machine than they will to you ... Somehow you get the feeling that the machine is better than you are. (Terkel, 1974, pp. 159–60)

Part of the alienating tendency of work is that it structures and controls time for us. Modern technology, since the Industrial Revolution, has ensured that productive work continues non-stop, and this has been interpreted by writers such as E. P. Thompson as a form of discipline and control (Clarke and Critcher, 1985, ch. 1). While the extent of such alienation may be tempered by specific technological and organisational arrangements which, for example, allow workers to halt or slow a machine, or to change tasks (see Grint, 1991, ch. 8) workers have less power than employers and managers, little control over their work situation, and are producing not for themselves but for the profit of others. These are the factors that are seen to create alienation.

This critical perspective assumes that, as social beings, we need control and autonomy; emotional, spiritual and creative activity; and a potential for self-directed activity. Psychological studies show that, in general, people's performance at work improves when these factors are improved (Karasak and Theorell, 1990). Psychologists have also argued that human beings have a basic need to play and satisfy needs for leisure, as an antidote to the privations and stresses of work (Haywood *et al.*, 1989). Sociologists too, have investigated this idea (see, for example, Sayers, 1988, pp. 736–38; Horne *et al.* (eds), 1987; Rojek, 1985; Rojek (ed.), 1989).

In such a context, work tends to be seen as being instrumental. The 'Affluent Worker' studies in the early 1960s showed that workers in the postwar British car industry did indeed have instrumental attitudes to work, which they perceived as a means to attain other goals, such as a more affluent lifestyle, holidays abroad and better life chances for children (Goldthorpe *et al.*, 1968–9). We may engage in work purposefully not as a goal in itself, but because it allows us to achieve other goals – and this is one of the reasons why, in a society where it is assumed that everyone will engage in paid work, being unemployed is often traumatic and demoralising for individuals (Glyptis, 1989).

Strategies and approaches by managers, oriented explicitly towards improving 'human relations' in the workplace, recognise implicitly that better relations at work increase production and management control over workers. We might note here that generic management training has a disciplinary base in the social sciences and therefore draws on the psychological, social and other issues emphasised by these disciplines, even though it often remains outside and frequently distorts them (Watson, 1994; Rose, 1989).

The famous and subsequently much criticised Hawthorne studies, conducted at the Western Electric Company in Chicago from 1924 through to the 1940s, are usually seen to mark the beginning of the so-called 'human relations' approach in management. Initially designed to show the relationship between productivity and physical, environmental aspects of the workplace (for example, lighting) they ultimately drew attention to the importance of 'the face-to-face relationships of the workplace – its micro-politics' (Rose, 1975, p. 106). These and later studies indicated that people at work are motivated and affected by a range of factors, and it is these that influence and are influenced by formal, including environmental, structures. Other research indicates that people take to work a range of attitudes and expectations which affect their experience of work (see Dex, 1988, pp. 50ff; and Watson, 1994, pp. 61ff).

Marx's view of alienated labour was rooted in a political view of the world which explained alienation as the outcome of exploitative class relationships and predicted that when there was equal ownership of the means of production, necessary labour would not be alienated. Whether because of capitalism, as Marx thought, or some other cause, the idea that meaningful life takes place outside work – for example, during leisure – is embedded in social-science views of work as a necessary evil. Alternatively, despite its alienating tendency, social science recognises that people still create meaning in and gain satisfaction from their work. Even within the alienating, exploitative and constraining structures of work, as social individuals we create and produce meaning (see, for example, Moorhouse, 1984; du Gay, 1996).

Unemployed people, on the one hand, do not have to work within these constraints yet, on the other, find it difficult to organise their days meaningfully without these imposed structures:

> I used to be interested in politics at one time, but I don't bother much now...Sometimes when we get up we've got no idea what time it is. We ask the man at the shop what time it is. It might be seven o'clock. Or it might be three o'clock in the afternoon. Sometimes I say, 'D'you know what time it is? D'you know what *day* it is?...We haven't much sense of time. Sometimes we'll be sitting here and we'll say 'Let's go down for a game of darts in the pub', and we'll go down to the pub and the pub will be closed, and we'll think, 'Christ, fancy the pub being closed'. (Marsden and Duff, 1975, p. 210)

As we have already illustrated from the classic study *Marienthal,* work helps to construct the meaning of time for individuals. Even for women who are not 'out at work' themselves, a working man or other family members finishing work each day is part of what structures *their* day (Jahoda, 1982, p. 39).

Despite their instrumental views of work, the car assembly workers mentioned earlier found ways of relieving the tedium and stress created by the technology of the assembly line and the attitudes of employers. There are many other examples:

> I miss the company [since being made redundant]...because working in a factory full of lasses, I think it was just a good laugh all the time really...

but ... I could never go back to that now, not that sort of job ... The same thing over and over again each day. I think that's why you have such a good laugh in a place like that, because if you didn't you'd just go loopy with frustration. (Coyle, 1984, p. 91; see also Burowoy, 1979)

Marx's term 'relations of production' refers to the way in which social relationships are embedded in the practices of work, and indicates that these relations form and shape our consciousness of the world. The meanings and satisfactions which we create within paid work stretch beyond work and organisations to domains, such as leisure, and to our notions of time. Indeed, they shape core elements of our identity, such as gender and age, so, for example, old age is constructed on the premise of non-participation in work.

Work cultures and masculinity

This focus on social relations and the shaping of our consciousness through work leads us to consider the *culture* of work. The field of cultural studies, incorporating some of Marx's basic insights, has introduced an explicit and theoretically rigorous approach to this area. It attempts to deal with the everyday cultural details of the 'relations of production'. By treating work as part of the fabric of culture, the approach emphasises the 'lived' nature of work – its meaning and construction by individuals as part of their daily lives.

'When we are at our most natural, our most *everyday*, we are also at our most cultural ... when we are in roles that look the most obvious and given, we are actually in roles that are constructed, learned and far from inevitable' (Willis, 1979, p. 185). Paul Willis explains that work is part of culture, arguing that cultural patterns and symbols make us social beings and that 'we are therefore most *deeply* embedded in our culture when are at our most natural and spontaneous: if you like at our most work-a-day' (p. 186). Since many people spend much of their lives 'at work', Willis argues, 'Work is a living and active area of human involvement – it makes, and is made by us. It affects the general social nature of our lives in the most profound ways' (p. 186).

In his famous British study, *Learning to Labour* (1978), Willis shows how the activities of a group of working class 'lads' at school, seen conventionally as 'underachieving' or 'dropping out', are, in fact, a preparation for a life of work with few intrinsic satisfactions. To subvert the formal school system and 'have a laff' is a preparation for the strategies and knowledge needed for coping and making sense of life on the shop floor. Describing this, Willis states that

> despite the dispossession, despite the bad conditions, despite the external directions, despite the subjective ravages, people do look for meaning, they do seek enjoyment in activity, they do exercise their abilities. They repossess, symbolically and really, aspects of their experience and capacities. (Willis, 1979)

For men in particular, there is pride in doing a hard, dirty job and mastering the skills required, even if the work is classified officially as 'unskilled' or 'semi-skilled'. Pride in doing the job, learning the skills, and gaining the acknowledgement of others, is in part what creates a gendered self. For working-class men, it 'provides the materials for an elemental self-esteem . . . The wage packet is the provider of freedom and independence: the particular prize of masculinity in work' (Willis, 1979, p. 196; see also Cockburn, 1983, ch. 5; and Collinson, 1992). For male managers too, in the areas of design, marketing, production and sales, masculinity is embedded in work, coming not from pride in hard manual labour but from control over the products of the manufacturing process – for example landing gear, timing belts on welding equipment:

> At one remove from the physical work of production, they seek masculinity instead from the fruits of manual labour. Control of the manufacturing process as a whole enables managers to 'steal' the psychic delights afforded by products. (Roper, 1991, p. 191)

M. Roper describes this as an 'interweaving of self and product'. Managers had offices decorated with models and graphics of their product: 'products helped engender a sense of selfhood and anchored male friendships' (p. 193). Managers identified with products that were the result of exercising their managerial function, and recounted their careers in terms of them: 'Skill was codified in products' (p. 197; see also Watson, 1994, chs 3 and 8). Technological change is an important aspect of modern working practices, and writers have commented on the way in which technology is frequently identified with masculinity and manliness (Wajcman, 1991; Cockburn and Ormrod, 1993; and McNeill (ed.), 1987).

So masculinity, seemingly such a personal quality, is in part created by work itself, or to put this in more theoretical language, it is created through what Marx called the relations of production. Being unemployed in a society where masculinity is embedded in work in this way has repercussions for men's self-esteem and for their personal identity as men (Connell, 1991). Studies of families where men are unemployed and women employed, indicate that there is no necessary or logical 'role reversal' of household tasks, and many unemployed men would feel their identity as men threatened even further by taking over 'private' roles identified as women's. As one man put it, what he really dislikes about being unemployed is that 'it takes you out of the manly role. I used to be the breadwinner with my meal on the table. It lowers you. I feel like a lodger in my own house' (Wheelock, 1990, p. 63). This was not the response of all men in this study. In some couples, for example, men did household tasks 'to fill the time', but many women too reaffirmed that men's self-identity was partly produced through the gender segregation of work roles.

Similarly, employed men's resistance to their wives' paid employment reflects the meaning that many men attach to their role as family provider through paid work. Their resistance may include an unwillingness to take a share in household tasks. An example of this is a husband who refused to bring in washing off the line, and was discovered vacuuming the living room on his hands and knees, in case he might be seen by neighbours (Sharpe, 1984, p. 182). This amusing incident makes a serious point about the way work is part of men's identity, and how this meaning is reinforced by others. In the same study, several women colluded in their husband's concern not to be seen doing unmanly work (pp. 182ff), but in a study of role changes brought about by the 1984–5 miners' strike, women wanted greater change than men did. This identification of masculinity with paid work clearly points to issues concerning power and dominance in gender roles. Criticism of such views by some feminist writers has perhaps not fully recognised the implications paid work has for men's personal identities, or the fragile nature of these (also see Chapter 4; Frosh, 1995; Ochberg, 1987).

Since masculinity involves '*différance*' (to use the postmodern term), that is, not being feminine, and a large part of men's masculinity and power are embodied in their public work roles, it is not surprising that researchers have recently 'highlighted the embeddedness of masculine values and assumptions in the structure, culture and practices of organisation' (Collinson and Hearn, 1994, p. 6). Such dominance is linked to the fact that men's self identity is constructed in large part from their role in the workplace. What is currently being researched is the variety of ways in which masculinity may be pursued in the workplace (Collinson and Hearn, 1994).

If there is a clear connection between paid work and masculinity, between the public world of men and their private and personal identity, is there a similar or different relationship between women's self-identity and their public working lives? It is possible to find examples similar to the ones above, which indicate women's pride in their skill and competence at paid work. For example, a woman who had been trained as a skilled worker, a 'through hand', stated that:

> They used to teach you everything about a pair of trousers. You'd to learn the whole thing through including the fancy machines, and you'd be about a year just learning. You used to be sort of trained for life, you could go and get a job anywhere, well I could even now because I'm an experienced trouser hand. (Sharpe, 1984, p. 84)

There is considerable evidence that much work in the late 1990s has become deskilled, although technological changes and changes in the structure of the labour market have also created a demand for new and different skills (see, for example Wajcman, 1991; and Purcell, *et al.* (eds), 1986). Because women and men are concentrated in different areas of work, and women as a group have unequal status in the labour market, deskilling is particularly likely to affect the work that many women do (see, for example, Westwood, 1984, pp. 45ff; Phizacklea, 1990; and Purcell *et al.* (eds), 1986). Once we begin to recognise that men and women do different kinds of work, and that the experience and meaning of work both mediate and create gender differences, we highlight further the issues with which we began this chapter: power and control, and the separation of public and private.

'Women's work is never done'

While commenting critically that more attention has been paid to work as production, rather than reproduction, this chapter has continued in a similar vein, and given considerable space to the meaning of work for men. Where we have looked at women's experience we have indicated this might be 'different' in some ways. While we emphatically do not wish to privilege men, we have examined both commonsense assumptions and the social science 'script' which, until recently, has been that work and 'public' life largely concern men. This gender script powerfully affects our perceptions concerning the nature and meanings of work, and it is time to examine why this is so.

In most societies there is a division of labour on the basis of gender, but there is no foundation for believing that such divisions are other than socially constructed. Although some aspects of the reproduction and nurturing of infants obviously have a biological base, the specific tasks considered to be men's or women's vary considerably in different societies. In 'postindustrial' societies, at the end of the twentieth century, women increasingly engage in paid work for almost as much of their lives as men do, but women are segregated in different areas of the economy and frequently work under different conditions from men (Dex, 1985). Even when such occupational segregation does not occur, women undertake the greater part of unpaid domestic labour if they live in a shared household with a husband or other male(s).

Introducing the idea of unpaid domestic work not only extends the definition of work, but uncovers the inherent 'masculinity' of its commonsense meaning, allowing us to see immediately that the experience and meaning of many women's work is likely to be different from that of men. In comparison with much of the work people are paid to do in a factory, office, shop or other public place, housework and child care take place in the private confines of the home. Consideration of domestic work, of unpaid work and homework (or outwork) does begin to blur the boundaries between the association of work with the public domain, and domestic life with the private: it challenges the idea that the world of work is differentiated from the private, domestic world.

Being masculine is identified for many men with being workers. Such paid work may also be a very important aspect of self-identification for women too, and is concerned, for example, with being independent, having money of their own and being a fully autonomous adult. None the less, it is not *necessarily* part of women's *feminine* identity as such. For many, it is their identity as mothers, in particular, but also as wives or carers, which is crucial to their identity as women, and there may be ambivalences and contradictions surrounding paid work and a woman's self-identity. Many social scripts for women's 'doing' are intricately bound up with their 'being', again blurring our original boundaries. A good example of this is the emphasis in women's magazines on the work we need to do *as women*, to be feminine – perfecting our figures, make-up, and sexual desirability. The 'work' of beauty is not defined as such: it is invisible, aimed at the appearance of 'being', *naturally* feminine and attractive (Winship, 1987). This difference of emphasis is part of the way men as a social group maintain power over women. Instrumental 'doing' is more highly valued than non-instrumental 'being' and takes place in the public world where considerable power and influence is exercised over others. This point was made by Bologh (1990), whose work was considered when we discussed rationality earlier in this chapter.

Although domestic labour is undervalued and frequently seen as menial, in contradiction, its products are highly valued – good food, comfort and being cared for. The contradiction is echoed in women's own reflections on their domestic work (see, for example, Sharpe, 1984; Oakley, 1974; Hunt, 1989; and Charles and Kerr, 1988). Domestic labour and a private world, away from the public, are essential if we are to 'be', rather than just to 'do' in modern or postmodern societies. The products of domestic labour are often seen as an entitlement, a reward for paid work, as several examples quoted earlier illustrate. Domestic labour is a general term that does not differentiate between work such as cooking, laundry and cleaning, which maintains us – and as Marxist writers point out, the labour force – and other types of nurturing, including child care, which are concerned with reproducing people (Murgatroyd; 1985). It is interesting to note that by describing a woman as 'being in labour' when she is giving birth we implicitly recognise the (unpaid) work involved in the production of children (Martin, 1987, pp. 65–7). Yet this work is made invisible because *professionals* do the work of gynaecology and midwifery. Similarly, work that is paid if men do it may be valued differently when done by women. For example, in Norway, butter produced by women for the market was seen as sideline or had a different ritual status (Nicholson, 1995).

Distinguishing between domestic maintenance and nurturing work appears to be useful, and women themselves frequently comment on the monotony and alienation of housework, distinguishing this from the satisfactions and self-identity invested in child care. For example, one of Sharpe's respondents stated: 'I never felt bad about relinquishing housework to . . . [my husband] but felt threatened about giving up my child-care role. My children were part of my womanhood, mine, not his' (Sharpe, 1984, p. 185).

Despite this, the identification of femininity with motherhood and nurturing means that even menial aspects of domestic work are frequently endowed with the emotional overtones of nurturing and caring, as television advertisements for detergents constantly remind us. Providing 'proper meals' for husband and children has considerable emotional significance for both providers and recipients (Charles and

Kerr, 1988). All women's work in the private sphere of home is perceived as an aspect of women's feminine identity, the social script here often implying, with various degrees of certainty, that there is something 'natural' about women's ability to change dirty nappies, iron and clean (Brannen and Moss, 1991; Collins, 1985; and Osborne, 1991).

It is significant that, while it is in our private world of home and family where we are most relaxed, most ourselves, it is also here where many unmentionable or even taboo events occur: child abuse, domestic violence and sex. It is also here, as part of domestic labour, often performed by women, that many private tasks take place: caring for ill people, tending to private bodily rituals, and personal hygiene. While most work that occurs in the home is private and concealed, it has a cultural script and often concerns the power relations between men and women, parents and children, and carers and the cared-for. Such power relations, including those that lead to child abuse and domestic violence, are part of the range of cultural scripts available, so in this sense our private world is part of the public one too.

Women 'at work'

Practices that blur the distinction between the public and the private, and the meaning of the relationship between the two types of work women do are documented in studies of women in paid work. While many women may gain satisfaction of various kinds from working outside the home, because their domestic roles are a major source of identity they transfer some aspects of this role to their paid work in a variety of ways. In Westwood's study of a knitwear factory, women resist the exploitative and alienating character of the work, and the paternalistic management, by domesticising the shop floor – the public workspace – with family photographs, by wearing comfortable slippers and using spare time and materials to make items for children and family (Westwood, 1984). Similarly, A. Pollert's account of tobacco workers shows a culture of romance, cosmetics catalogues and friendship that feminises the boring, noisy work, which many of the women see as temporary and ancillary to their main role as wives and mothers (Pollert, 1981).

Domestication of workplace culture is not the only way in which paid work for women both echoes and gives meaning to their private domestic role. While many women have instrumental attitudes and economic as well as personal reasons for engaging in paid work, much of the paid work they do is an extension of their caring and domestic roles. Some of this work is actually paid domestic labour, in other people's homes, in caring institutions and in hotels, in the catering industry, and catering roles in a range of organisations (Crompton and Sanderson, 1990). Sheila Cunnison's study of wardens in a British sheltered housing project, for example, shows that work done by these women goes beyond what they are officially paid for. They act as 'family proxies', caring for the needs of residents beyond the call of duty because they see caring as a moral imperative for women. Not to act in a caring manner, whether or not this meant that they were exploited workers, would have contravened the strong sense of moral obligation that many of these women felt (Cunnison, 1986). Home helps, secretaries, teachers and nurses are frequently called upon to show feminine nurturing traits in their work. Outwork, or homeworking, an increasing type of employment for women, blurs the boundaries between private and public even further. While paid for at piecework rates, as in a factory, this work is done in the person's own home. (see, for example, Allen and Wolkowitz, 1987; and Phizacklea, 1990).

Sociological studies cited in this section emphasise the exploitative nature of women's paid work and demonstrate how a female culture helps to perpetuate women's entrapment in both their domestic and subordinate labour force role. These studies also indicate that women may resist and refuse to collude in such exploitation. Our emphasis is on the way these two aspects of women's work 'scripts' – the 'double shift' they are expected to work – both structure women's identity and are structured by women themselves.

Emotional labour: public and private work

Examining the importance of gender and power in creating the culture and meaning of work shows us that work has a wider meaning than simply paid employment. Introducing the concept of 'emotional labour' continues to move us away from simple definitions, but returns us to concerns raised in our discussion of distinctions between rational and non-rational social action. Some of the work, the tasks of social life, which take place within the structures of organisations and institutions are concerned with the organisation and management of people's emotions and feelings. It is only relatively recently that sociologists have recognised this explicitly, the emphasis previously having been on the importance of rationality and scientific modes of thought and action. The notion that emotional labour takes place within both the private and the public spheres (James, 1989) echoes Bologh's critique of Weber's masculinist notion of what constitutes rational social action, which we examined earlier in this chapter.

Some of what we have described as the nurturing and caring aspects of domestic labour, usually carried out by women, also comes under the heading of emotional labour, as does much of the paid work that women also do. Nicky James argues that emotions and feelings are part of everyday life, constructed and managed socially, as well as individually. The activity and labour put into this construction and management is as instrumental and 'rational' as other forms of activities. However, as the previous section of this chapter shows, the work undertaken by women is undervalued and, where emotional labour is concerned, this coincides with an over-emphasis on rationality in Western and modern societies. As children, we learn, for example, that we should be brave and not cry when we fall down, and, as adults, that we must keep emotions such as grief under control, for expression in private. Individuals none the less continue to express and explore their emotions, and it is usually women who manage this process:

> Emotional labour is organised and managed both in the private domain of home and the public domain of the workplace. The forms it takes are affected by the dominant organisation so that the form of emotional labour within the relatively pliable routines in the home differs from that which is possible within the rigidity of workplace organisation. (James, 1989, p. 29)

It is often believed that women are 'naturally' better than men at dealing with and managing emotions, but also that women are 'more emotional' – that is, less rational. A counter argument is that managing emotions for ourselves and other people is skilled work, that women learn such skills and are then expected to use them, often unpaid, both in private, as part of their domestic labour, but also in paid work, where it is structured by the needs of organisations and the powerful individuals in these organisations (see James, 1993).

'There is a sense in which every woman [in an organisational setting] is seen as a receptionist – available to give information and help, perennially interruptible' (Tannen, 1995, p. 117). That such skills are perceived as being feminine and not rational, that they involve intuition and sensitivity, are reasons they are devalued. These are also reasons why men are often seen not to possess such skills, whether or not this is actually true (Williams (ed.), 1993). The consequence of this 'feminine' connotation of emotion and feelings, and thus of emotional management skills, is that the emotional labour carried out in the workplace is frequently hidden, and not identified as productive labour. The hidden nature of emotional labour by women in the workplace derives from the assumption that emotions and feelings are about 'being', and that work concerns the imperative of action, of 'doing'. As we have seen previously, this is underlined by the ideological split between the private and the public:

> An alternative view is that emotional labour is productive work. It is hard work and can be sorrowful and difficult. It demands that the labourer gives personal attention which means they must give something of themselves ... Its value lies in its contribution to the social reproduction of labour power and the social relations of production. (James, 1989, p. 19)

Gender work scripts

Gender scripts are not simply stereotypes or narrow discourses: there is a range of femininities and masculinities, but they are defined only in relationship to each other – what postmodernism terms *différance*. The gendered perception of work and the division of labour affects how we as gendered individuals perceive our own skills and those of others, how we are treated and treat others in the workplace, and how we achieve satisfactory identities through work. Women with emotional management skills are often seen as less decisive than men; they are more likely to admit their mistakes and to suggest courses of action to subordinates rather than issue directives (see Tannen, 1995; and Court, 1994).

Gender discourses create work cultures in which it is difficult to cross gender lines and for women to be promoted to senior posts (see Court, 1994; Collinson and Hearn, 1994; Mumby and Stohl, 1991, pp. 325–9; Cockburn, 1991; Collinson *et al.*, 1990; Hearn *et al.* (eds), 1989; also Williams (ed.), 1993). Institutional and organisational practices perpetuate gender-specific cultures or discourses, and as individual women and men we also identify ourselves in these terms. We can apply Althusser's notion of 'hailing' here, to explain how the structures or ideology of gender operate through the way we think about the world and ourselves, and the way we recognise or 'hail' ourselves as filling a certain socially-constructed work role – 'I am a man with leadership qualities', or 'I am good at managing people'; 'I am a caring person and therefore not interested in money'; 'I am ambitious'; 'I've always been interested in what makes things work'; 'This is my trade'; 'I need work which will fit in with the children'; or 'I am the breadwinner'. However, we do not need to see ideology as totally determining work roles. Foucault uses the term 'discourse' to indicate the dominant practices and beliefs through which we act and which, in turn, create oppositional discourses. The concepts of ideology and discourse are both more fully explained in Chapter 1. The notion of discourse is certainly useful in the current debates surrounding gendered work roles, and in explaining the fact that gender scripts are always changing, although we must recognise the structural economic and social factors that perpetuate existing arrangements and continue women's subordination to men in this area.

Working metaphors

In his analysis of the development of rational capitalism, Weber identified as a key factor a particular form of ascetic Protestantism that prescribed hard work and effort, according to a person's 'calling' – their occupation in life – as a way of achieving religious salvation. This set of attitudes led to economic activity that encouraged capital accumulation and other rationalising processes conducive to the development of capitalism (Weber, 1978, pp. 138ff; and Lee and Newby, 1983, ch. 12). Weber described this 'Protestant ethic' as a particularly individualistic set of attitudes to life and in Chapter 2 we saw that the idea of a separate 'self' is not a neutral term, but is comparatively recent and peculiar to Western societies. By examining the importance and meaning of work we have recognised its centrality to social life in general, and the ways in which people identify themselves and their social roles. Given this centrality, it is not surprising that the metaphor of work is so powerful in a range of contexts and situations. We use the term to refer to activities that do not fall into any of the categories examined in previous sections.

Modern societies are imbued with the 'work ethic': work is valued as an imperative, and this spills over into many other areas of life, including leisure, fitness and health, marriage, intimate personal relations and children at school. Once the work metaphor is extended to areas of life such as health, issues of power are also raised. Current medical opinion emphasises the importance of healthy eating, keeping fit and avoiding activities such as smoking and too much alcohol, in order to maintain good health. The implication here is that there is a moral obligation on individuals to work at being healthy, and failure to do so means that we are partly to blame for our own ill-health (see Willis, 1991; Coward, 1989; Bunton *et al.*, 1995). Similarly, we are led to believe that we should 'work' at our marriages and family relations, and it is a mark of late-twentieth-century society that fufilling sex and intimacy are now 'projects' that must be worked at (Giddens, 1991 and 1992). Ironically, though, as we have seen, the skills involved in such emotional labour are not highly valued.

It appears contradictory to apply the term 'work' to leisure, since leisure is normally taken to mean activities that occur when we are not working. In a profound way, however, we can see leisure as the ultimate goal of work: we work in order to be able to enjoy our leisure, including the means to pay for it, since many leisure activities involve spending money (Clarke and Critcher, 1985; Rojek, 1985; and Rojek (ed.), 1989). Many of the activities some people list as leisure would be considered 'hard work' by others. Indeed, they are seen as hard work by the participants – for example, gardening or DIY, or sports and other physical activities, as the phrase 'working-out in the gym' indicates. Similarly, many people engage in 'voluntary' work when they are not 'at work'. People gain satisfaction from engaging in these activities, particularly, we might argue, if they gain little satisfaction from their 'real' job. It is the fact that such activities are *chosen* that defines them as leisure. On the other hand, the work ethic impels some people to work at and in their leisure time, and such activities are an important part of their self-identity.

Conclusion

In this chapter we have explored the notion of work and its construction through social organisation and roles, constantly returning to Marx's concern with labour as a necessary part of social life, and to Weber's concern with rational, instrumental action. We have also elaborated the notion of the reproduction of social life, and seen that work metaphors are part of the 'work' of constructing and reproducing ourselves in society. Work is intricately bound up with individuals' idea of self, self-esteem and personal identity, and the concept of work as purposeful gives meaning to much human activity. To the extent that the worker is controlled by the processes of work, rather than being in control of them, they may create a sense of alienation. But, similarly, in a world where it is through work that both meaning and economic necessities are created, the absence of work, because of unemployment, retirement or disability, may also create a loss of self-esteem and self-worth. This construction and reproduction is a gendered process, and consideration of this raises questions concerning the notions of private and public identities; and indeed about the fundamental meaning of work itself. It is through work of various kinds that some of the most important aspects of personal identity – masculinity and femininity – are largely constructed and reproduced. Work can be understood in its commonsense meaning, but it is also a statement about ourselves. Thus it is a fundamental aspect not only of culture, but also of the way in which the tasks of social life are conducted.

7

The Wider Context

Foreigners abroad

Earlier chapters of this book have concentrated on individual identities and selves, and on issues closest to individual and private concerns. In a sense, we have examined some of the 'micro-aspects' of social life, although always with reference to and in the context of wider social structures. When examining work, in Chapter 6, we recognised that organisational structures and social institutions are both constructed by and contribute to social identities and roles, and that the organisational structures in which work takes place are part of social structures that powerfully affect how individuals live their lives. In this chapter we shall begin to examine more explicitly some of the ways in which these wider social structures are conceptualised, and how such conceptualisations are part of our identities and, as such, construct and constrain us. Concepts such as community, nation, state, citizen and ethnicity are simply abstract ideas 'out there' – they are social constructs, part of how we understand our own identities and how others perceive and treat us.

When I go away for holidays to Europe, I am conscious of 'being abroad', of being a foreigner. My passport cover bears the legends 'European Community' and 'United Kingdom of Great Britain and Northern Ireland'. Inside it states that I am a 'British Citizen'. While abroad, despite being dressed in what appear to be the inconspicuous clothes of a middle-aged, middle-class, woman, I notice that people frequently address me in English, even before I have spoken. During a stay in the USA which, despite the dominance of the English language, felt 'foreign' to me, I was approached in shops and other places by people who noted my English accent, welcomed me to America, told me about their trips to England and, sometimes, their English ancestors. A sizeable audience for a university lecture I gave was explained to me in terms of the novelty of hearing a 'real English accent' ('standard English' with no regional accent)! Formally asked my nationality, I usually reply 'British'. Asked to describe myself to people of other nationalities I say I am English. If asked to write an autobiographical piece I probably would not include either of these identities.

This account of one author's experience and observations 'abroad' raises a broader range of questions and puzzles significant for the major themes of this book. If we 'go away', what do we go *from*, what do we leave? What does being a foreigner mean? Of what significance is the possession of a passport with its designations: European Community, and a United Kingdom which implicitly includes Wales and Scotland, but explicitly refers to Northern Ireland? How is being British different from being English? There seem to be several meanings to the word 'English'. What is it that makes America a different culture from ours, despite the fact of a common language and that the origins of the modern USA lie in the UK? What are the cultural clues we gather from people which indicate to us that they are 'foreigners'? Why does it seem important to distinguish ourselves as a group from others and what is the significance to individuals of being identified as members of one group, rather than another?

These questions relate to the idea raised in previous chapters, that outside the sphere of our own lives and personal identities there is a range of 'others' to whom we are connected in various ways, although they may be unknown to us. While knowledge of these individuals and groups may be imperfect, part of our identity is formed by recognising that we are similar to or different from them. Agnes Heller uses the term 'particularity' to describe a person's orientation to the world, which links the self to specific groups of others, and which is something distinct from the individuality of the self:

> Particularity therefore takes two related forms: it applies to the interests and endowments of the self but it can also be held in common as the cultural perspective of the group in which one comes to self-understanding. (Wright, 1985, p. 9)

When abroad and outside the boundaries of the culture and community in which we usually live, we make explicit part of our taken-for-granted identity – our nationality. It is the taken-for-grantedness of our own culture and surroundings that we leave to 'go abroad'; a temporary transition, but similar to the example we used in Chapter 3, of Laurie Lee leaving home in the transition from boyhood to manhood. Feeling 'at home' describes a sense of ease and comfort, rather than challenge. Significantly, we talk of being 'at home' as the converse to being 'abroad'. 'At home' refers to our identification with a particular group, for example the English, and identifies the French and the Belgians as 'others'. When there is an air or rail crash or other disaster involving people from a range of countries, the news media announce the number of *British* dead or injured, the implication being that it is our own compatriots, those who 'belong' to us, who are our main concern. This identification of 'them' and 'us', can be seen as an extension of the 'private' versus 'public' dichotomy discussed previously.

As foreigners abroad, a range of subtle differences concerning cultural procedures and styles, mark us out and subjectively identify us as members of a different cultural group. Similarly, as travellers we are aware of a range of cultural practices and customs that inform us that we are not 'at home'. A. P. Cohen talks of the 'boundaries of commonality within which meaning is shared and communicated in idiom and social organisation', and defines cultures as 'experiential worlds of meaning' (in Cohen (ed.), 1982, p. 9). He argues too, that while a person might identify themself as British, or a Scot or a Shetlander, it is at the level of the local community that people's identity is clearest and at which culture is most 'real'. It is at this level he says, 'I present myself through increasingly informed and complex pictures' (p. 10).

Boundaries between ourselves and others exist at an individual level and at the level of groups. The metaphors people use to describe themselves and others, and their relationships to them, are often instructive. In English, people's private home and native country, for example, are made synonymous: they 'go out' to work, the shops or the pub. Traditionally British people also went 'out' to India, Australia or other parts of the British Empire. The strength and meaning of such boundaries varies, and those between the public and the private are not always distinct, as we saw in the previous chapter. Everday life is a constant process of relating our inner selves to our outer selves and attempting to feel 'at home' in the world (Wright, 1985, p. 11). The outer self or public aspects of life may exercise a power over the private and personal that feels oppressive. Boundaries between different cultural groups and national communities may also be oppressive in ways we shall examine later.

In this book, discussion of sexuality and gender, health and illness, work, and major life transitions, has emphasised the importance and significance of 'society' for the construction, development and maintenance of our identities. As we explained in Chapter 1, by 'the social' we refer to something beyond the individual, but at the same time part of what we construct as human beings (Durkheim, 1982, ch. 1). National, regional and ethnic identities and communities are social constructions located in time, and may or may not have a geographical location. By examining these constructions we hope to be able to find answers to some of the questions we raised at the beginning of this chapter.

Community

Young children's drawings contain representations of the comparatively small and enclosed world in which they live: mummies, daddies, grandparents, brothers and sisters, family pets and immediate surroundings such as houses, trees and flowers predominate, then gradually things from outside are incorporated into the pictures. As older children and adults, we are aware that the world is larger than our family and our street. As we move beyond the boundary of home we learn to identify ourselves as belonging to a range of other groups. Neighbourhood, schools, shops, the doctor's and dentist's surgeries, clubs, sports facilities, neighbours' and friends' houses all gradually become part of an expanding world. As adults we often refer to this wider environment as 'the community'. In four Northern Irish villages this sense of community was expressed by the norm that people should act 'decently' towards and 'get on' with people who lived in the same locality, despite the sectarian divisions that existed (Cohen (ed.), 1986, p. 96).

There is considerable debate among sociologists and social anthropologists about the definition of community beyond its commonsense meaning. Here we can take it to have three meanings, which may overlap in reality. It can refer to a local, human settlement in geographical space; to a local social system and a set of social relationships (rather as we have just described); or it can mean a type and quality of relationship and sense of shared identity which may or may not be linked to a spatial location (Worsley (ed.), 1987, ch. 7).

So, for example, we may bemoan the decline of 'community spirit', indicated by increasing vandalism and petty crime in a particular neighbourhood. Alternatively, we may talk of the Afro-Caribbean community, the scientific community, or a community of scholars, none of which are defined by geographical location. Using the third definition of community introduces another source and focus of identity. A woman's personal identity and sense of self may incorporate the roles of mother, wife, sister, daughter and, friend, but she may also feel that she belongs to the academic community and the community of feminists. The latter example is interesting, as many feminists would use the term 'sisterhood' to describe their sense of belonging together, implying family – a stronger and more personal bond and sense of identity. Similarly, trade unionists have traditionally used the term 'brother' (and belatedly, 'sister') to indicate group solidarity and identity, and the American black power movement in the 1960s and 1970s used the same metaphor.

These examples illustrate that a sense of self, of personal identity, involves identification with a wider group, and this may have a political dimension; it is concerned with the relative power position and common interests of that group. Once we move beyond primary groups such as our family, we begin to identify with others on the basis of interest. In the nineteenth century the sociologist Ferdinand Tönnies used the terms *gemeinschaft* and *gesellschaft* to indicate the difference between relationships people have in rural societies from those in urban societies. Traditional and rural societies were *gemeinschaft* communities, he argued, where people have no choice but to identify with each other on the basis of kinship and emotional ties developed through the small-scale, face-to-face quality of relationships. In modern and urban societies, relationships are based on the large-scale and contractual nature of human association – *gesellschaft* (Lee and Newby, 1983, pp. 41–66). Community in Tönnies' sense included an almost automatic sense of identification with neighbours and kin, in the same way that Durkheim saw people in pre-industrial societies linked together by the social bonds or solidarity of 'likeness'. As we indicated in Chapter 1, however, Durkheim saw this diversity in industrial societies, as the source of social solidarity, social identity, because it was based on interdependence created by the division of labour (Durkheim, 1984). So manufacturers, for example, are different from people who run transport systems, but each need the other in order to thrive. We are, of necessity, involved with groups outside our primary kinship group.

When we use the term 'community' in the late twentieth century to indicate a sense of shared identity between people living in complex modern societies, we mean that people feel they belong to a group of other people; the community in this sense is an *imagined* one. We are able to identify subjectively with other neighbours, residents of our village, schoolchildren, feminists, black people, gay people, or whoever, on the basis of an imagined relationship, although we may never have a face-to-face relationship with them. Throughout this book the term 'we' has been used to indicate not just the three authors but also an imagined relationship with our readers who are, we hope, following our arguments! Implied here is what might be called a 'we-feeling', an identification with fellow travellers in intellectual exploration.

Insiders and outsiders: similarity and difference

It seems...incontrovertible that if people in one milieu perceive fundamental differences between themselves and the members of another, then their behaviour is bound to reflect that sense of difference: it means something to them which it might not mean to others. (Cohen, 1982, p. 3)

Underlying notions of belonging to a community or a nation is the designation of some people or groups as 'insiders' and others as 'outsiders'. Such a distinction exists in all communities and societies, between those who belong, who are part of 'us', and those who may be experienced as foreign or alien. Using language to exclude another group may be a powerful way of underlining this.

'Your own' refers at one level to kin or relatives but at another to those who are like you, or on the 'same side' (see Cohen (ed.), 1986, p. 92). The basis on which groups or whole societies make such distinctions is subjective and embedded in their culture and history. People who have always lived in an isolated rural community having very little contact with other areas might see anyone outside this community as being 'other'. In an urban environment, where there is more frequent contact with a range of different people, there is more choice in deciding which groups to identify with. However, it is in urban societies such as Britain, France, the USA and South Africa, with histories of colonialism and/or slavery, where insider/outsider status may be based on 'race'. In all these societies people who are black or Asian, and in the USA, Hispanic or Native American, are defined by some white people not simply as outsiders, as not belonging, but also as inferior. We shall take up some of the issues raised by 'racial' and ethnic identification later on.

Boundaries between insiders and outsiders, and between self and others, are not necessarily fixed. In Graham McFarlane's study, previously cited, the boundaries between Catholics and Protestants did not always operate. People were identified, and identified themselves, as neighbours too, and 'getting on' with people at this level was considered to be important. There are also degrees of belonging to a community, ranging through, for example, being 'born and bred' within it, marrying into it, and so on (Cohen (ed.), 1986).

Insider/outsider identity may be conscious, or articulated only in certain situations. In the opening example, the writer felt English in America because her accent was identified as not-American, and Americans underlined her difference from them, while some simultaneously noted a common ancestry. We can assume that for Americans with British ancestors, conversation with an English person reminded them of this aspect of their identity. In the same way that the cultural boundaries of belonging or not to a community, group or nation may constantly shift, so there may be 'a multiplicity of . . . idioms through which people present themselves to themselves and to others as they organise, adapt and make sense of their everyday lives' (Phillips, 1986). Phillips' study of Muker in the Yorkshire Dales examines inhabitants seeing themselves as part of a wider 'Dales life' but presenting themselves to outsiders as sharing

> a sense of belonging to a distinctive parish community whose families, dialect and history are *different* from those of the resident incomers, *different* from those of other Dalespeople in neighbouring Dales, and *different* from those of towns and cities further afield. (Phillips, p. 143)

In conversations *within* the community people qualified their 'belonging-ness', indicating their place on a 'scale' of belonging, involving the number of generations who had lived in Muker, and differentiating new incomers from old incomers.

Small-scale and traditional societies studied by social anthropologists illustrate some of the ways in which groups may establish their identity and differentiate themselves from others. The Nuer (from Sudan) for example, showed a pattern of 'fission and fusion' – that is, considerable in-fighting among groups which made up the ethnic group, but a fusion of these groups in the face of an outside 'enemy'. A rather different example is the way that people in residential care, categorised by outsiders as 'the elderly', differentiate themselves clearly from one another by categorising their fellow residents as 'confused', 'incontinent', 'badly brought up' and so on (Hockey, 1990).

Identifying ourselves as belonging to a group and perceiving some as 'other' or 'outsiders' has profound effects for ourselves, for the structure of society, and for those who are defined as others or outsiders. Many of the injustices and inequalities within societies, and the oppressive practices surrounding these, are intricately bound up with these processes.

State, citizenship and nationality

It is time to address the concepts with which we began this chapter – 'citizen' and 'nationality'. Nationality is a function of the modern nation-state, a relatively recent historical political development. The origins of many modern nation states are associated with an hereditary monarchy, whereas many societies studied by social anthropologists are 'stateless', government and regulation being carried out by smaller, often kin-based groups (Held, 1992, p. 71). Within the boundaries of the nation-state, certain kinds of power are exercised over a population and its activities, which constrains personal identity in many ways. Sovereign political power is invested in a political system claiming legitimacy on the basis of its history. Such power may be disputed and is ultimately maintained through control of the means of coercion through the legal system, the police and the armed forces (Weber, 1983).

Nationality is a formal, legal category: a person is identified as 'British', or 'French', or 'Canadian' because their passport states they are. The designation 'British Citizen' or 'French Citizen', or citizen of wherever, will be accepted as part of a person's formal legal identity abroad. At home it bestows on them a legal status and entitles them to a range of 'rights'. Some of these ensure that a person is able to retain aspects of their self which constitutes their personal identity. Thus, for example, in Britain or France or Belgium, as in other democracies, citizens may legally marry, vote and expect protection from the judicial system; they are at liberty to undertake legal employment and entitled to certain kinds of health care. Nationality and citizenship also impose on people a range of duties and restrictions, and constrain them in a variety of ways. In Britain at the time of writing, for example, a male citizen under the age of eighteen may not legally engage in sexual intercourse with another male, and gay citizens of either sex cannot marry each other. Similarly, no one can be legally married to more than one person at a time, build a house wherever they like, or practise as a doctor, lawyer or accountant without the training and qualifications required by those professions. We should note too, that Britain, like many other nations, recognises the crime of treason – betraying one's country.

However, the formal legal identity of nationality and citizenship does not ensure that all citizens are treated equally, and not oppressed. In Britain certain forms of sexual identity are not accepted; people with disabilities do not have free access to a range of facilities; the average pay for women is considerably less than that for men; and people of Jewish, Irish, Asian or Afro-Caribbean origins are likely to be the subject of jokes denigrating their ethnic identities. Similar inequalities exist in many other European societies and in the USA. The ways in which citizenship constructs and also *de*structs our identities will be pursued further in a later section. The main point to note here is that whatever their precise meaning, and however this meaning is contested, nationality and citizenship are part of the social structures that construct aspects of our identity and deny us others.

Formal, legal identity does not necessarily accord with how we identify ourselves. That I am a 'British citizen', does not mean that I identify *myself*, except for formal purposes as 'British'. Other British citizens might identify themselves as Welsh, Scottish, Afro-Caribbean, Punjabi, Bengali, or Irish, although others *would* describe themselves as British. Although the UK is part of the European Community, most UK citizens would probably not identify themselves as 'European'. These distinctions are not merely semantic but indicate the subjective nature of those aspects of our identity stemming from the fact that we live within the boundaries of a nation-state.

Nationality as imagined community

Earlier, we defined the idea of community as describing a subjective and imagined relationship with others we perceive as being similar to ourselves. Benedict Anderson has argued that all communities larger than those where people have face-to-face contact are imagined. It is the way in which 'nationality, or . . . nation-ness, as well as nationalism' are imagined that distinguishes this cultural construction from other types of community (Anderson, 1983, pp. 14–15). Used in the sense of identification, a 'we-feeling', rather than a geographical location, the boundaries of community are often fuzzy, but the idea of nation and nationality involves the idea of boundaries – each nation is limited, however large, even if some members live outside the geographical boundaries, which may in turn be disputed with other nations. Arguably,

> If many traditional and community-based forms of cultural integration
> have been eroded, the nation which replaces them is not simply abstract;
> it works by raising a dislocated and threatened – but none the less locally
> experienced – everyday life up into...the lustre of the idealised nation.
> (Wright, 1985, p. 24)

This process can be seen clearly in the late 1990s in many former
Communist societies, once part of the Soviet bloc (Calhoun, 1994,
pp. 304ff).

A nation is an imagined political community consisting of other
people with whom we have an affinity on the basis of a range of
historical factors (Anderson, 1983, p.15). Defining nationality and
nation as involving imagined relationships, however, raises the thorny
issue of whether the political boundaries of a nation state, a political
entity, in fact coincide with those of the imagined nation. Historical
political changes lie behind this complexity and are an indication that
national identity is not fixed or unchanging. In European societies that
have retained a monarchy, the changes have incorporated monarchs of
foreign nationality. In the case of Britain, the royal family had a foreign
surname until the First World War (Anderson, 1983, p. 80). Identifying oneself as Welsh or Scottish (or English) implies nationhood (or
'nation-ness', as Anderson terms it) for each of these groups, but
sovereign power over them all is held by the government of the United
Kingdom.

In the case of Scotland and Wales, which are regions within the
UK, constitutional and administrative arrangements do recognise some
elements of distinctive nationhood. These are likely to be strengthened
in the light of recent referendums aimed at increasing further
the devolution of power. At present Scotland has a separate
legal and educational system from England, Wales and Northern
Ireland and the Welsh language is officially recognised for administrative purposes. In the case of Northern Ireland, the historical
partition of British-ruled Ireland in 1922, after a civil war, into the
Republic of Ireland and Ulster resulted in the formation of a separate
administrative structure for the part of Ireland remaining outside
the Republic. Partition created new issues concerning nationalism.
Conflict between Protestant Ulster loyalists and Catholic Irish nationalists has continued ever since, escalating into almost continuous
violence since the 1970s. On a less political level, Northern Ireland,
Scotland, England and Wales are recognised as separate entities by the
Football Association for the purposes of the World Cup competition.

While the histories of Scottish, Welsh and Irish nationalisms are different in detail, as are those of of other nationalisms, they are all the outcome of complex political processes in which territorial, cultural, and in some cases colonial, relationships were vital factors in their formation.

Nationalist identities have arisen from the power relationships between different countries or states. The ways in which, accepting a *particular* national identity, we perceive and relate to members of *other* nationalities reflects these origins. At one level 'it is common-sense that the world is 'naturally' divided into separate nations' (Billig, 1992, p. 35). Imagined relationships of nationalism are often difficult to specify, and people may be unable to articulate their consciousness of such relationships. Many aspects are expressed symbolically and through anecdotes and stereotypes. McFarlane's study of a community in Northern Ireland comments on the stereotypes through which Protestants and Catholics described each other and on the historical explanations they gave for these (Cohen (ed.), 1986, pp. 92–3). 'Nationalism involves more than depicting one's own nation; it involves depicting the nation's place amidst the world of nations. Here, a sense of superiority can be invoked' (Billig, 1992, p. 35).

So, for example, the British and the French, who have been at war many times in the past, often express mutual and stereotyped contempt for each other: the French are depicted by the British as a nation that eats frogs' legs, snails and too much garlic; and the British are depicted by the French as stuffy, inhibited people with no tradition of good food. Each of these stereotypes also says something about the identity of the group expressing it. This particular example indicates that each nation sees itself as different and rather superior to the other but, while prejudices persist, there is a sort of equivalence between the two. If we look, however, at the stereotyped views the English express about the Irish, through jokes that label Irish people variously as dishonest, uneducated, simple, peasant-like and illogical, we see the oppressive legacy of a colonial relationship and an expression of the power one group has held over another. This example illustrates how some aspects of nationalism constitute racism and ethnic conflict, which we shall discuss later, rather than just prejudice.

Any nationalism may contain a whole parcel of meanings, some of which are contradictory. It may also be that, as individuals, national identity is only consciously recognised or acknowledged in particular circumstances when we are made aware of our difference from others, or theirs from us, as the example at the beginning of the chapter illustrates. Expressions of nationalist identity are flexible and vary with the situation. Specific ways in which the imagined community of the nation is symbolised may take a variety of forms, and as individuals we may incorporate only some of these as part of ourselves and way of life. For example, the discussion of Northern Ireland above identified Protestantism with Ulster loyalists (who reject all identification with republican Ireland), and Catholicism with Irish republicanism. The nationalist conflict in Northern Ireland is often symbolised in these religious terms. Yet there are many Protestants in the Republic of Ireland, many citizens of Northern Ireland identify themselves as Irish, rather than British, or Ulstermen [*sic*], and some people marry across religious boundaries. Knowing each other at a local level as members of the community may also cut across boundaries that exist at another level (Cohen (ed.), 1986, p. 97).

Public ceremonies and celebrations for the fiftieth anniversaries of VE Day and VJ Day, marking the Allied victory over Germany, and the defeat of the Japanese army that ended the Second World War, took place during the writing of this chapter. In public rituals of remembrance for those who died during this war, and in the media coverage of these events, explicit connections were made between the actions and sacrifices of individuals and the preservation of the nation. British condemnation of Japanese treatment of prisoners of war and reluctance by the Japanese government to make public apology for this treatment underlines the distinctive nationalism of each nation. Leaving aside the moral and humane issues involved in the treatment of prisoners of war and in the nuclear bombing of Japan by the Americans, the condemnation of the Japanese by Britons is an expression of solidarity with fellow Britons who engaged in military service on behalf of the nation. In Japanese terms, the surrendering of British troops was interpreted as being dishonourable, and Japanese reluctance to make public reparation for their treatment of prisoners of war must be seen as an expression of *their* nationalism and culture and support for *their* members' war service. Overall, fiftieth anniversary celebrations in Britain of the end of the Second World War symbolised aspects of the nation's history, and individuals' roles in this, as the Queen's speech at the VJ commemoration illustrates:

> The Second World War was the most destructive in history. We fought it against an evil which threatened our freedom and our way of life. Our dogged endurance left our resources much depleted. Yet in the end we came through triumphant. (*The Times*, 21 August 1995)

There are many instances where religion symbolises the nation, although there may be sizeable religious or non-religious minorities. In Britain, people with no formal religious affiliation often state they are 'C of E' (Church of England), or are entered on official forms as such, because this is the established national religion. In legal proceedings the oath to tell the truth is still sworn on the Bible, and people who have other or no religious affiliations must ask especially for the right to affirm instead. Ritual state occasions usually have a formal religious component and the national anthem calls on God's help for the preservation of the monarch as the symbol of the nation.

Seeking a social rather than psychological or theological explanation of religion, Durkheim argued that when people came together and engaged in religious or other communal rituals it symbolised their worshipping of society: the group. Participation in such rituals allows each individual to feel connected to others in the group, and their individual and communal identity is reinforced (Durkheim, 1915). Large public funerals in Northern Ireland attended by hundreds of either Protestant or Catholic mourners for those killed during the violence since the 1970s appear to have served this function.

American Nationalism is symbolised by what appears to be a contradiction. There is no established or official religion, but American schoolchildren, regardless of creed, begin the day by saluting the American flag and pledging allegiance. Nevertheless, a Judeo-Christian religious identification is an important aspect of American national identity. Although decreasing recently and divided by fundamentalist-versus-liberal orientations, there is still a high level of religious affiliation. This individual religious affiliation is mirrored by American 'civil religion', as it has been termed, evidenced by public presidential references to religious allegiance and prayers at major political events. This civil religion

> portrays its people , often in comparison with people in other countries, as God-fearing souls, as champions of religious liberty, and in many instances as a nation that God has consciously chosen to carry out a special mission in the world. (Wuthnow, 1989, p. 244)

A different type of relationship between nationalism and religion may be found in other states. Like Judaism or Christianity, Islam is an aspect of personal identity, but, in some Islamic states, to be a Muslim is synonymous with membership of the nation. Muslims also identify themselves in some contexts with Muslims in other parts of the world.

There is a parallel here with Judaism. To be an Israeli is also to be identified as a Jew, and the state of Israel was founded by Jewish Zionists as a result of their history of persecution and oppression, although many Jews outside Israel are not Zionists. Thus religious affiliation may be part of one's personal identity and nationality. Nationalisms in secular states often assume at least a residual religious identification and are expressed through religious symbolism.

Although it might seem obvious that speaking a particular language indicates an individual's national identity, the issue is not straightforward. It is through language that we are able to express ourselves and communicate with others; we think in the language we learn as members of our culture, and to be unable to communicate in our language threatens our sense of self. Significantly, the language people learn as children is referred to as their 'mother tongue', and links with our nation or culture are affirmed through this 'family' metaphor.

Languages, like nations, have histories, and are one way in which ethnic groups and nations distinguish themselves from others, but this is not so in every case. Scottish nationalism, unlike Welsh, for example, is not symbolised by a distinctive language (although there are Gaelic speakers). Flemish is spoken only in the region of Belgium known as Flanders. French is spoken in other parts of Flanders and the rest of Belgium, and there is considerable antagonism between Flemish and French speakers, reflecting the history of this country. To an untutored ear, Flemish sounds like Dutch, but to Flemish speakers their language identifies a culture distinct from that of the Netherlands. The examples of Belgium, also Switzerland and Canada, as nations where there is more than one major language, indicate that while language may be an important part of cultural identity, it is not necessarily synonymous with nationality. Historically, French was the common language of the European aristocracy and upper classes, allowing these groups to transcend any national identity when convenient.

There are many instances where language *is* a symbol of national identity, particularly where an indigenous language has been suppressed by a colonial power (for example, the British Ordnance Survey changed Irish place names), or where the official language is that of colonial or imperial rulers. Late-nineteenth-century attempts to revive the Irish language were a deliberate expression of nationalism, and in the late twentieth century, using Irish names is an expression of Irishness (Brown, 1981). The Basque language also, symbolises the fight for a separate Basque nation within Spanish territory. As noted earlier, Welsh has been accepted as a second official language, after considerable pressure by Welsh nationalists. Fighting for recognition of a minority language – for example, by painting over English street signs in Wales – or deliberate retention of one in the face of ruling opposition, may be important symbolic elements in retaining the identity of small nations or groups.

Since nationality and nationalism concern imagined communities, the outcome of centuries of historical and cultural change, it is not surprising that they are not simple to understand, contain contradictions, and may be interpreted differently by different groups within the nation. British nationalism has been largely a function of its status as a colonial power, now lost, but it is a relatively flexible concept, allowing citizens to identify themselves as English, or Scottish, or Welsh (but not perhaps as Pakistani, Bengali or Afro-Caribbean), while remaining 'British'. Identifying oneself as specifically British today may indicate a reactionary and racist political orientation; for example, a neo-Fascist political organisation calls itself the British National Party, but many expressions of British nationalism are more complex, as M. Billig's study of the royal family shows.

Similar to the way that Durkheim equated religious worship with 'worship' of society or the group, Billig argues that, for many people in Britain, the significance of the monarchy is that it symbolises the nation:

> The equation of monarchy with nation implies that an attack on monarchy is an attack upon the fundamental uniqueness of the nation. If 'our' selves are equated with the nation, then the attack is also a threat to the unique identity of 'our' national selves. To imagine the imagined community without a monarchy is to do more than de-imagine the nation: it is to de-imagine 'our' selves. (Billig, 1992, p. 34)

One of his respondents uses the metaphor of 'we', the citizens, as the branches, with the monarchy as the 'national root' that must stay alive in order for our collective selves to survive. The metaphor has symbolic meaning: a distinctive part of our identity as a nation would disappear with the monarchy, and the collective 'we' would change, become more like others – for example, a republic like America.

Individuals feel connected to and part of the wider society in a way we express symbolically. Billig's research shows that people are interested in and identify with the Royal Family, despite simultaneously having ambiguous and cynical feelings about them. By 'identify', Billig refers to a complex process he calls 'double-declaiming': when people make claims about the Royal Family they are actually making claims about themselves. The 'royals' represent aspects of family life and 'doing a job' well; they have some magical qualities but are also 'ordinary' and like 'us' (Sue Townsend's novel, *The Queen and I* illustrates this). In imagining what royal life is like, people are drawing on their own experiences of life and projecting this on to the Royal Family. Billig quotes Marx to the effect that a monarch is only a monarch because other people imagine they are subjects, and subjects imagine they are such because there is a monarch (Billig, 1992, p. 87). This is a particular example of how individuals both construct and are constructed by society.

The 'job' of the Royal Family is to present publicly an idealised version of the private, including its gendered nature. By affirming the life of the Royal Family through showing interest in and discussing it, including, we would suggest, its recent marital problems, we are affirming our own selves, our own lives. Thus identification is an ideological process. Official symbols of the nation are part of our ideological heritage and, as Althusser argues, ideology is not just 'out there', we think in it too (Billington *et al.*, 1991, p. 25). This is clearly expressed by Billig, writing of his respondents, who were interviewed as family groups:

> As speakers used the common-places of common-sense , so also were they expressing their own individuality. No two voices had identical tones, nor did they say the same things. The family members were doing various bits of family business, as they spoke. In consequence, the discussions gave glimpses of lives being uniquely led. (1992, p. 202)

The unprecedented and prolonged grief and mourning by many thousands of 'ordinary' people at the death of Diana, Princess of Wales, seems to confirm this complicated process of identification as an ideological one. For example, interviewed about why she had joined the crowds in Hyde Park for the funeral procession one young woman stated that the Princess 'brought out all my Britishness. I felt a national pride in her'. This was despite having some criticism of Diana's personal behaviour (*The Times*, 8 September, 1997).

At a national level the Princess's death has been emphasised and perceived by the media, in particular, as a national calamity and loss, because she was both the mother of the future monarch and an effective worker for charity. At a personal level thousands of individuals and families have publicly and movingly expressed their own grief at an intensely personal sense of loss, as they might for a member of their own family. Diana was in one sense a charismatic and beautiful 'fairy-tale' Princess, yet at the same time a charity worker, a member of her family, and a divorced mother in conflict with her ex-husband's family. These complex and sometimes contradictory roles and the fact that her young sons are now bereaved emphasise that she was both like and unlike 'us'. It is both her ordinary nature as one of 'us', with marital and personal problems, and her extraordinariness as a Princess which have aroused so much emotion.

The breaks with royal protocol and tradition for the funeral, including flying the union flag, the symbol of the nation, at half-mast over Buckingham palace underlines the identification of royalty with the nation, but also the shifting and precarious nature of this. The death of Princess Diana and the direct involvement of ordinary people in her funeral also illustrate the complex blurring between what is 'private' and what is 'public'. They continue the controversy about the private and marital problems of the Royal Family which are publicly discussed in a way similar to that in which we discuss problems in our own families.

The significance of the Royal Family as an affirmation of 'ordinary' life has replaced the older symbolic significance of royalty as divinely appointed to rule. During the VJ celebrations the Queen Mother openly shed tears and in her VJ speech, quoted above, the Queen mentioned that Prince Philip had been on active service in the Far East on VJ day (*The Times*, 21 August, 1995). Both these incidents underline the 'ordinariness' of the Royal Family; even during wartime they suffered 'like us'. Similarly, the Royal Family is suffering through the death of Princess Diana, made more difficult because of her divorce from Prince Charles and conflict between the Royal Family and Diana's family of origin. Tensions within ordinary families too are often exposed at times of bereavement. Billig interprets this ordinariness as a sign of postmodernism and the demystifying of traditional ideologies (see Chapters 1 and 9 in this volume).

This analysis of the Royal Family is complicated by the fact that many people in Britain who might identify themselves favourably with certain aspects of British life would exclude any identification with the Royal Family. Many are republicans favouring abolition of the monarchy as a costly anomaly symbolising outdated aristocratic privilege. However, in expressing this viewpoint there is still concern with a collective 'we', albeit a very different one. Even entering into the debate about royalty, and familiarity with media discussion about them, in some sense acknowledges their symbolic significance for Britain as a nation. Such debate simultaneously outlines alternative identities for individuals – for example, 'republican'. Popular culture reflects this, containing jokes, 'send-ups' and caricatures at the expense of various members of the Royal Family. Good examples here are the photographs available as cards with captions that denigrate whichever 'royal' is portrayed, and the immensely popular TV show *Spitting Image*, which used puppet caricatures and worked because of our shared knowledge concerning the 'royals' and prominent politicians. Children's jokes such as: 'What does the Queen do when she burps?' 'She issues a royal pardon!' illustrate the same point. Were the 'royals' no longer significant, such subversions would cease to be pleasurable.

That such cynicism and open hostility is common indicates both the relative strength and flexibility of British nationalism. Britain has never needed any institution performing so crudely the function of the Un-American Activities Committee of the US House of Representatives during the Cold War period. In societies such as France and Italy, which no longer have monarchies, nationalism is symbolised in different ways. There is insufficient space here to indicate the range of alternative ways in which people can express their national identity, but sport is an obvious example of what J. Hargreaves calls 'constructing the nation' (Hargreaves, 1986, esp. pp. 154ff). Hargreaves comments on the masculine qualities glorified through sport. Much of the symbolism of nationalism is masculine, particularly the way it integrates the experiences of power and war, including colonial wars (Barthes, 1983). This has implications for the specific aspects of nationalism with which women might identify, and Billig's study shows that it is women who are most interested in the British Royal Family. The gendered nature of the symbolic representation of nationalism reflects the gendered nature of other aspects of power in modern societies.

Myths of national identity

The symbolism of rituals surrounding the British Royal Family and events such as the Opening of Parliament, changing the guard, and 'Beefeaters' guarding the Tower of London are expressions of national myths that involve making sense of the past in terms of the present. Accounts of the wartime activities of the nation, including those involved in the commemorations of VE Day and VJ Day discussed above, are also myths. In comparison, we might mention the American myth of the Frontier and, in socialist societies, perhaps, the myth that society can be perfected (Samuel and Thompson, 1990, p. 5).

Myths are not untruths but accounts or narratives of events which develop through official records, academic writing and media coverage to create a collective memory that is constantly being rewritten and reinterpreted: 'Myth is a system of communication, a message with a characteristic structure which fulfils a specific social function: it offers a model of behaviour' (Cabezali *et al.*, 1990, p. 162). What we called earlier 'cultural scripts' contain such myths. Nationalist myths are the outcome of 'negotiation between the . . . symbolism of the idealised nation and everyday life' (Wright, 1985 p. 25). As we saw earlier, for example, in Britain, where emphasis has recently shifted from the monarchy as such to the Royal Family.

Myths play an important role in creating shared identities at different levels in society. Families have their own myths concerning origins and characteristics that help their members make sense of who *they* are. Historical and cultural myths containing heroes and heroines present us with elements from which to create our own identities. An example here might be Florence Nightingale, less popularly known for her creation of professional nursing in nineteenth-century Britain than for her experience of nursing the troops during the Crimean War. Thus to be a female nurse today is not simply to be a carer or a healer, but also has an association with patriotism and service to one's country.

Part of everyday life is an historical consciousness or 'historicity'; the capacity of a society to construct a system of knowledge that provides an account of where we have come from and where we are going, which makes sense of the past and the present (Wright, 1985, pp. 14–16). History, then, can be defined as a shared mythology that helps us to link our family and individual biographies to those of the wider community or nation. The Queen's speech at the VJ commemoration, quoted earlier, made these links explicit, paying tribute to 'the vast number of men and women who had fought for, and saved, the future of the free world' and recalling

> the qualities which brought us through those terrible years: the courage, the comradeship and, above all, the sense of common purpose. They are still with us, and we must cherish them, for they have served us well down the centuries. (*The Times*, 21 August 1995)

As members of our nation we develop a sense of our own *historical* existence, and the VE and VJ celebrations in Britain underlined this.

Television commentary drew attention to the varied elements of the British nation, including its distinct Scottish, Welsh and Northern Irish components, and also those of what was the Commonwealth. Participants and spectators of the events were shown caught up in very strong emotions, including many veterans in tears. Even the writer of this chapter, born during the Second World War and remembering her own family myths about life in wartime, felt a strong sense of national identity on this occasion, notwithstanding the fact of having a German grandfather and real distaste for nationalist rituals.

We can begin to see here, the significance for subordinate or minority groups if *their* history is excluded from the collective national history if, as P. Gilroy has phrased it, 'there ain't no black in the Union Jack' (Gilroy, 1987). If the heroic cultural myths feature only white, able-bodied men, then it is correspondingly more difficult for those of us not in these categories to identify ourselves. It is this which explains attempts by subordinate groups across the world to write their own histories, and the importance of the collective myths of such groups for their survival (see, for example, Samuel and Thompson, 1990, pp. 17ff). In order to make sense of our own individual past and present lives, we construct our own histories or memories, our own myths, arguably leaving out those that are contradictory or painful. Although this would appear to be an individual, private process, our 'material' is drawn from the public accounts and myths which exist: 'Our memories are risky and painful if they do not conform with the public norms or versions of the past' (Thomson, 1990, p. 78). We shall explore this further in a later section.

This chapter began with the theme of being a foreigner abroad, and for some people this role is an increasingly familiar one through the growth of tourism and holidays abroad, although, as the next chapter shows, there are many world changes which mean that we are all *global* travellers in a variety of ways. In what appears to be a contradiction, tourism increases cultural vocabulary and knowledge of other societies at the same time as it helps to perpetuate national myths. The great museums and art galleries of the world, the historical and 'heritage' sites visited by tourists in their own countries and abroad, and tours and guides provided by the tourist agencies, all present particular interpretations of the historical myths of a country. The reconstruction of colonial Williamsburg in Virginia, USA, for example, presents an idealisation of colonial America which says little about native Americans, or the black Americans who were slaves during the period. Most of the great museums and art galleries of the world are concerned with aristocratic and bourgeois culture, as are the country houses and historical sites that UK visitors usually see. Package tours to the Caribbean or safari trips to African countries do not reveal the domination of local economies by multinational corporations, or the poverty of local populations. As tourists, it is difficult to see beyond the cultural myths so carefully constructed. We bring these experiences to the way in which we view our own and other societies and, in turn, this affects how people view themselves as being similar to or different from others.

In earlier chapters we argued that in complex modern societies there are increasing choices of role, of cultural scripts, and of how we recognise and negotiate major life transitions. The question arises now, of how much freedom we have to choose our community or national identity, to define and be defined as insiders or outsiders, and to control the consequences of such categorisations. The apparatus of government and state ensures that we cannot escape a range of legal identities; we may wish to eschew all connections with the European community, but as British citizens this designation is on our passports. Neither can we simply choose to be citizens of other countries without fulfilling a range of legal requirements. Similarly, we must send our children to school and meet formal legal obligations as parents and taxpayers. In many countries, even where there is no conscription, men cannot escape military service in wartime without being scapegoated as cowards, as were pacifist conscientious objectors in Britain. American 'draft-dodgers', who refused to fight in Vietnam, were seen as disloyal to their country, and in the British army during the First World War desertion during battle was a capital offence.

We cannot shed these obligatory formal and legal identities. Neither can we easily think outside the ideological discourses of our society, including those of nationalism. Althusser used the term 'ideological state apparatuses' to explain that beliefs, values and ideas about ourselves and our society constrain us because they are developed and reinforced through a range of social institutions – in particular, the family, the Church, the educational system and the mass media. Since we are involved inevitably in these institutions, it is difficult for us to ignore their discourses. To this extent, then, we have a limited choice concerning the ideas and roles prescribed by these institutions.

Governments become particularly concerned to express a coherent nationalism in the face of external threats, and there are interesting examples of this for Britain, some of which illustrate the gendered nature of nationalism mentioned previously. During the First World

War, women were needed as an emergency labour force, in direct contradiction of the traditional ideology of motherhood. The prevailing assumption was that high infant mortality rates and the poor health of working-class mothers and babies was a result of the fact that women worked outside the home. State reaction to the contradiction created by the labour shortage was through a range of welfare campaigns aimed at improving the health of mothers and babies, and 'the idealization of motherhood became a powerful unifying factor during the war' (Rowan, 1984, p. 156). While some real improvements were made, it was as difficult for working-class women to escape the moralising of welfare agencies concerning the care of their children, as it was for them to escape the necessity to work in a range of occupations such as munitions, where conditions of work were particularly arduous. We can recognise here the constraining force for women themselves of the argument that they should work in both roles to ensure the continuity of the nation, since men were already protecting the nation in their capacity as members of the armed forces.

Myths concerning sexual morality, while they may be concerned with gender roles, do not at first sight appear to have much to do with nationality, but during both world wars such myths were important. Sexually transmitted diseases were represented as dangerous to the nation's health and morale. Government campaigns in Britain emphasised that men should beware of prostitutes and 'good time girls' who endangered the nation by spreading disease (Bland and Mort, 1984). Policies of the former Conservative government in Britain, aimed at reducing the numbers of single mothers with 'illegitimate' children, indicate a similar concern with women's sexual morality. It is linked symbolically to the preservation of the nation, with the nuclear family as its foundation.

A different gender myth in many nationalist ideologies symbolises women (and children) as the nation to be protected. British propaganda posters from both world wars portray women as needing protection from rape and defilement by the enemy (Higonnet and Jenson (eds), 1987). The complex way in which nationalisms symbolise the life of the nation, including its intimate personal relationships, is illustrated horribly by the historical frequency with which women have been raped and sexually abused by invading armies, the case of Bosnia occurring in the 1990s. This disturbing fact indicates how identification of the group or country being invaded or fought against as 'other' may motivate extreme action. Ill-treatment of prisoners of war by the Japanese, and by groups involved in the conflict in the former Yugoslavia, are other examples. The attempt by the Nazis during the Second World War to exterminate all Jews is the most extreme example of a nationalist mythology that involved the construction and treatment of one group as 'other'. Nazi nationalist mythology, which aimed at preserving and perfecting the purity of the so-called 'Aryan races' was potent enough to motivate sufficient men and women to staff the concentration camps where millions of Jews died.

'Race' and ethnicity

It is apparent that the boundaries of nation may coincide or conflict with, or crosscut, the boundaries of ethnicity and/or 'race', as an important aspect of group and individual identity. Ethnicity, like nationality, and locality or community, is an awareness of likeness and difference, and 'it is at the boundaries of ethnic groups that ethnicity becomes meaningful: that is, that groups become aware of their ethnic identity when they engage with others' (Cohen, 1982, p. 3). Ethnic identity may include language and religion and, like nationality or community, has a history. Discourses of nationalism frequently suppress or ignore histories of ethnic minorities and the power conflicts that created minority status. The historical reasons why we call a sense of Welshness 'nationalism', for example, rather than ethnicity, are obscure, but in general the minority and often oppressed status of ethnicity originated in the politics of colonialism and imperialism. We can trace the origins of the destructive ethnic conflicts in the former Yugoslavia to historical changes that created and re-created empires in this area. Many of the conflicts within modern African states are ethnic conflicts, in part the legacy of colonial rule by European powers. Territorial boundaries of many modern nation-states cut across and complicate older ethnic boundaries.

Ethnicity is a major aspect of identity for many people living within modern European nation-states, but such an identity may include the oppression of racism (see, for example, Scheff, 1994, pp. 276–303). For some, ethnic identity is a relatively free choice – for example, for people of Polish origin in Britain, or Italian origin in the USA. But for people of Asian or Afro-Caribbean origin in Britain, or black and Japanese Americans, while their ethnic identity may be a source of pride, it is also an identity created out of engagement with dominant cultures that have insisted on their 'otherness' (see Wiley, 1994, pp. 131–49). Physical appearance – skin colour, type of hair, shape of eyes – is construed in 'racial' terms. Historically, most European societies, the USA, and other nations too, have discriminated against non-white people on the basis of ideological beliefs concerning racial superiority and inferiority. These developed as different societies came into contact through colonial and imperial expansion from the seventeenth century. There is considerable debate among sociologists and others concerning the different implications of the terms 'race' and 'ethnicity' (see Billington *et al.*, 1991, ch. 5). Here it is sufficient to note that 'race' is not a scientific but a cultural construction. Ideologically, the concept of 'race', often based on the notion of inherent biological differences, has been used by dominant groups to justify various types of exploitation, including slavery, forced labour, sexual coercion, segregation, and lack of civil rights such as voting and education.

Such behaviour towards ethnic or 'racial' minorities by ruling or dominant groups has consequences for the identity of people in the subordinate groups. Franz Fanon, for example, argued that Western colonial cultures, through their denigration of the indigenous cultures of colonised societies, created the 'colonised' black personality, and increasing awareness of a distinctive black culture was a reaction to this (see Billington *et al.*, p. 71; also Hall, 1995). It has also been argued that black slaves in America internalised and identified themselves as having the characteristics attributed to them by white people. While there is little evidence for such psychological generalisations, these theories draw attention to the problems of identity created by suppressing subordinate cultures (see Elkins, 1959; and Boskin, 1986). So, for example, at the same time as the struggle for civil rights was occurring in the 1950s and 1960s other 'coloured' Americans were content to 'pass for white', or to de-emphasise their *négritude* by straightening their hair (Gates, 1995).

Categorisation of minority ethnic or racial groups as 'other' implies a homogeneity within the group that may not exist. Concentrating on Britain, Gilroy illustrates the *diversity* of racial and ethnic identities that make up the non-white population of the UK, but most white Britons fail to recognise such diversity (Gilroy, 1987). Racial discrimination may deter ethnic minorities from identifying more closely with the dominant British culture, but the assumption that ethnic minorities 'should become more like us' denies the validity of ethnic or 'racial' identification. Such denial may result in the strengthening of particular aspects of ethnic identity such as religion or language, the pride felt by many Afro-Caribbeans in their African origins (see for example, BBC,

Radio 4, 1995) and the development of new cultural identities which challenge the status quo. For individuals with origins in a minority ethnic group, their struggle concerning personal identity may focus around ethnicity. In order to be accepted by those of the dominant culture it may be necessary to speak their language and conform to their customs, but what does this mean if a person can no longer converse in their own language with grandparents, or is frowned on by family and friends for marrying outside the ethnic group? It may feel increasingly difficult to withstand pressures to identify publicly with others of similar ethnic or racial origin, since *not* to do so is seen as a betrayal. Blackness or whiteness, or other easily recognised physical symbols of distinctiveness, are cultural constructions, not givens, but they have real consequences for the identity of individuals and groups. A person who is continually identified by others in terms of such a cultural construction may have less choice of cultural identity.

Citizenship and the nation-state

In an earlier section, the role of the modern state and citizenship in defining issues of personal identity was examined briefly, and this section takes up the theme again. Like the notion of the importance of an individualised 'self', which we discussed in Chapter 2, the political and philosophical notion of individual liberty is essentially Western: 'we have come to regard liberty as something that, firstly, should be granted to everyone and, secondly, as being intrinsically valuable' (Foster and Kelly, 1990/1, p. 73). Individual liberty is usually linked to notions of citizenship and democracy and underlies the idealised nation-state, as illustrated in our discussion of perceptions of Britain's wartime role (see also Marshall, 1983). However, all these concepts are contested and must be examined in the context of the relationships of power and subordination that also underly the nation-state.

   Citizenship entails our political relationship to the state. It endows us with certain rights and it is usually argued that citizenship guarantees us individual liberty or autonomy (Foster and Kelly, 1990/1, p. 73). This freedom may be overridden by the state, however. In Britain in the late 1960s and early 1970s, for example, there was considerable debate over the racist connotations of restricting immigration by residents of some of British colonies, despite their British citizenship. More recently, a similar debate has taken place concerning Hong Kong Chinese people. The British Nationality Act (1981) excluded some

British born people from citizenship (London and Yuval-Davis, 1984). Thus the autonomy of certain groups of people to identify themselves in certain ways may be quite severely curtailed by the state.

Western societies are democracies – that is, citizens may engage in the political process through their right to elect the legitimate government – but we do not have a direct voice in all the legislation that affects us or in the distribution of economic resources. The state has a range of powers in areas that limit our autonomy in material ways. State involvement in welfare of various kinds, particularly health, housing and education, and its economic policies, including areas such as taxation and state benefits, affects what Weber called the 'life chances' of individuals (see Marshall, 1983). Life chances include 'cultural capital' and all those resources that enable us to acquire many of the rewards and resources of our society, including, health, education and a good income.

In most modern Western societies the welfare state provides a minimum of resources in most of these areas, although this has diminished during the 1990s. Because of inequalities of wealth and 'cultural capital' (for example, a family tradition of educational achievement) which exist, some individuals already have more resources than others (Bourdieu and Passerant, 1977). Life chances affect what Weber referred to as an individual's 'market situation' – that is, the types of skills they acquire, and their occupation (Weber, 1978, pp. 43ff). In Chapter 6 it was emphasised how important work may be for the identity of individuals. Some individuals can buy better education, health care and so on, all of which give them greater choices in the organisation and direction of their lives, including the work they do. Marxist views of the state see it as an instrument of ruling or powerful classes who benefit from the economic system of capitalism (Hall, 1983, pp. 243–7). Thus, the social class structure on which capitalism is based is a source of social inequality and of the social identifications arising from this. Whether or not we accept this analysis, state policies which redistribute life chances do have a direct effect on the lives of citizens.

Recently, attention has focused on the gendered nature of citizenship and the effect of social policy on women. Citizenship is often conceptualised as part of the public world of politics but, as we have already indicated, the public and the private overlap and what happens in one area affects the other. Using the terms 'citizen' or 'women' or 'men', to indicate some monolithic group obscures the way that the various identities of any particular person cross-cut each other. Thus a person's identity as a citizen 'will be mediated by other factors such as "race", class, poverty, sexual orientation and age' (Lister, 1991, p. 66). In the area of social rights, women citizens are not treated equally with men, particularly in the area of employment. Recent policies aimed at reducing the number of children in Britain born outside marriage and making biological fathers responsible for financial maintenance of their children curtails the autonomy of the mothers of such children to be single mothers. The regulations surrounding a range of welfare state benefits, pension laws and taxation also restrict women's autonomy in different ways from men's. Despite the connotations of liberty and freedom attached to the status of citizen, the state has power to interpret this status and this has consequences for the identity of its citizens.

Conclusion

Answers to the questions posed in the first section of this chapter have proved complex. These were questions concerning what we mean by 'being abroad', by 'foreign', and how such concepts are perceived as part of individual identity. Examination of these questions led us to look at a range of commonsense concepts that are used to describe the world outside our own private 'home': community, nation, state citizen, ethnicity or culture. Such concepts were discovered not be simple at all. Rather, they are open to various and often contradictory interpretations of a complex and symbolic nature. Because they are beyond our own immediate and private world they concern imagined relationships with other individuals and groups whom we do not know as we know our family and friends. Beyond the boundaries of our primary relationships we are identified as, and identify ourselves, as members of wider groups. Through the imagined qualities of these groups, we are citizens and members of the community, the nation, the ethnic group, although we have varying degrees of freedom to reject these identities. Identification with one group involves categorising others as outsiders, which has consequences for *their* identity. Our feelings and identification as part of these wider groups depends on the historical circumstances of their formation and on our own experiences of the complex relationships of power that take place within and between them. Overall, the powers of the nation-state define and mediate our autonomy within these various identities. The next chapter moves outside the boundaries of nation and state to look at how our identities within these boundaries are challenged by the postmodern trends of globalisation.

8

Globalisation and Identity

The global framework

In Chapter 7 we went further in examining the ways in which the self and self identity are understood. Examples were the experience of the self in relation to a foreign 'other' during travel, and the role of national myths or mythic figures, such as the Royal Family. As noted, experiences of this kind can provide a point of identification in knowing oneself as, for example, 'English'. In the present chapter we ask some questions about those aspects of life that no longer seem to be bounded by or contained within our own societies or nations. We shall be exploring what is meant by the concept of globalisation, focusing on the way in which cultural and political changes throughout the world have meshed with one another. The question of whether or not the world has become a single social system will be addressed, and we shall be exploring the ways in which colonialism brought previously very separate parts of the world together, but in relationships of marked inequality. Finally, we shall examine the ways in which *localised* self-identities are shaped by the consumption of objects from different parts of the world.

In post-war Europe, foreign travel has increasingly come to be seen as an uneventful, ordinary activity, rather than a thrilling or threatening voyage into the unknown. In the UK, its new status has been symbolised, for example, in the building of a tunnel under the English Channel, a development that is represented by the tourist industry as a convenient and speedy rationalisation of a previously awkward journey across a narrow strait of water. Its status is none the less ambiguous in that it has also been seen as a threat to a centuries-old representation of the United Kingdom as a single, bounded island entity. Without the surrounding seas as a marker of British separateness, national, and therefore personal, identity ceases to be as clear-cut. For some, therefore, the 'Chunnel' has been a welcomed development which is indicative of the end of outdated political, economic and cultural divisions. Others have shown considerable resistance to the adoption of aspects of a European lifestyle – from metrication to social policy to a common currency.

Developments such as these are not confined to Europe. They are shared with members of societies throughout the world. Lives are no longer lived in localised isolation, but rather within some kind of global framework and it is relevant to ask how this affects our sense of self and identity. What the nature of that global framework might be, however, is open to debate, and it is this debate that provides the core focus for the present chapter. Thus, for example, the relationship between global connections that are primarily military, political or economic, and those that are cultural is far from clear-cut. E. Zaretsky has argued that global cultural connections cannot now be separated off from what were traditionally seen as political linkages (Zaretsky, 1995). The reason why the two had previously been seen as separate was that prior to the 1960s the social sciences had relegated culture to the private sphere of life. That is to say, gender relations, sexuality, the family, ethnicity, and religious and racial identity were seen as lying outside the capitalist economic realm. However, after the emergence of 'identity politics', where active campaigns were fought against oppressive 'race', gender and sexuality-based social inequalities, such a distinction no longer held sway. Zaretsky argues that the coming together of political movements based on 'race' and ethnicity with other movements based on gender and sexuality in the 1960s and 1970s – the Women's Movement and Gay Pride, for example – had the effect of challenging a previously taken-for-granted separation between the public world of politics and a private world within which the individual's sense of self-identity is fostered.

> The result was a realignment or reorganisation of the division between the public and the private, which brought the private sphere, the sphere of culture but also the sphere of the family, to the fore in a new way. What had previously been the taken-for-granted background of political life, the process of identity creation, now became foreground and was politicised. (Zaretsky, 1995, p. 246)

This chapter develops the focus on the politics of self-identity and the relationship between self and society that has been sustained throughout the book. When we address issues of globalisation we therefore continue to examine the ways in which the cultural and the political domains of life might be linked – just as we did in earlier chapters. Examples here are the emergence of the idea of individualism with the development of capitalism (Chapter 2), and the way in which freedom to work, marry and so on are determined by the legal framework of the state (Chapter 7). Zaretsky's work on identity politics is very much in keeping with the arguments we have been developing in that he challenges the usefulness of making any kind of separation between culture and politics.

Mapping a global landscape

The discipline of sociology has grown up using a model of society that resembles the nation-state (Featherstone, 1990, p. 2). In the 1990s what we now find is a body of work that seeks to make sense of something called 'society', but on a global level. In earlier chapters we examined some of the differences and similarities between Western and more traditional societies, but we said little about the fact that they cannot now be seen to exist in isolation from one another. We are none the less familiar with the notion that there are issues that concern every nation, or indeed every social group, within the world. *Global* issues range from the damage to the planet's ozone layer and possible climatic changes, to the testing of nuclear weapons and the reduction of the world's forests. Intertwined with these environmental concerns we also have political and economic concerns that can be understood only when examined from an international or global perspective – for example, the meeting of women from all over the world in Beijing in 1995 to discuss the politics of gender.

Central to this chapter are questions that ask how we might think about the self and society when the boundaries of the individual's social context are no longer clear-cut. Thus, while nationhood no longer provides the location for our sense of self, this does not mean that we have a sense of living in a global village or an ethnic 'melting pot'. When we refer to society and to self-identity, what is it, therefore, that we have in mind? In order to make some sense of this kind of contradiction we shall first examine some of the ways in which social life has ceased to be shaped purely by national-level issues and decision-making. In the second half of the chapter, we shall contrast the apparent 'globalisation' or 'internationalisation' of society with evidence to suggest that social identity continues to reside within a whole series of highly localised social contexts.

First, however, we examine arguments which suggest that the individual now finds themself living within a world that has become a single social system. Few of us can claim to inhabit social settings that are not interconnected on very fundamental levels with the rest of the planet. As Giddens notes, events and issues that take place completely outside our immediate daily lives none the less have effects upon us (Giddens, 1989). While we must recognise that the members of European societies have had access to raw materials from across the world since the eighteenth century – cotton, coffee, minerals, tobacco, for example, – in the 1990s many individuals living in the West have a diet increasingly made up of fresh foods produced in many different parts of the world. Leisure pursuits, such as watching TV, expose us to images of peoples whose lives unfold at great distances from our own, *often at the moment at which activities are actually taking place.* Our economy, and therefore our individual standard of living, is affected by world markets and international political developments. While colonialism and international trading are by no means new phenomena, current events reflect a far more complex set of links between the peoples of different societies.

Prior to the sixteenth century, however, the world was indeed characterised by diversity, its constituent societies knowing little of one another's existence. The boundaries of what they saw as human society lay at the point of contact with neighbouring settlements. Anthropological accounts indicate that the members of hunting and gathering societies which have maintained their traditional lifestyles into the twentieth century often refer to themselves by a tribal name that translates as 'human being'. Their neighbours represent the 'other', peoples who are different and 'not-like-us' (Hart and Pilling, 1964). As we began to show in Chapter 7, it is through the comparison or opposition between social groups that are territorially close that social identity or difference has traditionally been constructed.

Western colonial expansion, which began in the sixteenth century, brought together members of societies from widely dispersed territories. The political linkages between countries produced as a result of colonial rule are, however, a more recent phenomenon, with most traditional societies coming under Western government only during the nineteenth century. Giddens describes the triple purposes of colonialism as political/military, ideological and economic (1989, pp. 520–2). Thus it was the setting up of military bases, the spread of Christian missionary work, and the access to raw materials that first brought the societies of Europe into contact with the rest of the world. The move towards globalisation therefore operated on three main levels – ideas; material wealth; and political power.

If we accept that these post-sixteenth-century interconnections are continuing to develop, this raises questions about how they affect the individuals who make up the societies concerned. Giddens argues that the forms of social association or connection that now span the earth have emerged in a fragmented and unequal fashion, which carries inevitable implications for the quality of lives of societies' individual members (Giddens, 1989). Here, therefore, we take up sociology's traditional concern with social inequalities and the economic under-pinnings of power by examining the material inequalities that occur at a global level. We then move on to examine their cultural implications for the individual's sense of self-identity.

The links between the countries of the world that came about as a result of colonialism are often characterised by inequalities that are now endemic and increasing. Broadly, we can divide up the world into the Western and the developing or Third-World countries, noting the vast difference in wealth between the forty richest and forty poorest nations. As Giddens makes plain, the value of all the goods and services produced in the richest countries, their gross national product (GNP), is twenty times that produced in the poorest countries (Giddens, 1989, p. 525). This can be explained as a result of the ways in which colonising Western nations encouraged developing countries to enter into trading arrangements based on cash crops, such as tea, sugar and tobacco and minerals such as diamonds and zinc. Produced under Western control from land appropriated from indigenous peoples, these goods were exported on terms set within Western money markets. They were given priority over the production of subsistence crops needed for everyday nutrition, and were often produced using traditional, labour-intensive methods. One of the results of this process is the lack of any developed industrial base in many developing countries, a circumstance which puts them at a distinct disadvantage in relation to the West, which has undergone nearly two centuries of industrial growth. While some developing countries, such as Brazil, Mexico, Hong Kong, South Korea and Taiwan, have undergone periods of very rapid industrialisation during the twentieth century, they remain tied in debt relationships with Western countries, their wealth tending to remain in the hands of small elites, while most of their populations live in poverty. Indeed, it is indebtedness which, crucially, binds many of the countries of the world to one another, Western aid having declined with the world recession, along with the prices paid to developing countries for their exports.

So great is the discrepancy of material wealth between Western and many developing countries that it is estimated that 700 million Third-World adults are seriously undernourished, while 10 million children under five are virtually starving. This does not, however, reflect a shortage of food on a global scale. There is enough food in the world for everyone. What we are describing is therefore a highly complex situation where that which is produced is not available for those who are in need of it. Here we ask about the extent to which sociology can help us understand the entrenched nature of this situation, arguing that it is by restoring the relationship between the political and the economic domains of social life that we can begin to make sense of what is happening.

Making sense of global inequalities

Giddens outlines three theoretical perspectives that have been developed to help make sense of this complex picture (1989). Imperialism, as envisioned by J. A. Hobson and later developed by V. I. Lenin, is an explanation of global inequalities which has a profoundly economic basis. Thus, in this view, imperialism describes the expansion of Western markets at the point when the production of goods began to exceed the capacity of the home market. New consumers and cheaper raw materials were the rewards sought in colonising countries outside the West. Having an established industrial base, the West was able to pursue this economic strategy successfully, thereby cementing its own advantage, to the growing cost of societies in other parts of the world. The argument that this process is driven primarily by business interests is lent credence by the fact that imperialism has been superseded by neo-imperialism, a set of relationships that continues to bind the former colonial empires economically, even though their political ties have been broken.

Dependency theory argues for the presence of a division between a metropolitan centre, made up of industrialised Western countries, and satellite countries in the developing world, which are reliant upon traditional subsistence agriculture and cash crops, a form of production that binds them in deepening dependency upon a wealthier West. Economists such as Andre Gunder Frank argue that the economic ascendancy of the West is directly proportional to the loss of resources and economic stability in Third-World countries. Giddens questions this view, arguing that it was primarily the development of an industrial base that secured the economic power of 'First-World' countries and, conversely, the lack of such bases that maintains poverty in the developing world.

World systems theory incorporates a deeper historical perspective, one which foregrounds the development of capitalism globally since the sixteenth century. Devised by Immanuel Wallerstein, it highlights the development of industrialised manufacturing, advanced agricultural production and centralised government within core states in the north-west of Europe. A semi-periphery of countries around the Mediterranean then came to be drawn into trading relationships with the core countries, with peripheral regions such as Poland often providing the raw materials for this kind of trade. It has therefore been only over a period of time that the periphery of the world system has expanded, and developing-world countries which previously represented an untouched, external arena have now come within a Western-dominated political and economic orbit. What Wallerstein offers us is an overview of a protracted process of capitalist growth.

In their focus on the globalisation of economies, all these theories assume a prior state of localised production. Globalisation is conceived of as an outward move which brings together societies that previously were separate. A. Bergeson, however, contests this view, arguing that we should not take it for granted that it is pressures from *within* which set in train processes of internationalisation. Rather, global relations of inequality are the outcome of military struggles, the conquered then being forced into disadvantageous trading relations with conquerors. Raw materials are sold cheaply to Western countries only because their producers have no choice in the matter. Thus, as Bergeson, argues:

> it was conquest which established the political framework of colonialism within which trade...took place. It was conquest and colonial relations which structured peripheral production and thereby created underdevelopment, and, since the colonial relations characterised most of the world (by 1914 some 84 per cent of the world was, or had been, under colonial rule), this made the colonial relation...the core–periphery relation for the world economy as a whole. (1990, p. 72)

According to this view, we need to think globally at a much earlier historical stage than much current social theory would suggest. Global relations of power between the conquered and conquerors can be traced back to the fifteenth century, there being a core and a periphery which long pre-dated more recent relations of exchange. The notion that we should see individual societies as the originators of a global or international system of any kind is refuted by Bergeson, who argues that it is only within a larger-scale system that social formations such as nation-states came into being: 'there was an international order which arose at the same time as states, such that one cannot separate out the state as coming first and the international system as coming second' (Bergeson, 1990, p. 78).

Bergeson finishes by arguing that economically-based theories tend to make the mistake of assuming that globalisation is a process which radiates out from individualised states because they ignore relations of military or political power, as well as issues of culture. What other theorists have tried to do is to sketch out the broader cultural landscape into which the state has emerged, a landscape which none the less transcends the limits of state boundaries. M. Featherstone, for example, argues for the existence of trans-societal cultural processes which have preceded the interstate relations within which nation-states are now embedded (1990, p. 1). Examples of these are independent diplomatic languages such as, initially, Latin, and later French; and the extensive networks of the Church and dynastic families during the Middle Ages. International cultural systems such as these underpin the current flow of goods, services, information and people within and across the boundaries between states.

In questioning the more materialist theories of imperialism, dependency and world systems, and looking at such connections in terms of overarching systems that are primarily cultural, we are beginning to tap into some of the domains that the individual experiences at first hand. Cultural connections at a global level have been a focus in the work of A. Appadurai (1990; 1993). Using the concept of global cultural flows, he invents the terms *ethnoscapes, technoscapes, finanscapes, mediascapes* and *ideoscapes* to explain what he means. The term *scape* is chosen because it suggests a kind of landscape or perspective that stretches across both local and national boundaries. His definitions of these terms help us focus on the ways in which society has gradually become global from the sixteenth century onwards. Thus *ethnoscapes* describe some of the people who, over the centuries, have increasingly come to make up the individual's social world – 'tourists, immigrants, refugees, exiles, guestworkers' (Appadurai, 1990, p. 297). Contemporarily, the shifts of international capital and immigration policies of different countries mean that finding an income or a place to live can involve major migrations for members of social groups from many parts of the world. The result is that we are now thoroughly accustomed to a social life comprised not only of long-standing local families or communities, but also of newcomers from different parts of our own country, or indeed other parts of the world. People from the Indian subcontinent, for example, may be familiar members of our immediate environment, whether as students, medical staff, textile workers or refugees. Alongside the flow of peoples between different parts of the world is the growing prevalence of the *idea* of movement as a desired or necessary possibility. No longer can we expect those around us to remain present throughout our lives, nor, ourselves, reliably anticipate a lifetime within the locale of our birth.

While migrations as a result of war, plague, famine and religious persecution have characterised global social relations for centuries, the movement of peoples is now increasingly linked with *technoscapes*, the diffusion of mechanical and informational technology across the world. Multinational companies, for example, bring Western technology to those parts of the world where labour is cheap, shifting location in response to changing local economies. Another example is the Internet, a computer-based information-exchange network which links individuals across the world in a more rapid and immediate fashion than any previous media exchange system. Currently without any centralised control system, it is anarchic in its organisation and organic in its patterns of growth. Whether we are speeding across the Channel in the Eurostar Link train, jetting from America to Europe, or 'surfing the Net', we are using forms of technology that transcend the boundaries which, formerly, served to maintain a clearer sense of distance, and therefore also *difference*, between nation-states.

This fluid spread of technology throughout the world is also connected with *finanscapes*, the rapid and unpredictable movement of money through 'currency markets, national stock exchanges and commodity speculations' (Appadurai, 1990, p. 298). *Mediascapes* and *ideoscapes* are also related to the other kinds of global cultural flow that Appadurai feels are now connecting the members of different societies. Thus his term *mediascapes* refers to the electronic capabilities and the kinds of information and images that technoscapes project across the planet. He argues that items such as news broadcasts, pop music and documentaries are transmitted in a variety of forms to all kinds of audiences, via a whole variety of technological means. This process has been referred to as cultural imperialism, though in Appadurai's view the meaning of any one image or idea is subject to multiple interpretations, depending upon who views it, in what form and via what means. We cannot therefore assume that Western sets of values are everywhere being imposed. However, people living in different social contexts begin to build up information and ideas about one another that are shaped by the ways in which *mediascapes* represent them, and these images and items of information can become the basis for fantasies which can bring desires for new acquisitions or new lifestyles (also see Billington *et al.*, 1991 pp. 75–80). *Ideoscapes* are similar to *mediascapes* but they tend to focus more on sets of political ideas or ideologies – for example, 'freedom', 'rights', and 'democracy'. They can be linked back to the ideologies introduced by Western missionaries during the nineteenth century and to the birth of independence movements. It is none the less important to recognise that while such ideas or concepts have a particular meaning within the framework of the dominant Western world view, they may take on a new life or be used for different ends when taken up in a contrasting political climate.

Though these cultural connections can be shown to bring people into contact of some kind with one another – whether through migration, technology, money or the media – Appadurai argues that they also serve to separate them. Local social worlds are constructed and experienced partly as a result of the presence of these kinds of multiple linkages, each one operating independently yet in tandem with the others. This, Appadurai argues, allows for an increased *diversity* of forms of social life. For example, in Bombay, the movement of wealthy Arabs from the Gulf states has raised the price of basic foodstuffs and influenced the design of hotels and restaurants. While this is an unwelcome connection for the people of Bombay, one that they feel endangers their 'local' lifestyle and identity, it is none the less a connection that enables members of that society to find employment in the Middle East, thereby bringing wealth and luxury goods back to Bombay society. Fuelled by the *mediascapes* of the West, such goods find ready markets among the members of that society. Bombay changes as a result of external influences, but in ways that are specific to local cultural and social norms.

On the basis of Bergeson's and Appadurai's work we can therefore question the idea that globalisation is an increasing trend towards tighter and more complex links between previously separate societies, something which, were it not for the presence of so many problematic inequalities, might lead to some kind of global or world state. In its place we can begin to conceptualise globalisation as: (i) a pre-sixteenth-century set of political, social and cultural conditions that provided the context within which nation-states could later emerge; and (ii) the cultural flows or *scapes* that transcend national boundaries – these include, for example, 'law factories' made up of international lawyers, international corporate tax accountants and management consultants. Neither of these versions of globalisation describes a world of separate societies that gradually became tied up with one another; both highlight cultural conditions that override social divisions such as nation-states.

A recent example of the cultural conditions that cast doubt on a purely materialist account of globalisation is the transformation of capital after the Second World War. By this, we refer to the rise of service and part-time work; the importance of 'educated labour'; emigration flows that were continuous and large-scale; and the growth of transient cultures and stateless corporations. Here we see some of Appadurai's *scapes* appearing – *ethnoscapes* , for example. The previous divisions between the public world of productive, industrialised labour and the private world of the family and personal life underpinned a Marxist preoccupation with the centrality of paid work within any model of society. Economic relations were therefore seen as the primary source of broad social divisions between the bourgeoisie, the owners of the means of production, and the proletariat – those with only their labour to sell. However, E. Zaretsky argues that the globalisation of capital and a global division of labour meant the entry of many previously marginalised groups into the labour force – 'women, racial minorities and new immigrants and previously peripheral nations' (Zaretsky, 1995, p. 252). As a result, gender, ethnicity and sexuality-based differences were made visible in *public* space. Indeed, they came to be 'lived' or 'performed' rather than being submerged, either within structural positions such as 'bourgeois' or 'proletariat', or within the private world of the family. Furthermore, what Appadurai describes as *technoscapes*, the flow of informational and mechanical technology across the world, meant that knowledge, information and communication – that is, the cultural rather than merely the material domains of life – came increasingly to the fore. Zaretsky argues, therefore, that culture, in forms such as the media, advertising, education, leisure and sport, has effectively transformed the boundary between the public and private spheres, organising rather than merely reflecting social life. Central to the breaking down of earlier divisions is the emergence of politicised group identities. Recognition was demanded within the sphere of culture for divisions based on 'race' and ethnicity; liberation was demanded for gender and sexuality issues which had previously been relegated to the sphere of the personal life (Zaretsky, 1995, p. 257).

We therefore need to recognise that globalisation cannot adequately be understood in terms of a network of economic interconnections that underpin a potentially homogenised global state where ideas, tastes, and indeed language, are shared. Globalisation requires us to take account of the complexity of interconnections which exist within a world where previous divisions between the economic and cultural realms no longer hold sway; where national or economically-defined identities are no longer primary but exist alongside identities based on gender, ethnicity and sexuality.

The following three case studies allow us to examine issues of diversity and difference within the context of globalisation. What will be argued is that, paradoxically, an understanding of globalisation requires that we start from the local view, a perspective which, like that of Zaretsky, challenges our existing divisions between work and family, between economically and culturally-based social identities and between the nation-state and a potential global state.

Diversity and difference: local identities

In this section we shall look at material that shows how global capitalism can play a part in localised identity formation, and we shall be focusing on patterns of consumption rather than relations of production as the source of social identity. However, this is not to say that patterns of consumption follow some kind of global cultural script, where Western manufactured goods and European fashions are of universally high status, and where cultural imperialism holds sway. Instead of this overly simplistic way of looking at what is going on in the world, we examine the diversity of ways in which the consumption of objects can play a part in the strategies through which identity is created and recreated.

Friedman's work on the People's Republic of Congo illustrates this approach (Friedman, 1990). He offers three case studies from this locality. The first concerns the *sape*, a member of a group of young men living in the Congo. While belonging to a low-status social group, the *sape* creates his high-status local identity by visiting Paris and returning with designer-label clothes that are worn with the maker's name stitched ostentatiously on to the lapel. Similarly, the display of cans of imported, rather than home-produced, Coca-Cola in one's car is also, significantly, constitutive of the high-status social identity of the *sape*. From a Western perspective, therefore, the *sape's* pattern of consumption is one that involves the purchase of high status, First-World items as a way of masking a social identity as a low-status member of a Third-World society. Friedman argues that this view misses the point of a set of local practices. Among the Congolese, appearance and identity are one and the same thing. Clothes are an immediate expression of the individual's life force, something that is thought to be external to the individual. Like Western medicine, clothes are not symbols of a desired source of power. They *are* the power: 'Consumption is a life and death struggle for psychic and social survival and it consumes the entire person' argues Friedman (1990, p. 316). The *sape* is therefore someone whose strategies for the formation of his social identity are entirely in keeping with those of his *local* culture, yet they involve the purchase of goods that carry high social status within a European society. To what extent can his pattern of consumption therefore be said to be local? Friedman argues that, in the West, the purchase of designer clothes is a way of infiltrating a higher social order; among Congolese youth the purchase of such clothing is an assault on the rank order of society. He who wears the designer label does not fabricate, but, rather, takes on the essence of high status. In sum, rather than seeing this as an example of Western domination or colonialist expansion, what Friedman presents to us is an example of the way in which Western goods, while recognised as being of high value, take on social power only to the extent that they are incorporated within the set of practices through which status is gained at the purely local level.

While the low status Congolese *sape* takes items from an external world market of designer clothes, dominated by European couture houses, in order to create an authentic high-status local identity, an indigenous Japanese people, the Ainu, seek to overcome their low social status by promoting a nationally-unrecognised identity as an attraction for foreign tourists. Thus, within Japanese society, differences of ethnic status do not exist. The Ainu are seen to be poorly acculturated, and economically and politically marginal within Japanese society. However, by developing an Ainu cultural movement, this group have sought to constitute for themselves an ethnic identity that will make them acceptable as the equals of other members of Japanese society. As Friedman argues, 'The presentation of Ainu selfhood is a political instrument in the constitution of that selfhood' (1990, p. 321). As such, participation in tourism is the precursor for demands that land be made available for the Ainu to grow their indigenous foodstuffs, that Ainu language and history be revitalised, and that Ainu rituals be revived. While the Congolese *sape* brings in items from an external world market in order to gain local status, the Ainu pursue a similar goal by inserting indigenous items such as food and ritual practices into an external tourist economy.

Finally, Friedman introduces the case of an Hawaiian cultural movement devoted to rescuing the state's indigenous culture from the depredations of the dominant American way of life and from the incursions of Asian plantation workers. When its plantation economy began to dwindle, tourism became a major economic asset. However, this has come to be seen as a threat to Hawaiian identity, rather than an opportunity, as was the case among the Ainu. While members of Hawaiian society had willingly identified themselves as part-American or part-white or part-Chinese up to the 1960s, from that time onwards, with the growth of identity politics, the Hawaiian cultural movement has resisted tourism, believing that its ethnic authenticity would otherwise be vulnerable to external misrepresentation. Friedman sums up the relative positions of these three localised identities as follows:

> Congolese consume modernity to strengthen themselves. The Ainu produce traditional goods in order to recreate themselves. The former appropriate otherness in order to create themselves while the latter produce selfhood for others. Hawaiians produce selfhood for themselves. (1990, p. 323)

What might seem to be occurring in these three examples is that groups and individuals are pursuing *local* cultural strategies as a way of meeting indigenous political and economic ends. All that has changed is the public arena within which these localised sets of practices are acted out. However, this interpretation overlooks the historical relationship which, in each example, links the local social setting with wider, global relations of power. Thus what is going on at a local level is an attempt to overcome cultural, social, political and economic disadvantages that have an external source.

Diversity and difference: cosmopolitans

The work of Hannerz on 'cosmopolitans' provides another example of the complex relationships between diversity and difference (1990).

Travel across national boundaries takes many forms. As noted, foreign tourism is increasingly thought of as an 'ordinary' event, to be undertaken without extensive planning and preparation. Bargain flight-plus-accommodation packages are often bought by holidaymakers immediately prior to their departure date. Indeed, within an industry that sells many of its products on the basis of convenience and reliability, there are subcategories of holiday for those who feel travel should retain a sense of challenge or adventure. Thus the advertising brochure of the company *Worldwide Journeys and Expeditions* includes 'a classical Kenya safari, a Himalayan trek, a yacht charter in the Galapagos Islands'.

The relationship between the individual who travels outside their country of origin and their destination is therefore likely to vary. For example, the cosmopolitan can be distinguished from the tourist in that they 'know' and participate in the culture of those among whom they travel (Hannerz, 1990). Thus the cosmopolitan is someone who is at home in more than one culture, who is aware of 'culture' as a concept and who can exercise choice over their role *vis-à-vis* someone who is foreign and therefore seen as different. In the cosmopolitan, therefore, we have the paradox of someone who travels globally while valuing the diversity of local social contexts and identities. Cosmopolitans differ from tourists, who often seek what Hannerz describes as 'home plus'. This may be home plus sunshine and/or cheap alcohol, as in Mediterranean resorts; home plus illegal drugs, as in Morocco; home plus prostitution, as in South East Asia; home plus *haute cuisine*, as in France. Alongside whichever 'plus' attracts the tourist comes a requirement that accommodation, travel arrangements and insurance are of the same standard as at home, and that extensive knowledge of a foreign language will not be required. The individual's local culture can therefore be said to travel with them, being preserved relatively intact in a different part of the world. In this sense, the tourist resembles the migrant worker, for whom the 'plus' is employment and a higher standard of living, but who also seeks to preserve the culture of home, either within the host country or through high levels of contact with 'home'.

For the cosmopolitan their experience of foreign parts of the world is constructed in a distinctive fashion. When abroad, they surrender to the culture of the foreigner, something that provides them with status at home. This is often made visible in what they eat, how they dress and how they decorate their homes. Television programmes such as *Auf Wiedersehen Pet* are therefore targeted at an audience of cosmopolitans, or would-be cosmopolitans. First shown in the early 1980s, and repeated in the mid-1990s, this popular programme derives much of its humour from the *lack* of cosmopolitan *savoir faire* among a group of British building workers who find employment in Germany. Each member of the cast has a different relationship with their German host culture, varying from those who are constantly in touch with home and resist contact with locals, to those who maintain an aggressive disdain towards a society they see as a defeated enemy, both politically and on the football pitch. As its audience, the viewer is positioned as a knowing cosmopolitan who can 'read' the situations that baffle the less worldly members of the programme's cast. Furthermore, the cosmopolitan's pleasure in diversity is satisfied by the characters' 'Geordie' identity, represented not only in their distinctive local accent but also in their provincial attitudes.

What Hannerz is trying to understand through his work on cosmopolitans is what happens to culture when relationships cease to be territorially bounded and instead take place across international boundaries. Like Friedman, therefore, he argues that we need to examine how the nature of the self and society is experienced at the local level in order to make sense of a series of global transformations. He sees local identity as being constituted through face-to-face relationships that occur in social contexts where there is little territorial movement (see also the discussion of Durkheim and Tönnies in Chapter 7). However, while Hannerz sees relationships as the locations or sites where culture takes place, he none the less distinguishes between different cultures in terms of how they are positioned within global social structure. Thus some cultures are located territorially, within nations, regions and localities; others are carried within what he calls 'collective structures of meaning by networks more extended in space, transnational or even global' (1990, p. 239). As such, cultures can co-exist, mingle and overlap, in terms of both their form and their location. Here we are getting at the kind of complexity that Appadurai has in mind when he describes the 'cultural flows' of his *ethnoscapes*, *mediascapes* and *ideoscapes*.

The cosmopolitan is therefore someone who is at the forefront of a growing process of interrelatedness that is creating new sets of connections between different cultures, connections that can perhaps be seen more appropriately as a kind of transnational culture. In some respects, therefore, Hannerz is anticipating the globalisation of culture, particularly in the form of the occupational or business cultures within which professionals often operate. As such, they may travel the world, but insulated from local cultures, sealed within a Western, metropolitan culture, using travel books or tourist manuals as guidance in their relationships with locals. None the less, in that the professional may share many aspects of the cosmopolitan's love of diversity, we can also argue that there can be no single global culture while cosmopolitans continue to place high value on knowledge of the cultures of others. Similarly, the locals' attachment to their own uniquely local culture helps to preserve its identity in the face of increasing contact with other parts of the world and their peoples.

Identity and consumption

Eating 'foreign' food often plays a central role in the formation of a 'cosmopolitan' social identity. Indeed, food is central to many of the debates associated with globalisation, as this chapter has already indicated. On the one hand, access to food from other parts of the world has contributed to trade relationships from the sixteenth century onwards: to eat 'exotic', expensively-imported foodstuffs has been, and indeed remains, a way of displaying high social status. On the other hand, as already argued, trading relationships are associated with the growing inequalities among the peoples of the world. Thus the lack of food in countries where land has been used to grow food for export rather than subsistence is seen as a global political problem. As a result, we have a situation where diet highlights both material inequalities and cultural diversity on a global level. Food issues can therefore be said to link the peoples of the world in a series of interconnected problems, as well as playing a part in the ways in which social groups differentiate themselves from one another. In the following example, we examine the argument that what is eaten in any one locality needs to be seen as an aspect of local identity, even though it may comprise dishes and foodstuffs from anywhere in the world.

Up to the 1950s, identifying oneself as British, for example, involved conforming not only to a distinctive national diet but also to a rigid daily, weekly and seasonal cycle of meals. Alongside these practices went an unquestioning wariness of food eaten in other parts of Europe. Indeed, even UK regional dietary variations – Scottish haggis, 'northern' tripe, black pudding and bull's bissom, Welsh seaweed (laver) bread, and cockney jellied eels – were shunned by those living outside the immediate region, being seen to be made from 'inedible' substances such as blood, intestines, genitalia or snake-like sea creatures.

M. Douglas explored many examples of the ways in which the 'edibility' of foodstuffs was closely tied to particular social identities (Douglas, 1966). Food items can therefore provide clear evidence of the strangeness of people living at any distance from the known world of the local. For example, earlier this century the culture of the UK's closest European neighbour was made known to children through playground tales of the French diet of frogs legs, snails and horses. This, coupled with the rumour that women and men shared the same lavatories, confirmed the view that this was not a properly civilised people. Indeed the term 'frog' is used in Britain pejoratively to describe French people, a connection thereby being made between an improper diet and a less-than-human status. This linguistic practice echoes the example of the Tiwi, whose name means 'human being', the implication being that the members of neighbouring social groups are not fully human (Hart and Pilling, 1964). Items of French diet – frogs and snails – are also to be found alongside puppy dogs' tails in the nursery rhyme which asks what the uncivilised *sex*, little boys, are made of ! Today the notion persists that food that is not British is likely to be greasy, too heavily seasoned, and made from 'inedible' items such as sheep's eyes, raw or even living fish, bird's nests and insects. In 1995 a television documentary on the relationship between animals and human beings showed cats being skinned alive for consumption in China, images which suggested extreme cruelty to a British audience – themselves inhabiting a country where living shellfish are boiled alive. Similarly, members of many European countries identify the British in terms of overcooked vegetables, thin coffee and a largely bland diet.

Alongside a persistent wariness of foreign food, Europeans none the less have a growing interest in 'foreign' food, something evidenced in the UK by the popular 1960s convenience food – 'Vesta curry' – as well as the still growing diversity of foreign food restaurants in British high streets. The eaters' response to the 'strangeness' of non-British or non-French food is, therefore, also indicative of the extent to which they might be described as cosmopolitans. For some its difference and diversity is an attraction, travellers' tales of the consumption of that which is normally 'inedible' granting status to the cosmopolitan on their return home.

We can therefore recognise a growing openness, and indeed attraction, to the diets of peoples among whom the local might be travelling, something that is matched by the availability of a diverse range of foods within local environments. In Western cities, towns, and even villages, the food of the world is available, either ready-cooked in restaurants and cafés or in the form of raw or pre-cooked ingredients in supermarkets as well as specialist stores. Can we therefore point towards evidence that local diets are losing their distinctiveness, that we are moving towards a globalisation of diet and eating patterns where almost any food is available, and indeed 'edible', if the individual has the wherewithal to buy it and the stomach to digest it?

A. James questions the evidence of a process of dietary globalisation (James, 1996). She notes the presence of a *Carrib-Northumbria* restaurant beside the main road north to Alnwick; the opening of an Indian restaurant in Northampton, complete with 'Taj Mahal'-shaped windows and air-conditioning, where the diner finishes their meal with an 'After Curry Mint'; the British Rail Intercity 'dishes of the world' menu which offers food from India, the Middle East, China, Greece, Italy, Scandinavia and France; and the emergence of the Chinese pizza. This apparent evidence of a process of globalisation raises questions about the nature of local identity. Is food no longer constitutive of a distinctively local or territorial sense of self? How can we know ourselves as members of particular communities when a core item of consumption – our diet – is now available almost anywhere in the world?

What James argues is that an apparently globalised range of foodstuffs is often put to local uses. Food items from around the world can become an aspect of local identity. It is, however, something that operates in a precarious manner, identity no longer having the stability it once gained from Sunday lunches of roast beef and Yorkshire pudding, and steamed fish dinners on a Friday. James uses ideas about edibility and inedibility, which anthropologists have shown as being central to the distinction between insiders and outsiders. Thus, as noted above, when French and Chinese people eat British domestic animals – the dog, the rabbit and the horse – we see one people eating food that another group find *conceptually* inedible, even though, in a dietary sense, such animals are entirely fit for eating. However, what we need to bear in mind is that these boundaries, marked out through concepts of edibility and inedibility, are susceptible to change. Over time, the effects of international trade have brought new items within the repertoire of apparently indigenous cuisines. James mentions the introduction of olive oil into the cooking of Provence in the late nineteenth century, an item that now characterises many of its apparently most traditional dishes. We cannot therefore pretend that food is linked in any simple kind of way with national identity. What we might think of as a traditional British diet in fact encompasses a diversity of regional dishes. It also includes items such as potatoes and tea, which are not indigenous but were introduced from abroad. There are similar variations in other societies. Furthermore, different foods are eaten within the same society depending upon the class, gender and age of the eater, and the nature of the social occasion. Thus the authenticity of particular cuisines – French, Chinese or Middle Eastern – is clearly a kind of construction, a melange of diverse ingredients eaten by the members of different social groups on different social occasions.

If we are trying to understand the implications of eating foods from across the world we should, perhaps, concern ourselves more with the organisation of diversity, rather than an apparent trend towards uniformity. Thus, rather than working towards some kind of universal statement, James identifies a range of dietary trends, all of which reflect issues to do with traditional localised identities. The first is *global food* and is expressed in the spread of Western products and food outlets such as McDonald's and Coca-Cola throughout the world. During the mid-1980s, for example, McDonald's increased its franchising by 34 per cent, and by 1992 was estimated to be serving a million customers a day, world-wide. She highlights several features of fast food restaurants such as McDonald's: they are uniform; they represent Western ideals; and they are a threat to local diets. In every restaurant of this kind, drinks and the food items are precisely and predictably packaged. How much they will cost, how they will be served, and how the customer should behave while eating them are all known to the individual before they enter the restaurant. As such, eating in this context becomes a way of managing an increasingly fragmented and unpredictable world within which individuals may be overcome by a confusing range of dietary possibilities. For those who venture away from their local environment, a McDonald's restaurant is a reassuringly familiar place to eat, a home-from-home when abroad.

For those living in newly-industrialising parts of the world, such as China and Eastern Europe, this environment is valued precisely because of its *différance*, because it represents a way of quite literally consuming high-status Western culture. McDonald's, like many successful businesses, is therefore able to maximise its appeal for apparently competing markets. It is both comfortingly local for those who are threatened by the diversity or foreignness of other eating places, and attractively transnational for those wishing to buy into the American Dream. Its blandness and predictability can, however, make it unattractive to those accustomed to a rich local cuisine. Indeed, local eating establishments can thrive on the new-found competition with fast food outlets (James, 1996).

James' second dietary trend is *expatriate food*, and by this she is referring to a cosmopolitan love of diversity, of the cuisines of other peoples. Central to this trend is authenticity, and she cites the work of Peter Mayle whose best-selling novel, *A Year In Provence*, quite literally fed the cosmopolitan's hunger for difference in an account of his expatriate life, which revolved around local Provençal dishes. Alongside accounts such as Mayle's, which give the reader a taste of authentic peasant food as eaten in a local rather than a touristic setting, can be placed the magazines and cookery books that enable the would-be cosmopolitan to fabricate these dishes within their own local environment. As noted by Hannerz, it is by displaying the capture of the culture of the foreigner that the cosmopolitan increases their local social standing (Hannerz, 1990). Highest acclaim goes to the cook who can bring together authentic ingredients and cooking vessels – for example, French cast-iron casseroles, Moroccan tagines or Chinese woks. The cheap, efficient import of these items is a constant threat to the cosmopolitan, for whom they once symbolised the penetration of exotic markets. As a result, cookery writers compete to introduce to the reader ever-finer distinctions of taste and texture in the products required for their dishes.

Food nostalgia is the third trend identified by James. By this, she is referring to the celebration of indigenous cuisines, something that can surface in the face of different kinds of foreign pressure. We have noted the growth of indigenous eating places when Western fast-food restaurants appear locally. In a similar vein, the food hygiene regulations of the European Union have put local foods such as mite-infested Stilton cheese under threat. They defend themselves with statements such as: 'Here is a product which has been English to the bone from 1700 onwards ... it has had mites on it ever since' (James, 1996, p. 88). In the face of apparently globalising trends we therefore have an assertion of diversity and difference, also manifested in the Great British banger, steamed puddings and real ale. As James notes, nostalgia for distinctively British dishes, like the search for authentic Provençal *daubes* and *terrines*, is often the prerogative of particular social classes. Such dishes are not acquired cheaply, nor prepared quickly and easily. As such they reinforce existing divisions, despite their appeal for those who would break down existing structures and embrace diversity.

While it is the authenticity of *expatriate* and *nostalgic food* that constitutes its appeal, James' fourth trend, *creolisation*, is about the transformation, or indeed appropriation, of the diet of one culture by members of another. She gives the example of the way in which Chinese restaurateurs produce English versions of Chinese food that bear no resemblance to what they themselves are accustomed to eating. Rather, such dishes are carefully adjusted to meet English dietary preferences, albeit oriented towards an apparently 'foreign' cuisine. It is argued that cheapness and ease of preparation have long shaped British culinary preferences. Creolised food may therefore be seen as a predictable formula – the dishes of the world made cheap and accessible in fast-food or convenience versions. Hence the bottled pasta sauces, the chilli baked beans and the prawn cracker crisps, all of which offer *safe* and easy access to the dishes of the world.

Conclusion

This chapter has shown how social scientists are trying to build models of a world where the once-stable boundaries of the nation-state no longer confine society's members, either culturally, socially or economically. We have reviewed some of the theoretical explanations that highlight the material connections between different parts of the world, both historically and in the present day. However, such accounts do not help us to understand the ways in which life within a globalised society is still experienced at the local level; neither do they help us to understand the increasing importance attached to the diversity of social identities that go to make up the world's human population. A focus on the formation of social identity does require us to take account of the growing links between different societies in a world where far-distant events can have an impact upon our everyday lives. However, as the detailed examination of the work of three authors has shown, we cannot assume that the growing influence of one part of the world upon another is leading to a more 'global' sense of social identity. For example, Western fashion clothes, trends in travel and tourism, and 'foreign' food are now available throughout the world. Yet, when individuals use them or consume them they do not seem to become 'global villagers'. Instead, such items take on meanings that are specific to the individual's local context. They become part of the social repertoire through which individuals and groups assert *particular* ethnic, gender or class-based identities. However, what cannot be overlooked are the external pressures that influence negotiations over power and status which take place at a local level. Thus a global setting of extreme political, social and economic inequality must be recognised as the wider context within which we discover the diversity and difference that has been the focus of the second half of this chapter.

9

Acting Human

Contemplating knowledge and action

This book began by noting similarities and parallels between, on the one hand, the way that individuals reflect on their private lives and social environment, both locally and globally, and, on the other, the disciplines we call the social sciences. Each of its chapters has focused on key issues in the everyday lives of society's individual members – for example, on health and illness, sexuality, self-identity, and work. These are areas that engage us constantly, both in thought and in practice. At times they are a focus for conscious thought or for explicit conversations with friends and family where we try to make sense of ourselves and our world. At other times they are an implicit concern, reflected, for example, in the way we may search for specific items when we shop, or ponder on the effects of our appearance, conversation or actions upon other people. Sense-making, or mapping, is therefore an almost constant focus within people's lives, whether they engage with it as a conscious practice (what Giddens (1984) calls discursive consciousness), or whether it is something that underlies activities apparently oriented towards other ends (Giddens' practical consciousness – see Chapter 1).

However, what this volume has not, so far, made its explicit focus are the implications for human social *action* of this kind of sense-making: what we do as well as what we think – our 'practice'. This is true both for individual map-making as well as for the maps or theories that social scientists construct. Yet, as noted at the very outset of this book, many people turn to the social sciences as a guide for action. When students complete application forms for

216

university places in the social sciences, they often state quite explicitly that they would like to find out more about why social problems exist in order to respond to those problems more effectively, to actively bring about social change. Similarly, when governments allocate funds for social science research, what they want is not just more 'maps' – they spend money with the aim of finding out how to remedy social problems such as a high suicide rate, a high juvenile crime rate, or a high rate of accidents in transport systems. As this book has shown, while part of the social scientist's work may involve asking how governments, and indeed society in general, come to define and perceive certain features of social life as 'problems', their engagement with these problems none the less reflects a pervasive concern to act within and upon society in ways which make it, for example, more just, safer, healthier and more organised. Our 'maps' therefore lead us into political and moral choices, not just about what they think and how we understand our world, but also about what effect we have on it. As individuals, this may express itself, for example, in whether or not we actively support the work of trade unions in our workplace, whether or not we challenge some of the opinions expressed by those around them, and whether or not we buy certain products or take holidays in certain countries.

However, a sense of confusion characterises many people's decision-making and action in these kinds of area. If we support our trade union it may be because (a) we always have; (b) we think our workmates expect it of us; (c) we feel personally threatened by our employers; or (d) because we have a broader commitment to the aims and beliefs of the trade union movement. Often, however, we may query the foundations of our choices and actions. Do we properly understand the issues, and can we really predict the outcomes of particular political strategies? Is there any way to ensure certainty about these things? This chapter takes as its focus the questions of not only how we come to 'act human', but also of how what we know and understand about our social world might relate to what we do, in our practice. It asks why, in contemporary Western societies, we may falter when it comes to translating thought into action or, conversely, when it comes to explicating the thoughts and ideas that underlie our practices. In so doing we will compare our situation as members of what have been called 'modern' or 'postmodern' societies with the more traditional social worlds that lie either in the past or outside the West, and where there is assumed to be less scope for choice and reflection.

Shifting realities

While this book has introduced you to some ways of mapping the social world which have been in existence since the nineteenth century, it has also examined some of the limitations of these various approaches. It has highlighted some of their inadequacies as sufficient or useful accounts of the complexities of social life, particularly when placed within the context of a rapidly-changing social world. We have adopted the metaphor of mapping to describe the activities of social scientists but we have moved away from the Enlightenment dream, noted in Chapter 1, of a 'modern' social science that will provide clear overall maps that represent the territory of society and social relationships accurately. In moving towards a view of social worlds as multiple, complex, shifting realities, we have inclined towards a 'postmodern' position which challenges the possibility of overall maps. Any maps we make can only be temporarily useful tools confined to specific localities.

As numerous examples have revealed, society is 'known' and understood both by its members and by social theorists through processes that not only draw on available sets of ideas but, in using them to negotiate social reality, in fact contribute to creating and changing that reality. Thus, when we make use of pre-existing knowledge as the basis for new sets of hypotheses or assumptions about the world – and this, of course, is the only knowledge we have available to us – what tends to happen is that our attention comes to be focused on those aspects of the social world that are relevant to our enquiries. This may well have the result of making these aspects come to play a more central role within the world we inhabit. For example, if women approach an institution such as a school or university and try to make sense of it in ways that are informed by a feminist perspective, what we will begin to engage with is the gendered nature of that social reality. A world where femininity and masculinity shape the nature of social relationships may become our experience of that institution, and this might result in changes in our practice as students or teachers. For example, we might challenge men's assumption that their voices will be privileged over those of women. As pre-1980s institutional studies show, social scientists whose research preceded the theories generated by the second wave of feminism, failed to 'see' gender as an organising principle which served the interests of men to the cost of women (see, for example, Eggleston, 1974; Reid, 1978).

Conversely, if our mapping is based on outdated or inadequate understanding of the world, we may be struck constantly by tensions and conflicts between our conceptual or imaginary schemas and the world we are experiencing. Thus social anthropologists who conducted research among the members of more traditional societies, using a Western model of the family, failed to 'see' how kinship and marriage linked people together into social groups. Drawing on Western assumptions about 'primitive peoples', they assumed that what they were encountering were 'native hordes' or 'bands' rather than societies organised in unfamiliar ways (Keesing, 1981). It is, however, conflict and tension between what we 'know' and what we experience that leads us to re-examine, amend or even discard the maps we are using. As a result, some form of new map comes into use. Road maps, for example, work well if we wish to travel quickly across a landscape by car. They show distances between towns and represent major roads with great clarity. For walkers, however, such maps are dangerously inadequate and are best left at home. They cover too much ground without giving the necessary detail of footpaths and contours. Roads are drawn mis-leadingly out-of-scale. Whether as travellers or theorists, the experience of using an inappropriate map may lead us to question assumptions about how the world actually is. If we stick to them, we not only go astray – but we also miss a lot.

Although we have found the mapping metaphor useful, we have also discovered its limitations as we have experienced the shifting nature of social worlds and social relationships and noted the various ways in which, as social actors, we participate in constructing, maintaining and reconstructing them. The very idea of map-making assumes a clear distinction between a map and the territory it maps, between the idea or theory and the reality it describes. This distinction is maintained in the metaphor even though we can recognise that using a particular map regularly will have an impact on the territory, some paths becoming more clearly defined whilst others get overgrown and disappear. As we have explored the importance of language and the way cultures can be understood as systems of symbolic representations which structure subjective experience and meaning, it has become increasingly difficult to maintain the distinction between social territory and how we perceive it. Social worlds *are* symbolic worlds, ideas and reality are not distinct spheres. Recognising this, we have been drawn increasingly towards an alternative metaphor, that of 'narrative'. The mapping metaphor, even when it is acknowledged that all maps are temporary and local, can perhaps be seen as being linked to a 'modern' conception of social science, while that of narrative facilitates a shift to a 'postmodern' viewpoint by putting more emphasis on the creation of meaning in the stories we tell and in which we live our lives as characters. What social scientists now contest is the idea of a social reality that exists independently of the frameworks through which we know it.

This chapter explores some of the implications of the view that social worlds are variously constructed and realised by individuals who are also differently located within social worlds. Thus it draws out parallels between the mapping and storytelling through which individuals negotiate their passage through life, and indeed the lifecourse, and the maps and stories that social scientists have devised and put to use as more theoretical or analytical accounts of individuals and their relationships to social and cultural worlds. In so doing, the chapter draws together some of the threads running through this volume and offers the reader a theoretical overview of the position that has been developing through the book. It provides a discussion of the problems and possibilities which a postmodern or post-structuralist position can offer us, both as individuals and as social scientists.

Knowledge into action

We began this book by acknowledging that many of us have first looked to the social sciences as a way of understanding a social world that seems to have lost direction or meaning, and to have become unfair, violent or impoverished. We seek understanding in order to decide how best that world might be changed, whether by our own hands or those we elect as our representatives. The book has introduced readers to some of the maps and narratives that have been used precisely for this purpose, by sociologists, social anthropologists and psychologists. In doing so, it has developed the view that the social world can be known only indirectly, via whichever theoretical map or story we have to hand. Not only is it differently understood and experienced by society's ordinary members as well as its policy-makers; it is also accounted for in a whole range of ways by those who study it from an academic position. So what are the implications of this for developing a view of social reality that can inform our decision-making and action as human beings who are also citizens, and perhaps professional practitioners of some kind? If there are multiple ways of knowing a world which itself is constituted through multiple voices, on what basis do we take action, and what is the role of the social sciences in informing action and practice? These are some of the questions posed from a postmodernist or post-structuralist position.

While it is important to recognise the inadequacies and problems inherent within some of the classical social science perspectives examined in Chapter 1, it is also important to be aware that a post-structuralist or postmodern perspective generates its own problems. It is worth noting also, that many of the ideas involved in post-structuralist and postmodernist thought have formed part of previous theories, but ones which for various reasons were discarded or forgotten in favour of those already discussed. In particular, it seems relevant to remember Weber's theoretical position that social science can only ever provide partial explanations of social life, and that these explanations will change with the focus or 'value relevance' of the concerns of the worlds in which the problems or issues are being defined (Eldridge, 1971, pp. 12ff; Weber, 1978, p. 21).

The conflicting senses of both liberation and confusion produced by post-structuralist and postmodern perspectives have engaged groups and individuals who espouse a whole range of political and practical agendas. How should we proceed when every aspect of the social world is known to be fluid and open to change, yet we possess no fixed knowledge to guide our reforms or revolutions? To illuminate this question, we can examine some of the dilemmas encountered by feminists with concerns about gender-based power and inequality. Feminism has not concerned itself simply with providing theoretical insights into the varying social processes through which gender comes to be produced; it is grounded in quite a practical agenda which includes the transformation of women's personal lives through political change. From what knowledge base, therefore, should decisions, and indeed actions, be taken?

Central to much feminist writing and activism has been a foregrounding of women's experience. This results from the view that many, if not most, aspects of women's lives – what they feel, think and do – are shaped, or indeed determined, by 'patriarchal' systems of thought, underpinned by male power. However, by side-stepping such control systems and making women's own thoughts, feelings and experiences the bedrock of knowledge, the desired political transformations have been imagined as a true reflection of women's interests and needs. It is this perspective that has underpinned a whole range of feminist initiatives. Women have written about their personal experiences using new literary forms, and indeed new language (Sellers,

1989). They have produced photographs and paintings that subvert the dominant modes of artistic production, so generating new forms grounded in women's own views of the world (Parker and Pollock, 1987). They have shared their private stories in consciousness-raising groups, where the threads of structural oppression rather than individual failure have been traced (Mies, 1983). Within academic life, feminists have questioned existing disciplinary boundaries, finding them inadequate as a framework for the kind of scholarship deemed necessary to illuminate and transform women's experiences of life (Oakley, 1974).

Much of this political activity, like that based on some versions of Marxist thought, is grounded in a view of social reality that assumes an essential or authentic human nature and experience. It assumes that women's problems are a result of patriarchal distortions of an essential or uniquely feminine experience. From a postmodern perspective, the apparent solidity, and indeed strength, of this approach seems to be put under threat. If the distinction between social worlds and the maps or theories we use to make sense of them disappears, if the stories we tell are indistinguishable from social realities, are we not robbed of any foundational knowledge for our attempts to act within and upon the world? Can one story claim more validity than another?

Various versions of Marxism and feminism, like structural functionalism, attempt to indicate some structural foundations upon which to build plans for action. So, for example, a classical Marxist view, while acknowledging the need for consciousness of class-based oppression, offers an essentially materialist account of how society's members are tied into the system. Such an approach assumes that, once released from external, material oppression, individuals will of necessity find themselves in a state of independence, freedom and autonomy. The same is true of radical feminist approaches, which advocate either the seizure of male power bases or the separation of women from men.

However, post-structuralism places more emphasis on the way in which, as individuals, we are not only disempowered, but also help to construct our own disempowerment. It is argued that a proper understanding of how power operates and how change can be brought about requires an enquiry into the ways in which, as members of society, we construct our subjectivity – that is, our sense and experience of ourselves and our worlds. The idea that human beings have a core self and the ability to know the world directly, through experience, itself has a history. This is discussed in Chapter 2. This historically constructed 'self-contained individual' underpins a humanist or individualist model of human nature and leads to the problematic theoretical dichotomy between self and society in the social sciences. As we have seen, what post-structuralism offers is a view of the individual that refuses the humanist notion of a core or essential self. The term 'decentring' refers to the idea that we need to look at how subjectivity comes into being. How is it constituted through the cultural and social processes that go to make up our everyday worlds, rather than as something given or inherent?

From a post-structuralist point of view, power relationships and inequalities must be looked at in the same way. They do not exist, as it were 'externally', in a social structure conceptualised as *suis generis*, or even in the 'pre-given' structure of language as conceived by structuralist theories. The social processes constructing power relationships are seen as being more fluid, and we have considered how the work of Foucault in particular conceptualises them as aspects of discursive practices – economic, cultural and political (see, for example, the discussion of the construction of sexuality in Chapter 4). It is within and through these practices that subjectivity takes shape or, more accurately, finds temporary, shifting forms characterised by inner conflict and fragmentation. Subjectivity is not fixed but shifts around as our social worlds change, the outcome of competing agendas and roles. For example, how we relate to the people we know as 'parents' shifts as we move within social time and space. We may experience ourselves as small and powerless in relation to large, omnipotent beings; we may experience ourselves as weighted by responsibility for frail loved ones; our comforters at bedtime can be sources of embarrassment at school concerts. This subjectivity is also the location for potential change, in that the individual's experience of contradiction within their social environment, when coupled with new frameworks of thought, can potentiate resistance and change. How people feel and what happens to them is no longer understood to carry an immutable set of meanings, but instead to be amenable to revisioning, to reinterpretation, and thence action to bring about change.

Post-structuralism was preceded by less radical varieties of social constructionism and by structuralism, which this volume has already introduced. Central to all versions of social constructionism is the view that human beings know the world and human societies as a result of the meanings they assign to its different parts. Things, objects and persons do not have any intrinsic meaning: they are brought into human society through the frameworks of knowledge in current use. This is the general position taken throughout this book in that it questions the notion of a fixed, objectively knowable, social reality. Where post-structuralism takes a more radical perspective is in fundamentally problematising the nature of the knowledge we have about the world. Recognising the 'swampy lowlands' of the social territory as our natural habitat, and the lack of any high hard ground from which we might gain a general picture or overview, it refuses the notion of an overarching, rational structure of ideas, or general theory, that can be used to map the detailed structure of the world.

Not Saussure

In order to understand this better it will be useful here to consider in a little more detail the work of the linguist F. de Saussure, who was so influential in the development of structuralist thought. He argued that social reality is constituted through a system of signs, made up of two parts – a signifier (that is, a sound or an image), and what is signified (that is, an idea or a meaning); the signifier stands as a symbol for something else. Thus, for example, when we see a metal disc on a pole beside the road with the figure 30 written on it, we are seeing an image, or signifier, that has an unmistakable meaning: what is signified. The image of the figure 30 refers directly to the idea that thirty miles per hour is the legal speed limit at which vehicles may be driven. However, driving speeds themselves are, of course, no more than ideas. There are no externally defined or intrinsically safe or unsafe limits. Thirty miles an hour in a built-up area represents an interpretation of driving speeds that is particular to British culture and society. A structuralist approach would see the road sign quite literally as a sign that gives us culturally specific but none the less fixed information about our social world. We have therefore come some distance from a positivist framework that would argue that what we know about the world has a direct and inevitable relationship with the way the world actually is. However, in highlighting the constructions or frameworks through which knowledge is made possible, structuralists none the less describe a system of fixed meanings that are shared by everyone. Indeed, in the case of the road sign, everyone is assumed to understand its meaning.

What post-structuralists all stress, however, is that there is no fixed relationship between signifiers – that is, images or sounds; and what is signified – that is, meanings or ideas. Theorists argue in different ways that signifiers – language, advertisements, styles of dress, for example – have plural meanings and remain ever open to new readings or to being linked with new things being signified. For example, the figure 30 on a metal disc on a pole is a signifier that carries no automatic link with a legal speed limit for someone who measures distance, and therefore speed, in kilometres rather than miles. Similarly, British people who drive on the other side of the Channel can only link the corresponding signifier and what is signified if they do some mental arithmetic, turning kilometres back into miles. The metal disc on the pole is a signifier that may not only be difficult to link with a specific signified meaning for the members of a different society. British people themselves may also link it with different meanings. Small children with catapults may see it as a target, as might drunken people wishing to smash an empty bottle; lorry drivers with wide mirrors might see it as an obstacle; and conservationists might see it as an eyesore.

What post-structuralism offers us is not only the possibility of assigning new meanings to aspects of our social environment; it also opens up the space between signifier and what is signified for examination. If we look into that space we find out how our knowledge is constructed. We find out how language and images – for example, 'commonsense' ideas about the 'nature' of women, and seductive photos of happy families – bind us unthinkingly into established and largely implicit systems of knowledge. Thus we need only a fleeting glimpse of a TV advertisement or a particular expression on our mother's face to read off unconsciously from that signifier an entire and systematic body of ideas (Barthes, 1983). Similarly, in responding to the speed restriction sign – in making the connection between signifier and what is signified – we are not just taking in the specific and limited idea that we should press down on the car brake with our right foot, we are also assenting to the notion of a legal system that has the power to restrict us in all kinds of ways. Hence the political implications of public vandalism. To deface a road sign is not just to waste a sum of public money; it is to flout the notion that citizens are governed by a legal system. However, as noted above, signifiers have plural meanings, and it is their scope for new meanings that provides us with the space within which to assert the need for transformation. They allow for the possibility of finding ourselves repositioned in such a way that we re-read the signifier and begin to make other connections. For example, images of alluringly slim women in advertisements, signifiers whose dominant signified meaning is that women find happiness when they make themselves attractive to men, may be read from a different position. From a feminist position, for example, a body of such dimensions might signify that these women lack personal choice, and may even be locked into the straitjacket of an eating disorder.

What this approach offers, it can be argued, is a more precise account of the relationship between agency and structure, a central issue in this book. For example, it explains how individuals imagine themselves to be authors of ideologies which are in fact the *source* of their own subjectivity. It shows the importance of the imagination in terms of the emotional and psychological force with which an individual identifies with their subject position. It also gives an insight into the ways in which change and contradiction can work powerfully to shift an individual's subject position. One example here stems from M. Mies' work around a project focused on domestic violence in Germany. The project was launched at a time, in the 1970s, when feminist awareness of domestic violence was far from fully developed. Mies and her colleagues took billboards on to the streets with slogans and information about violence in the home (Mies, 1983). The result was the bringing together of a whole group of women who had suffered domestic violence. What they did was to spend time sharing their individual accounts, then going on to trace the common threads that pointed towards a larger-scale structural problem. This material was made into a play and in this way subjectivities began to shift. The women were encountering their own experiences through a completely different set of meanings. Mies highlights the importance not just of this consciousness-raising work but also of rupture or discontinuity within the lives of women. For all the time that they remained within an abusive relationship, violence and humiliation were signifiers that could be linked with signified meanings such as: 'I'm a sloppy housewife'; 'men have quick tempers'; 'he has a hard time at work'; 'he doesn't really mean it'; and 'women should stick by their men'. Once a pattern alters and, for example, a woman removes herself and her children from the marital home, fearing for their personal safety; a woman is hospitalised after severe injury; or an influential relative discovers for the first time what is happening, this rupture of domestic arrangements can have ideological as well as practical consequences. It can provide the circumstances that make a break with the woman's customarily dominated position possible. The signifier of domestic violence can then be linked with new signified meanings. For example, 'no one ever deserves to be hit'; 'violence should never be tolerated'; and 'society empowers men in a way that condones abusive relations of power'. The woman then finds herself positioned as a member of a social category, 'woman', which is vulnerable in a whole multiplicity of ways not just to men, but to the patriarchal principles that inform most aspects of the cultural and social organisation of life – from the language available to us through to the laws which govern us. Once a woman ceases to experience herself as a blameworthy and helpless person, her subjectivity shifts.

What post-structuralism argues is that she is not the same individual. It refutes the notion of a core self which might be amended or go through some surface changes. Instead, it argues that women are who they are by virtue of how they are positioned within discourse. A woman who reneges on her marriage vows, on the conventional 'wisdom' that sees the family as the prime site for human happiness and fulfilment; who discovers people outside her family who not only see her differently but also give her practical and emotional support; who finds autonomous economic security and a home of her own; such a woman is differently situated within a whole range of discourses and discursive practices. Post-structuralism would see her as a different person with a radically altered subjectivity.

Relativism versus totalitarianism

The above example demonstrates both a useful way of conceptualising a social issue and a way of translating insight into political action. However, the central danger of post-structuralist and postmodernist positions can be seen as that of relativism. The women in Mies' project were enabled to create new meanings and ways of seeing themselves that empowered their political action. Nevertheless, their strength lay in their shared experience and solidarity as a group rather than in a claim to 'truth' in any 'objective' sense. The Enlightenment project, on the other hand, engaged in a search for well-founded 'scientific' knowledge of the social world. Based on such knowledge, demands for fair treatment or justice might be claimed by rational arguments rather than in power struggles. Post-structuralism and post-modernism strip away the rational foundations of knowledge and, if we have no grounds on which to choose one explanation or account rather than another, we seem to be left with the old equation of might with right.

We shall return to this fundamental problem, but first we shall consider the opposing danger inherent in the project of modernity itself. We have already noted that Lyotard saw the 'modern' search for overarching theories as containing the seeds of terror and totalitarianism (Lyotard, 1984, pp. 81–2). The more we appreciate the impossibility of achieving a god-like, external, 'objective', or even disinterested, view of any human social world, the easier it is to see Lyotard's point. Any overarching theory or 'meta-narrative' seeks to impose consensus and conformity, and we can see how these may be no more than the powerful ideological systems serving to legitimate dominant interests, suppress difference and oppress those defined as 'other'. The twentieth century is not short of examples of terror and totalitarianism, from Stalinism to the Ayatollahs, but the extermination of Jewish people in the Nazi 'Holocaust' is, for most people, the most distinctive and horrific, perhaps because it was nurtured in the heart of modern Western civilisation and raises the most fundamental doubts about its central belief in social progress.

Zygmunt Bauman argues that the Holocaust cannot be dismissed as an interruption to the normal flow of history, a cancerous growth on the body of civilised society, a specific event in Jewish history, or something to be accounted for by particular aspects of German history (Bauman, 1993, pp. viii ff). Instead, he links the Holocaust to the central characteristics of modern society itself. The Holocaust, he argues, was not an inevitable consequence of modern society, but rather a possibility contained within it. Modernity was a necessary, if not sufficient, condition for it to occur, and so it is important to look at the specific historical and cultural circumstances under which it happened. Nevertheless, we must also look at the characteristics of modern society that held the Holocaust as a realisable potential within it, 'not the antithesis of modern civilisation and everything it stands for', but another face, 'comfortably attached to the same body' (p. 7). The Holocaust, Bauman argues, was 'normal' 'in the sense of being fully in keeping with everything we know about our civilisation, its guiding spirit, its priorities, its immanent vision of the world' (p. 8).

It is precisely the characteristics identified by Weber as the tendencies of modern society that created the possibilities for the Holocaust. Rationalisation, the development of bureaucracy, the principle of efficiency, and scientific thinking that separates itself from values are what it requires. The technological developments of the modern factory system were exactly those necessary for the mass production of death in Auschwitz, and these were coupled with the ethically blind bureaucratic pursuit of efficiency, in terms of which Weber describes modern administration:

Precision, speed, unambiguity, knowledge of the files, continuity, discretion, unity, strict subordination, reduction of friction and of material and personal costs – these are the optimum point in the strictly bureaucratic administration ... Bureaucratisation offers above all the optimum possibility for carrying through the principle organising functions according to purely objective considerations ... The objective discharge of business primarily means a discharge of business according to *calculable rules* and 'without regard for persons'. (Bauman, 1993, p. 14)

Once the objective 'to get rid of the Jews' was set by Adolf Hitler, it was set about rationally and efficiently. In selecting those units that would be closest to the actual killings, special care was taken to weed out any over-emotional or ideologically zealous individuals. Obedience, impersonality, efficiency and organisational loyalty were at a premium. The 'overcoming of animal pity' in the ordinary Germans who were to carry out the extermination was achieved by authorisation (official orders), routinisation (rule-governed practices), and the dehumanisation of the victims. The first two bring to the fore what Weber calls the 'honour of the civil servant'. This is the ability to execute the orders of legitimate superior authorities, even when the orders seem repugnant, and discipline is substituted for moral responsibility.

A crucial, if unintended, consequence of this rational, impersonal bureaucratic structure of modernity, then, is to locate actions themselves at a distance from moral evaluation. Agents of direct action do not engage in struggles over moral issues, because they are positioned at the end of a long chain of decisions in a system where identification with the organisation, obedience and self-sacrifice are emphasised as virtues. Those who did the shooting and gassing were 'just obeying orders', while at the other end of the chain, giving the orders or passing them on, most of the participants in the genocide sat at their desks composing memoranda and drawing up blueprints. The victims were invisible to them. They did not shoot Jewish children or pour gas into the gas chambers, but participated in conferences and spoke on the telephone. Moral distancing was combined with obedience, and Bauman notes that, confronted by the shattering truth of the Holocaust, 'Dwight Macdonald warned in 1945, we must now fear the person who obeys the law more than the one who breaks it' (Bauman, p. 151). All of this is chillingly confirmed by Stanley Milgram's controversial experiments on obedience, to which Bauman refers in his book.

Milgram instructed volunteers to administer 'electric shocks' of increasing intensity to subjects in a bogus learning experiment. The volunteers were convinced that the shocks were real. Nevertheless,

Milgram found that a frighteningly high proportion of the volunteers found it very hard to disobey instructions given by the 'scientist' in authority over the 'experiment', even when they firmly believed that their actions could seriously damage the health or even result in the death of the subject. Milgram's experiments also showed clearly the increasing ease with which we inflict pain upon a person we only see at a distance, only hear, or neither see nor hear. Milgram notes that one of the most frightening lessons of the Holocaust is not that this could be done to us, but that we could do it ourselves. Echoing Dwight Macdonald, he quotes C. P. Snow:

> When you think of the long and gloomy history of man, you will find more hideous crimes have been committed in the name of obedience than have been committed in the name of rebellion. If you doubt that, read William Shirer's *Rise and Fall of the Third Reich*. The German Officer Corps were brought up in the most rigorous code of obedience. (Milgram, 1974, p. 2)

Post-structuralism and postmodernism are perhaps rightly seen as being on the side of disobedience, challenging all forms of authority.

Little narratives of social life

One of the liberating aspects of postmodernist thought is that, in rejecting the totalitarian tendencies of overarching theories which seek to encompass explanations of all of social life, it points to the significance of what Lyotard calls 'little narratives'. This steers us away from potentially dangerous conformity and consensus and introduces greater fluidity. It opens up possibilities of significant change within the small social worlds we inhabit. As we have seen in the examples already given in this chapter, feminist 'narratives' can re-map or reconstruct previously dominant 'masculine' narratives. We do not have to wait for *the* revolution; it is possible to make small revolutions. We have seen that Foucault conceptualises power as part of any discourse – for example medicine, law or gender – and as such is always likely to be challenged and opposed. By examining alternative discourses, or the multiple 'little narratives' of oppressed or minority groups, social scientists may be helping to challenge and reconstruct oppressive discourses or structures, as our example of feminism shows.

In her work on explanations of health and illness, discussed in Chapter 5, Wendy Stainton Rogers argues that not only is there a diversity of such accounts within social science, but also among medical professionals and among ordinary people (Stainton Rogers, 1991). Previous research found that people attribute blame and responsibility for their health and ill-health. Significantly, in the context of our position in this chapter, Stainton Rogers rejects a previously influential research tool – the Multidimensional Health Locus of Control scale (MHLC), used by psychologists to 'measure' how people attribute such blame and responsibility: the 'locus of control'. She rejects the scale because it makes a range of assumptions about how ill-health 'ought' to be explained, and therefore how people 'should' make health-related decisions, but is not sensitive enough to discover how people are in fact making sense of health and illness in the shifting contexts of their everyday lives (Stainton Rogers, 1991, pp. 175ff). For example, Stainton Rogers makes the assumption that people might have one explanation for how to prevent illness and a different one for how recovery takes place, and that there is no necessity for such explanations to be consistent.

She is highly critical of the ideological bias contained in findings using the MHLC scale; for example, that separatist lesbian feminists were more likely to be 'fatalistic' about the locus of control in medicine being held by 'powerful others'. Rogers argues that labelling this group as 'fatalistic' signally fails to recognise that such a perception of the locus of power constitutes part of the world view of this group of feminists, rather than an inability to understand the world properly (Stainton Rogers, 1991, p. 170):

> Put crudely [the MHLC Scale] . . . assumed that the kind of account salient to a small group of Western psychologists at a particular historical period would . . . explain why people act in particular ways, or why they construe the world in the way they do. (Stainton Rogers, 1991, p. 207)

Stainton Rogers' own research, using a different methodological approach and based on different assumptions, allowed her to discover that people's own narratives or accounts contained complex individual explanations not necessarily shared by others:

> Explaining health and illness is a lot more complex than separating out just three loci of perceived control. However strange or unfamiliar the accounts identified, each of them is clearly predicated upon active cognition, a theory-about-the-world, or a moral system, and often a complex mixture of both. (Stainton Rogers, 1991, p. 206)

The example of Stainton Rogers' study illustrates very clearly the implications, for our consequent action, of our conceptual or mapping tools and the ways we conduct research. If, for example, as social scientists in the area of health care or illness prevention, we ignore the experience and have an inadequate understanding of the meaning of health and illness for those in our care, our action, our practice is likely at best to be ineffective and at worst to be patronising and oppressive.

Alternative narratives

Nicholas Fox has made a systematic attempt to take a 'postmodern' approach to the whole area of health and illness by examining the discourses of what he calls the 'politics of health talk' (Fox, 1993). This approach, Fox argues, draws attention to the consequences of these discourses 'for power, control and knowledgeability' (p. 19). In particular, Fox is concerned with the 'small designs' – what we have already called 'little narratives' – of how people explain, experience and deal with health and illness. Fox utilises the notion of *différance*, drawn from the work of Derrida, an important postmodern philosopher. This notion involves the idea that the meaning of things – for example, ill-health, or masculinity – is constituted in terms of its difference from other things – in the case used in the last section, good health and femininity. We know them not as absolutes, but rather in relation to other features of the same system of knowledge. The concept of *différance* draws our attention to the slippage and deferral of meaning in any symbolic system, and to the emphasis in postmodernism on 'deconstructing' particular narratives and texts, rather than taking them as given or as truth. An example of both *différance* and deconstruction was given earlier in our discussion of the meaning signified by the signifier of the roadside traffic sign.

Using a postmodern theoretical approach in examining health and illness, Fox rejects the notion that there is a 'real' or 'true' explanation for health and illness, showing, for example, how the human body is 'constituted through discourse'. By explaining the social construction of the thin, young female body or the sexually unattractive, ageing body we move away from the medical model of the 'truth' of biology. We saw in an earlier chapter how an emphasis on biology as such gives rise to a particular conceptualisation of sexuality. Once the search for unmediated knowledge or explanations of health, or indeed anything else, is abandomed we also begin to examine the power involved in, for example, biological explanations of sexuality, or biomedical explanations of ill-health.

Fox also uses the concept of 'intertextuality'. By this he is referring to the way in which different narratives or texts – for example, those of the carer and the cared for, or the doctor and the patient – affect each other, and what actually happens in a residential home or a hospital. Stainton Rogers' research, mentioned earlier, shows just this process. Fox uses the work of other researchers to show that people construct their own stories or narratives about their bodies, and about biological processes such as menstruation, or about chronic illness. Such narratives may be used to resist the powerful discourse of professional medicine, the control by men of women's bodies, or the acceptance of chronic illness as disabling:

> Post-structuralist theory discloses that everything is *political*. Texts are written for reasons of power, and every reading of a text is an act of power, maybe empowering the reader, maybe causing disempowerment. (Fox, 1993, p. 122)

Fox argues that it should be the task of sociology to construct a postmodern social theory of health which in its deconstruction of dominant narratives creates a resistance and alternative to them which is ultimately political.

Many of the issues raised by Stainton Rogers, Fox and other postmodernists have also been raised by feminists, as we have seen. These issues have implications for the methodology of social science – that is, how we actually go about our research; not simply what questions we ask, but also who is asked and how we make sense of the stories which we get in reply. In her feminist study, *Investigating Organisations* (1991), Gillian Coleman shows that women's views and experience of working in organisations are different from men's. But she is only able to show this by defining her research as a piece of feminist action, and therefore choosing to work collaboratively and co-operatively with a small group of women, drawing on the research model developed by Reason and Rowan (Coleman, 1991, pp. 27ff). It is the women's accounts on which she bases her findings, having conducted her interviews using a counselling skills model. Positivistic approaches have dismissed such research as 'subjective' – that is, not scientific and reliable, but Coleman concludes that:

using this method has gone some way towards enabling a more authentic form of expression...[By] validating what is known experientially [it] highlights the *censoring* function of the formal, the objective, that which organisations articulate. It therefore points to the possibility of alternative subject positions – the possibility of 'being' differently (p. 68).

Coleman allows her informants to reflect on their experience of being in organisations by using counselling techniques designed to facilitate this process during her interviews. The women's accounts, their 'little narratives', are the outcome of this reflection, perhaps a more structured version of Giddens' discursive consciousness again. To use the language or discourse of counselling, the individuals in Coleman's study 'owned' their stories.

Similarly, in attempting to construct a postmodern social theory of health, Fox deals with the way in which patients' accounts of their illness may be part of their therapy. In other words, the process of making sense of, and attaching meaning to, their experience is part of their process of illness and recovery (Fox, 1993, pp. 111–14). Some social workers' and careworkers' training increasingly involves the recognition of the therapeutic aspects of helping client groups such as elderly people and children to tell their own stories (for example, see McLeod, 1996).

It is significant, too, that many people are turning increasingly to individual counselling or therapy as a way of understanding and creating meaning in their lives in what appears to be an increasingly chaotic and uncertain world. However, like other discourses within the health and illness professions, those of counselling and psychotherapy frequently construct 'reality' in ways that might oppress particular clients or client groups. We saw, for example, how psychoanalytic discourse, very influential in some approaches to therapy, constructs a reality in which homosexuality may be seen and experienced as being immature (Chapter 4). Furthermore, by concentrating on the individual's 'pathology', or need to develop strategies for 'coping' with stress at work, marital disharmony, bereavement or whatever, therapeutic discourses locate problems within the individual. This can distract attention from wider social structural forms of oppression such as 'race', class and gender, and organisational sources of stress such as working conditions. None the less, underlying many humanistic theories of counselling and psychotherapy is the assumption that the individual's (the client's) process of reflection and recognition, naming or 'owning' the feelings and emotions around themselves and events in their lives, allows the person to 'move on', to resist oppression, to make decisions, to change and to take control of their life (see Strawbridge and Woolfe, 1996). In this sense, then, therapy too pays attention to the authenticity of 'little narratives' in the creation of meaning and subjectivity, and in facilitating action on the basis of this.

Answers to relativism?

There is much then that is positive and liberating in post-structuralism and postmodernism, but what is left of our ability to make reasoned judgements and to make claims in the name of justice? Those who would throw out the Enlightenment project entirely must, it seems, face the consequences of relativism. If there is neither resort to reason nor any checking of maps and theories directly against 'reality', then the only standards are those of consensus and tradition, and the only challenges are those based on strength in numbers, loudness of voice, or sheer force. Any belief in the capacity for critical reflection and principled debate must be abandoned as illusory. This is a concern of some post-structuralist and postmodern thinkers. Certainly Foucault, in his later works, struggled to rescue critical reflection, and Lyotard contends that justice as a value is neither outmoded nor suspect, and that what is necessary is to arrive at an idea of justice that is not linked to that of consensus (see Lyotard and Thebaud, 1985).

   We cannot pretend to offer an answer to the problem of relativism. Even to explore the possibilities in any depth would take us into philosophical technicalities beyond the scope of this text. Nevertheless, we can indicate directions and suggest lines of argument that seem promising to us as people trying to make enough sense of our social world to engage in actions for which we can give good reasons. In order to do this we must venture beyond even the extended framework of social science that we have allowed ourselves in this book. We have recognised that value judgements and evaluative processes are internal to social scientific research. Nevertheless, although the descriptions and explanations sought through systematic research are always from one point of view and contain evaluations, it is not within the scope of scientific or social scientific reason itself to judge the quality and justification of those evaluations. We have suggested that one consequence of the Enlightenment and the enormous success of the 'scientific revolution' it made its own, has been the elevation of 'scientific' rationality to the model for all reason. We have already explored the limitations of the picture, painted by Schon, of this form of rationality, of a god-like vantage point from high hard ground overlooking a swamp (in Chapter 1). Another important characteristic of this model of rationality is that it is dedicated to calculating the most efficient means to realising pre-given ends. It is the model that was termed 'instrumental rationality' or *zweckrationalitat* by Weber (see Chapter 6), and as 'technical rationality' by Marcuse, who describes it as concerned with the

> production and transformation of material (things and men) through the methodical-scientific apparatus...Its rationality organises and controls things and men, factory and bureaucracy, work and leisure. (Marcuse, 1972, p. 205)

We have considered above the part played by this form of reason in creating the necessary conditions of the Holocaust. It is usually taken to be a model of reason that excludes consideration of ends and values. These are external to the structure of the reasoning process, although Marcuse identifies the values presupposed by this form of reason (for a more extended discussion see Billington *et al.*, 1991, pp. 180ff; see also Chapter 6 above for a feminist critique of this model).

If the dominant model of rationality available to us is one that does not provide us with the tools we need for reasoning about ends and values then Western civilisation, which puts such great store by reason, has no legitimated means for meeting the moral and political challenges of a technological society:

> Our culture elites are often in bondage to technocratic and scientific knowledge. We can best describe technocratic thought by the discrepancy between its claims and its consequences. It claims to be a full description of reality but its consequences frequently entail a systematic inhibition of the moral imagination. (Scott, 1983)

The difficulties in meeting problems generated by the Internet, issues about the environment, genetic engineering, food production and distribution, international justice, human rights, and the general poverty of much current political debate, are perhaps symptomatic of this inhibition. In the swampy lowlands, which are the 'indeterminate zones of practice' of all kinds, the canons of technological rationality do not apply. Uncertainty, uniqueness and value conflict are the order of the day in much of our everyday social action as well as in more explicitly-defined professional and political practice. Yet we seem bereft of the rational tools necessary to engage in complex debates involving the weighing of both evidence and values.

In professional practice situations such as a client's consultation with a social worker, or a patient's with a doctor, the limited applicability of formal knowledge – 'the case is not in the textbook' – brings into focus such value conflicts, together with the responsibility we have to others. John Shotter has taken up Schon's stress on the value dimension of practice (Shotter, 1993). In the indeterminate zones of practice we are at least required to give good reasons and be accountable to others for our actions. But what might count as good reasons? Shotter argues that in privileging technical rationality it is practical–moral knowledge and language that has been neglected. This he seeks to reinstate, arguing that the prime function of language is not to represent the world but to move people. Its role is essentially 'rhetorical'. In other words, it is the skilful use of language in argument, in persuasion and in justifying action that is crucial. There are no right answers, no cut-and-dried solutions in social life. Key concepts such as 'health', 'welfare' and 'justice' are complex and laden with value, and we can see that social life is radically open and 'essentially contestable' (see Gallie, 1956). Nevertheless, the actions of professionals have consequences that make significant differences in other people's lives. For example, one doctor's decision to regard myalgic encephalomyelitis (ME) as a disabling illness, and another's to discount it, will affect their respective patients' rights to benefits. While this may appear to be purely a matter of medical judgement of the evidence, it is not difficult to see how issues of resource allocation, beliefs regarding the use of welfare benefits, and value judgements about patients are also relevant, especially when there is no clear professional consensus regarding the 'disease' status of the sufferer. Under these conditions, complex skills are needed to engage in arguments involving the relative merits of differing value positions.

This is all very well, but in addition to skills we must ask what are the social conditions that must prevail for this argumentative process to work. Shotter recognises that it presumes the existence of democracy, and Michael Billig, who has done much to develop this position, explicitly acknowledges an ideal or utopian vision at the heart of the turn to rhetoric. Billig draws on Habermas's utopian vision of an 'ideal speech situation' in which undistorted communication is possible (see Habermas, 1984):

the practice of argumentation forbids any thoroughgoing relativism [it is not] an abandonment of ideological critique... a moral vision can be placed at the centre of the rhetorical perspective to enable such critique. The turn to rhetoric can be formulated as a celebration of argument. At its core can be placed the utopian vision of everyday philosophers arguing in conditions of enjoyment and freedom... This celebration of argument would express the wish for conditions of undistorted communication. This wish is an argument against present conditions, in which forces of power control the means of disseminating images. (Billig, 1991, p. 26)

This unashamed return to moral vision does not sit easily with the conception of a dispassionate social scientist sifting and analysing evidence in the light of cool reason. However, utopian or transcendental critiques of society reveal a form of reasoning which, although it may have been eclipsed by science, is equally respectable and has a long history. The questions being asked are about the conditions under which communication, undistorted by oppression and injustice, might take place. What Habermas has termed an 'ideal speech situation' represents a standpoint from which a critique of existing practices might be made, and an ideal towards which we might aspire. The concept of an 'ideal speech situation' points towards practices of communication which might be shared in any *possible* community. It would mean that no one voice or group of voices would automatically carry weight by virtue of its accent, or the gender or skin colour of the speaker. This might even go some way to defining the very meaning of 'community' itself.

From a different political perspective we can discern a similar structure of transcendental reasoning in John Rawls' classic attempt to develop a liberal theory of justice (Rawls, 1973). He imagines a group of people with no prior knowledge of their own or one another's abilities, tastes, religious beliefs, desires, social positions and so on. He asks what principles of justice would be agreed upon by these people, from behind this 'veil of ignorance', as binding upon them until 'eternity', no matter what course their individual lives might take. From this 'original position' he thinks they will agree on the principle of 'fairness', which he subjects to a detailed and lengthy examination. Again, Rawls presents us with a standpoint of critique from a definition of justice derived by rationally structured argument of a quite different type than that of technical rationality. So utopian or transcendental arguments suggest at least one model of rational critique of ends and values. They perhaps also force us to recognise that all those who argue from a relativist position do at least argue, and in doing so acknowledge, at least implicitly, some structure of reasoned argument within which they make their case. Absolutes and definitive answers may be impossible, but reasoned arguments and good cases can and must be made for actions that affect the lives of others.

A different form of critique, with a long and equally respectable history, recognises the influence of the context in which argument is taking place without entirely losing rationality. Internal or 'immanent' critique relies on exposing internal contradictions in any form of reasoning, knowledge or social life; it does not rely on arguing from an external or transcendental viewpoint. R. Geuss, in his study of the critical theory of the Frankfurt School, associates this form of argument particularly with the work of Theodor Adorno. What is accepted as valid criticism is only that which is internal and which could therefore be accepted as self-criticism:

> For Adorno we must start from where we happen to be historically and culturally, from a particular kind of frustration or suffering experienced by human agents in their attempt to realise some historically specific project of 'the good life'... a critical theory gives them knowledge of what changes would result if they were to apply the standards of rationality they tacitly accept in a consistent and thoroughgoing way. (Geuss, 1981, p. 63)

This form of critique plays an important part in counselling and psychotherapy, where the process of self-exploration may reveal sources of distress in the internal conflicts and contradictions experienced by clients. It is also at the heart of more socially-oriented forms of 'consciousness-raising', such as those engaged in by women, black people and others who struggle to make explicit the contradictions in their lives.

In the work of Sampson introduced in Chapter 2 we find an example of a critique that combines immanent and transcendental forms of reasoning. The form of immanent critique he employs is to bring into consciousness what is implicit. What is implicit or hidden, although apparently absent, is, in fact, crucially active in what is present and available to consciousness. Sampson examines the 'self', seen as an integrated whole or 'self-contained individual', which is the subject of Western psychology. This notion of 'self', which is taken for granted in psychological theory and sets standards of normality, is constructed in relation to a 'serviceable other', which is implicit or suppressed from consciousness. A 'serviceable other' is one constructed in relation to the needs and interests of the dominant group. So, for example, women and black people are cast in identities that serve the interests of the dominant white, Western, male identity by providing a construction of what it is not. Women and black people have to struggle to find their voices and a sense of difference that is not experienced automatically as being inferior. Alongside his immanent critique, Sampson sets a transcendental critique. This represents a utopian moral vision of genuine dialogue, in which difference can be egalitarian rather than oppressive, and the 'other' is therefore celebrated. This vision does not seem very different from Habermas's 'ideal speech situation'.

We can see, therefore, that it is feasible to abandon the possibility of finding one true picture of 'reality' without abandoning reason altogether. There are forms of reasoning and argument, such as immanent and transcendental critiques, which can recognise the force of social constructionist challenges to overarching theoretical narratives without jettisoning completely the human capacity for reason and judgement. We can see possibilities of holding on to some aspects of the Enlightenment project, ways of constructing and recognising good arguments, and engaging in reasoned critique, while also seeing the value in letting go of some of its old certainties and over-confidence, the aspects of the project that breed totalitarianism.

The promise of postmodernism lies partly in the creative energy that might be released. D. H. Lawrence, writing in 1928, commented:

> Man [*sic*] must wrap himself in a vision, make a house of apparent form and stability, fixity. In his terror of the chaos he begins by putting up an umbrella between himself and the everlasting whirl. Then he paints the umbrella like a firmament. Then he parades around, lives and dies under his umbrella. Bequeathed to his descendants, the umbrella becomes a dome, a vault, and men at last begin to feel that something is wrong...then comes a poet, enemy of convention, and makes a slit in the umbrella; and lo! the glimpse of chaos is a vision, a window to the sun. (Lawrence, 1964, p. 90)

And we might agree that:

> Paradoxically the order that we create and live through should not simply be there to keep us safe from chaos. Though we certainly need to feel safe, but also, if we are to do and dare, we need to keep in touch with the energy of the chaos and all the risks of creativity. Perhaps we need to find a balance between these states. And for that we need grace. (Powley, 1992)

So we feel excited in recognising the liberating potential of 'little narratives'. The equally important promise of postmodernism is for us in the lesson of humility it can teach, and if we leave you with more questions than answers, this is in acknowledgement of an increasingly sophisticated awareness of complexity by late-twentieth-century persons. Perhaps in the words on a greetings card one of us bought recently, 'Anyone who is not confused, really doesn't know what is going on' – and, after all, whatever Hitler was, he was not confused.

Glossary

This Glossary contains brief definitions of terms we use in this book that are specific to social science. Some of the definitions contain words in italics to indicate that these terms are also defined elsewhere in the Glossary. The meaning of many of the terms is difficult, and in some cases there is disagreement among social scientists concerning their meaning.

Agency
A term indicating the importance of human activity, human action, in determining and shaping social life. The agency/structure debate in sociology concerns the extent to which the *structure* of society determines the *consciousness* of individuals or *social actors* and the extent to which human action alters the structure of the social.

Alienation
Used by Karl Marx to argue that, under *capitalism*, what he saw as human-kind's essentially creative, aesthetic, spiritual and emotional aspirations, were thwarted. In his view, people were alienated by the exploitative relationships and *division of labour* operating within *capitalism*. Workers did not own the *means of production* and so felt separate from what they produced, and because of the control exercised by the pace of machine production, also from the processes of production. Workers were alienated from their fellow workers, with whom they were in competition, and finally from themselves, because of their lack of autonomy and inability to realise their human aspirations. Interestingly, when the sociologist Emile Durkheim described what occurs when the process of industrialisation is not properly and fairly regulated for the benefit of all (see *anomie* and *division of labour*) his description is very similar to *Marx's* one of alienation.

Anomie
Literally this means a lack of norms, a lack of social regulation. It is *Durkheim's* term to describe the *social structure* of *Industrial society* which had developed in

242

an unregulated way that led to a lack of *social integration and cohesion*. This also leads to a lack of a sense of identity and belonging among individuals. See also *functionalism* and *division of labour*.

Attachment theory

Within the *psychoanalytic* tradition, theorists have in different ways argued that many life problems are grounded in developmental problems of childhood. Attachment theory is particularly associated with the work of John Bowlby, who split with mainstream psychoanalytic theorists in the 1950s. It hypothesises that the baby and young child is attached to its mother, and that the process of separation which must be achieved, is painful. The child's experience of early relationships of attachment and separation, it is argued, shape our adult relationships. The popularisation of Bowlby's work in the 1960s led to the notion that young children should not be separated from their mothers, and created considerable argument by feminists and others.

Biomedicine/ medical model

The predominant or orthodox set of ideas or *discourse* for conceptualising health and illness. It is based on the rational scientific *discourse* that emerged during the *Enlightenment*. Michel Foucault argues that the power inherent in the knowledge defined by the medical discourse is a form of surveillance: that is, we are watched and controlled by it, and society has been affected by the process of *medicalisation*. Alternative *discourses* for the explanation of health and illness might be traditional, religious or holistic.

Capitalism/capitalist societies

A type of society characterised by industrial production based on the rational accumulation of profit or capital. All the *founding fathers* of sociology in the late eighteenth and early nineteenth centuries were concerned with the emergence of this type of society from the remnants of *feudalism,* and the profound effects *capitalism* had on human relations and organisation.

Citizenship

See *democracy.*

Colonialism

From the sixteenth century onwards, western European societies explored the world and 'discovered' new societies. Initially exploiting the raw materials they found here, their political, military and cultural (including religious) power was eventually extended to colonise these societies. Colonial expansion sowed the seeds of racism in the Western world, and the economic and cultural imperialism (power) exercised by *industrial* and *capitalist* or developed nations over modern so-called 'under-developed' or 'Third-World' societies. Colonialism and economic and cultural imperialism also formed the foundations of what today we call *globalisation*.

Commonsense

Everyday or taken-for-granted explanations about the world. Ordinary or lay people's explanations of, for example, why someone is ill, will differ from those of medical professionals. Similarly, commonsense explanations of how society works will be different from those of *social science*.

Community

The *commonsense* meaning of this term usually refers to our sense of belonging to, being part of a group that is wider than our immediate family, which may have a geographical or spatial location. It may include some form of ethnic or cultural identification, and often has a moral connotation. A sense of belonging to a community which includes people we do not personally know or meet face-to-face involves an imagined relationship with others on the basis of what we believe to be common interests and identity, and this may extend to a group as large as a nation. The *subjectivity* of the term means that its use in *social science* is often problematic. See also '*other/others*'.

Concepts

We cannot understand or make sense of the world around us without ideas that classify and categorise experience and what we observe. The *conceptual tools* of social scientists are ideas or terms, like *social class, social structure, discourse,* or *ideology* which we use to describe and explain aspects of the way the social world and social processes work. The terms in this glossary are concepts commonly used by *social science*, but many of them are contested – social scientists do not agree on their definition or utility. Other disciplines use different concepts. A set of concepts that are related together in a systematic and logical way into a set of propositions which can be used to examine the evidence constitute a *theory.*

Consciousness

In social science, *consciousness* refers to the assumption that it is the human activity of reflection and being aware that makes social life possible, by bestowing and creating meaning. It indicates that the social world involves human perception and understanding, and it involves subjectivity, based on interpreting experience. It implies that human action is both purposeful and *reflexive*, rather than, for example, simply instinctual (also see *practical consciousness* and *discursive consciousness*). The notion of self-consciousness indicates that an individual has a sense of 'I' separate from 'others', that we have a sense of a *self* that is not society, but which at the same time is part of society (see *symbolic interactionism*). Some sociologists, such as Marx and Durkheim, use the term *consciousness* in a broader sense too, to indicate a collective set of values and beliefs, or *culture* (also see *ideology*). Durkheim's *concept* of the *conscience collective*, a French term which combines the notions of both 'conscience' and 'consciousness' indicates that human consciousness concerns values and ideas about what 'ought' to be: that is, it is evaluative.

Culture

The beliefs, values, customs, practices and ways of living in a society. Often used interchangeably with the term 'society', the most useful definitions of culture emphasise that it is about 'lived experience', and that *social actors* are both shaped by and in turn shape culture. Cultural or social 'scripts' or *discourses* are those ways of feeling and behaving prescribed by our culture. Ethnography and ethnographic method in the *social sciences* are those ways of studying cultures that attempt to 'get inside' and experience them as participants might. The social anthropologist Geertz's term 'thick description' is an attempt to emphasise that to understand cultures we need not only describe them, but also make interpretations of the feelings and meanings they involve for their participants. It is this the sociologist Max Weber emphasises in his advocacy of the *Verstehen method*. Marx's use of the term *consciousness* is very similar to the definition we have given of culture. The Marxist term *cultural capital* (Bourdieu) is used to indicate that culture reflects the material inequalities of society, and that some aspects of culture (for example, education) may bestow a material advantage on people who have access to them.

Democracy

Organisation of the political system of a society on the basis of the right of participation of all citizens in the selection of a legitimate government. Citizenship in a democracy also assumes a whole range of human and social rights and obligations.

Différance

Drawn from the work of Derrida, this notion is used by some postmodernist writers to indicate that the meaning of something, for example, masculinity or health, is not inherent but lies in terms of its difference from other things: that is, in this case, femininity and illness. We can only understand things, therefore, in terms of their relationship to other things.

Discourse

A systematic set of beliefs, ideas or knowledge and practices specific to particular situations or locations; for example, the discourse of medicine, the discourse of gender. The philosopher Michel Foucault argues that power lies within discourses themselves, rather than in the structural arrangements of society. Discourses and discursive practices shape and limit the way in which we experience the world, and therefore our subjectivity. However, Foucault argues that discourses are not fixed and they have the potential for the development of oppositional discourses. In the discourse of *social science* the concept of *ideology* has recently tended to be replaced by that of *discourse*. This has altered the way in which social scientists perceive the social world, and emphasises practices as well as ideas.

Discursive consciousness

A term used by the sociologist Anthony Giddens to describe the way in which human beings, human 'actors', have the capacity for *reflexivity*: that is, they constantly reflect on and monitor their activities. *discursive consciousness* is the way in which human 'agency' affects and changes the patterns and regularities of social life that *practical consciousness* reproduces.

Division of labour

Characteristic of *industrial* and *capitalist* societies., it means the increasing specialisation and differentiation of productive tasks. The sociologist Emile Durkheim saw this process as an evolutionary one in which each of the institutions of society became more specialised in function and differentiated from the others, and in consequence created greater interdependence in society. If this process was unregulated then a state of *anomie* occurred. He used the concept of the forced division of labour to describe the situation where division of labour was accompanied by social inequality and lack of choice by individuals concerning their role. Karl Marx also recognised the importance of the division of labour and but saw it as inherently unfair and as a cause of people becoming *alienated* from each other, from what they produced and from social relations themselves.

Durkheimian theory

Emile Durkheim, a nineteenth-century French sociologist whose basic assumption was that all societies are integrated or cohesive, and that they function as social wholes made up of interdependent parts – individuals and social institutions. See *functionalism, division of labour, consciousness, anomie, social integration, social structure.*

Economic base/foundation

The basic assumption underlying *Marxist theory* is that human beings are essentially producers and must produce in order to live. Thus all human societies are structured around the purposive economic activity that forms the base or foundation for the *superstructure* of politics, law, religion, beliefs and values (*ideology*). It is this economic base that ultimately shapes social relationships (*relations of production*). Also see *historical materialism, mode of production, capitalism, alienation.*

Enlightenment, The

Intellectual changes or movement in eighteenth-century western European societies in which magical and religious beliefs gave way to belief in rationality and science and in progress based on this. *Modernity* is usually seen as stemming from this intellectual ferment and the rejection of traditionalism. The *social sciences* were part of the new definitions of knowledge that emerged at this time.

Ethnicity

Indicates cultural origins and differences between groups which may be a very important aspect of identity for individuals and groups. It may be the basis of national and political identity. Ethnicity may be loosely used interchangeably with '*race*' to indicate social inequalities based on difference, but such usage may ignore the particular political and power dimensions of discrimination based on 'race'.

Ethnography/ethnographic method

See *culture.*

Ethnomethodology

Theoretical and methodological approach in sociology based on the assumption that in each social situation the participants have to create 'structure' for themselves. Thus the researcher has to uncover the rules and structures constantly being created. Also see *interpretative social science.*

Feudal societies/feudalism

The type of society which many of the *founding fathers* saw as preceding *industrial* and *capitalist* societies. Feudal societies were based on landownership by a limited number of 'lords', including the monarch. Such landowners owed allegiance to the monarch and were in turn owed allegiance by their 'serfs', – agricultural labourers who were able to work land only in return for certain duties, including military service and labour. 'Feudalism' is often used loosely to indicate largely agricultural and peasant societies where there is not a free market in labour and goods.

Feminism

A movement and set of ideas that date from the late eighteenth century, based on the assumption that women as a group are structurally subordinate to men: that is, that they are disadvantaged through *gender*, and that such an unequal situation must be altered. Feminism has affected both intellectual knowledge and *commonsense* ideas about the relationships between women and men. In the *social sciences* feminism has led to a radical rethinking of many basic *concepts* and the recognition that *gender* enters into all social situations. Feminist writing and research foregrounds women's experience.

Founding fathers
Usually refers to late-eighteenth and nineteenth-century European male writers who wrote the first works that could be called social science. These would include Henri Saint-Simon, Auguste Comte, Durkheim, Marx, Herbert Spencer, Weber and many others.

Freudian theory
Sigmund Freud, late-nineteenth-century/early-twentieth-century Viennese founder of *psychoanalysis*.

Functionalism/structural functionalism
A theoretical approach stemming from the work of Emile Durkheim. It assumes that a society is made up of interdependent parts, each of which has a purpose or function for the cohesion of the integrated whole, and that if a society is working well it is in equilibrium. An influential variation of this approach is the *structural functionalism* of Talcott Parsons, who argued, for example, that the modern two-parents-plus-two-children type of family is functional in an *industrial society*. Also see *division of labour, anomie, social structure, social integration*.

Gender
Social differentiation, inequality, and sometimes discrimination and prejudice based on the perceived differences between the two sexes. Gender is a major aspect of an individual's social identity. Similarly, we can argue that many aspects of society are 'gendered', for example, sport, health and illness are experienced differently by individuals of each gender. Also see *sex, sexuality, social inequalities*.

Globalisation
The idea that there are complex cultural, economic and political connections between societies and nation-states, which means that they can no longer be seen as separate and independent entities, but constitute a global society. It is in one sense our increasing familiarity with the diversity of cultures, through the mass media and electronic communication such as the Internet, which creates a global culture, but the heritage of inequalities bestowed by *colonialism* means that such globalism is not synonymous with global integration.

Hermeneutics
See *interpretative social science*.

Historical materialism
Karl Marx's term for the historical and social process through which the structure of a society changes from one type to another. He classified societies

acording to their *mode of production*, the type of productive system in operation: for example, *capitalism*. In Marx's theory he argues that the material, the real economic base or foundation of a society, resulting from the type of productive system, determines the shape and direction of the rest of society and the processes of social change. See also *superstucture, ideology, relations of production, concepts, theories* and *economic base/foundation*.

Ideal-types

A concept developed by the sociologist Max Weber, who argued that we need tools to help us observe society and understand what we observe. An ideal-type includes the essential features that can be said to define something such as capitalism or bureaucracy, and is a kind of yardstick against which to measure what we study. Weber is assuming that as social scientists we cannot observe the social unless we already have some ideas about what we are studying – for example, that bureacracies are governed by set rules, but that we then need to test these ideas against what we observe.

Identity

The knowledge and understanding which *social actors* have of who they are and how they relate to others in their group or society. Identity involves both *subjectivity,* our experience and feelings about ourselves in relation to others, and the ways in which we are categorised by others. See also *self.*

Ideology

A much contested and difficult *concept,* it is Marx's term for the ideas and beliefs that stem from people's consciousness based on their real material situation. Ideology is part of the *superstructure*. More generally, it can be defined as a set of beliefs and values that works in favour of some and to the disadvantage of others, while at the same time concealing the conflicts of interests underlying it. Thus it is difficult to challenge ideology because it shapes our thoughts and understanding of the world around us. The Marxist writer, Louis Althusser, argues that ideology is a set of symbolic representations through which we interpret the world. His *concept* of 'hailing' refers to the way in which we recognise or 'hail' ourselves in socially constructed ways or *roles*: we *are* caring women, men who are breadwinners and so on.

Industrial societies

Developed first in western Europe. Organised on the basis of an economy characterised by mechanised manufacturing industry conducted by specialised labour processes and centralised in large-scale factories. Its characteristics also include centralised government, the rule of law and, in Western societies, a *democratic* political system. The term '*capitalist*' society is sometimes, confusingly, used interchangeably with 'industrial', even though industry need not necessarily be organised according to capitalist principles – state capitalism in

Communist societies is an example of this. Many social theorists argue that Western societies have now reached a late-industrial, postindustrial or post-modern phase of development. See also *postmodernism*.

Instrumental rationality.
Use of calculable and technically most efficient means to achieve a goal, what Max Weber called *zweckrationalitat*. See also *rationality/rationalisation*, *social action*.

Interactionism
See *interpretative social science* and *symbolic interactionism*.

Interpretative social science
An alternative perspective to *positivism*, *interpretative* approaches in social science argue that subjective experience and meaningful activity are the defining characteristics of human beings and that *social science* methods of studying the social must take this into account. Max Weber took this approach in developing his *concept* of *social action* and used the term *verstehen* (understanding) to describe the way in which sociologists should interpret the meanings which people give to the actions they take. A range of other theories and approaches are usually included under this heading: *phenomenology*, *interactionism*, *symbolic interactionism*, *ethno-methodology*, *social constructionism*. *Interpretative social science* is also referred to as the *hermeneutic* approach: that is, concern with the interpretation of meaning.

Kleinian theory
See *object relations*.

Life-chances
See *social inequalities*.

Lifecourse
The different age-based social categories a person may pass through between birth and death. Although associated with biological changes, such stages are also socially defined and most societies recognise, and mark with some sort of ceremony, the occasions of birth, adolescence, marriage, old age and death. Lifecourse transitions refers to the public rituals or *rites of passage*, for example, Christenings, bar mitzvahs, funerals. Ceremonies and rituals surrounding these types of event usually involve a range of *symbolic representations* concerning the meaning of the event for the individual, the social group and the wider society. It can be argued that *rites of passage* help the individual to adjust psychologically to their new *identity*.

Little narratives
See *postmodernism.*

Marxist theory
Theories stemming from the work of Karl Marx, a nineteenth-century philosopher, political economist and sociologist, have been important in the development of *social science.* *Marxism* and *Marxism/Leninism* are the political ideas and practice set up on the basis of some of the theories of Marx and his followers. See *mode of production, economic base/foundation, superstructure, ideology, historical materialism, relations of production, alienation, social class.*

Mechanical solidarity
See *Durheimian theory, social integration/solidarity, division of labour, functionalism, anomie.*

Medicalisation
See *biomedicine/medical model.*

Methodology
The aims, principles and methods or procedures of a discipline. The *concepts* and *theories* of the *social sciences* are thus part of the way in which they investigate the social world; for example, underlying the *agency/structure* debate within sociology is also a methodological debate. Also see *Verstehen method.*

Mode of production
Karl Marx's classificatory term for societies based on the type of economic and productive system in operation: thus he distinguished the ancient, the Asiatic, the *feudal* and the *capitalist* modes of production.

Modernity/modernism
Knowledge, culture and social organisation based on belief in rationality, science and the ability of humankind to bring about change and progress. Such knowledge and culture, and the *modern societies* structured on this basis, stem from the intellectual changes of the eighteenth-century European *Enlightenment* and the rejection of traditional beliefs and knowledge. The 'project' of the Enlightenment was the formation of societies and the development of human progress based on rational knowledge and organisation. At the same time that societies progressed, the freedom of the individual from the constraints of traditional society was guaranteed. By the end of the nineteenth century a range of intellectual and cultural movements known as modernism had developed in Europe. These celebrated the new and *avant-garde,* and

challenged the conventional and traditional. The *postmodernism* of the late twentieth century is now challenging the conventions of modernity and modernism.

Modern societies
See *modernity, industrial societies, capitalism.*

Non-literate societies
See *traditional societies*

Norms
These are the social rules that indicate how we should and should not behave. Normative behaviour is human behaviour governed by ideas of what should be, rather than, for example, by desire or physiological need. We may be driven by physical need to eat, but what we eat is governed by the norms of our society, which define what is safe and appropriate.

Object relations theory
Largely through the work of Melanie Klein, *Freudian theory* has incorporated assumptions concerning the importance of past childhood experience stored and in the *unconscious*. As infants and children, we form relationships with 'significant others', in particular a mother or mother substitute, and as adults we repeat the patterns of behaviour learnt in our earlier relationships.

Organic solidarity
See *Durkheimian theory, social integration/solidarity*, also *division of labour, functionalism, anomie.*

The 'other'/'others'
People or groups who, from our own limited cultural interests and perspective, we identify as being different, and sometimes alien or inferior to ourselves, not belonging to 'our' group. We see ourselves as 'insiders', and others as 'outsiders'. This identification of 'ourselves' compared to 'others' is a subjective judgement and may be used, as in the case of 'race', as the basis for prejudice, discrimination and unequal treatment. It may also unite and strengthen a group that is discriminated against.

Oversocialised view of humankind
The assumption that it is *social structure* rather than human beings that determine *social action*, and that we are simply actors on a pre-determined social stage. The sociologist Denis Wrong coined the phrase 'oversocialised view of man'. Also see *agency* and *roles.*

Personal construct theory

Kelly's social psychological theory assumes that, rather than simply reacting to the world, people act upon it on the basis of how we make sense of (or construe) each other and the world around us. Through our experience in a particular family, group, social position and so on, we learn only a limited range of constructs with which to understand and experience the world.

Phenomenology

Stemming from the philosophy of Edmund Husserl, in social science phenomenology is associated with the work of Alfred Schutz. It is concerned with the study of subjective experience, particularly the experience of everyday social life. In contrast to *positivism* it is argued that social phenomena do not exist in themselves, outside our awareness and interaction. See also *interpretative social science.*

Positivism/positivist-empiricism

The assumption that to be true, knowledge must be based on objectively observable facts that can be verified. Thus, in the nineteenth century in particular, the assumptions and methods of the natural sciences, for example physics, were transferred to the social sciences. The idea that rational knowledge is based on direct observation or experience is called the 'empirical' method. *Empiricism* is a term usually used in a critical way, to indicate an overreliance on this method, and the assumption that knowledge can be objective. In opposition to the assumptions of positivist-empiricism are those of the *interpretative* tradition.

Postmodernism/post-structuralism/post-industrial

Terms used to indicate both societies in the stage of late capitalism at the end of the twentieth century and also the types of ideas and theories that characterise them. *Postmodernism*, compared to the *modernity* that emerged with the European *Enlightenment*, has rejected the belief that overarching theories and solutions (such as *Marxism* or *structural-functionalism*) can provide universal answers to human problems. Postmodernism in social science has led to an emphasis on small-scale theories and the use of more subjective and experiential accounts of the social world – what Lyotard calls 'little narratives'. Postmodern culture, it is argued, contains no overall integrating vision and encourages cultural and theoretical eclecticism and relativism. See also *différance.*

Practical consciousness

A term used by the sociologist Anthony Giddens to describe the way in which social life continues, in part, because we simply 'get on' with it and know how to 'do' it. Practical consciousness is *social action* without the *reflexivity* which is involved in *discursive consciousness.*

Psychoanalysis

A body of theory and clinical practice initially developed by Sigmund Freud, many psychoanalytic *concepts*, particularly those concerning *sexuality*, are now part of *commonsense* understanding in Western societies. *Freudian theory* assumes that individuals are motivated by *unconscious* desires that are constantly frustrated (repressed) by the interactions of social life, and which are part of the development of the 'normal' individual. Although Freudian theory is concerned with the individual, it recognises the important influence of the social in the development of individuals from childhood to adulthood. *Attachment theory* and *object relations theory* are later developments in the psychoanalytic tradition.

'Race'

A social category based on perceived biological differences. In particular, it has been, and is, the foundation for unequal treatment of and discrimination against people who are black, or of Asian or Jewish origin in societies where the dominant groups are white and/or Christian. *Ethnicity* is sometimes used as an alternative term to indicate differences between cultural groups, but at the expense of overlooking the economic basis and power relations of 'race'. See also 'other'/'others'.

Rationality/rationalisation

By *rationality*, the sociologist Max Weber meant *social action* directed toward the achievement of a goal. He also saw the process of *rationalisation* as the defining characteristic of modern societies. By this he meant the displacement of traditional ways of thought, based on custom, religion and magic by science and technology. Increasingly formal or *instrumental rationality* – action or decisions aimed at achieving a specified goal by the most technically efficient means – replaced *substantive rationality* based on the desire to realise a value. See also *social action.*

Reductionism/reductive thinking

Explaining something by reducing it to its basic elements: for example, reducing the social and psychological meaning of sexuality to the biological components of sex. In arguing that society exists in itself (*suis generis*) rather than simply being the sum total of the psychological needs of individuals, the sociologist Emile Durkheim was attempting to avoid reductionist thinking (see *social structure*).

Reification

To make concrete something that exists at the level of ideas or symbols. To state, for example, that Durkheim reified society, means that he saw society as something real and concrete and outside human construction.

Reflexivity

The capacity of human beings to reflect upon their own actions, and as a consequence to alter their behaviour in future actions.

Relations of production

In *Marxist theory*, all social relations are seen to stem from the fact that human beings are essentially producers who must produce in order to live. Thus, the whole of human societies are structured on the basis of purposive economic activity, including the *relations of production*, which form the base or foundation for the *superstructure* of politics, law, religion, beliefs and values (*ideology*).

Rites of passage

See *lifecourse*.

Roles

Social *identities* based on the social scripts which we learn during the processes of *socialisation* and take on at different times. Some roles, such as girl/woman and boy/man are adopted early, although they may alter over time, but some, such as occupational roles, are acquired later in the *lifecourse*. While social roles or scripts may imply identities that are fixed and therefore constraining, we may also see them as being open to continual construction and reconstruction through *reflexivity* on the part of *social actors*.

Self

The concept that each person has a 'self' – a personal and individual identity – separate and different from 'others' is a specifically Western concept. It stems from the humanist/individualist tradition in Western thought. It can be also connected to the notion of *reflexivity*, the idea that as human beings we are able to reflect on and alter both what we do and what we are – we can be self-conscious. This reflexive capacity also results in a shifting *subjectivity*, our experiences of the social constantly alter and our selves change. The sociologist Anthony Giddens refers to the 'project of the self', meaning that the shifting and rapidly-changing nature of modern life and the flexibility of our social roles requires constant work by individuals on their personal identity and their sense of self. See also *identity*.

Sex

Biological differences, including reproductive capacities, between males and females. Biological sex is not synonymous with *sexuality* or with *gender*, although it is an aspect of both of these. Our biology, including our sex, includes both potentialities and limitations on our social action, and the social sciences are increasingly paying attention to the fact that social actors are embodied; that is, we live in our bodies. The way in which we interpret and give meaning to our embodiment and conceptualise our bodies is part of social action.

Sexuality
A social, historical and cultural construction that includes biological capacities, psychological desires and gender identity, all of which in themselves do not determine human action, but are endowed with meaning and significance by and through social relations.

Small-scale societies
See *traditional societies*.

Social action
The sociologist Max Weber argued that the starting point of analysis for social science is the *concept* of *social action*. By this he meant human action directed towards other people which has meaning for the *social actors* involved. He identified two types of *rational action*: (i) action employing the technically most efficient means of achieving a goal; and (ii) action aimed at achieving a specified value Also two types of non-rational action: (i) traditional action, based on custom or habit; and (ii) affective action based on emotion. Weber saw modern societies as being dominated increasingly by rational-legal action – that is, action based on written law and regulations, applied regardless of the person. Also see *rationality, roles, agency*.

Social actors
Used to indicate that human beings can only operate – that is, act within a social context – and that there are social scripts that we follow in order to play a given *role*. *Interpretative approaches* in sociology give human beings an instrumental part in constructing society, yet at the same time seeing them as social agents, constrained by the structures of society. Some theorists, for example, Erving Goffman, extend this notion of a social actor playing a role with the world as their stage.

Social scripts
See *social actors, roles*.

Social class
Usually theorised as a person or group's structural position compared to other individuals and groups. Official statistics such as the population census classify people on the basis of occupational position and income, but there are many disagreements within social science concerning both the basis, meaning and consequences of social class. For Karl Marx, it was the major motor of social

change and essentially antagonistic in character. For the sociologist Max Weber, it was one aspect of *social stratification*. See also *Marxist theories*.

Social constructionism

The assumption that, for example, health, illness, sexuality and work – that is, the social world – do not exist in themselves, outside of individuals, but are constructed through the perceptions and bestowal of meaning by *social actors*. As social actors, we know the world only through these meanings.

Social inequalities

Inequalities of wealth, status and access to social facilities and privileges that are created by the structural arrangements of society. Individuals and groups of individuals therefore have different structural positions. Max Weber saw these as giving people different 'life chances', and the term 'cultural capital' is also used to indicate the way in which people's structural position may mean they possess certain advantages. Such inequalities or social divisions may be assigned and reproduced on the basis of *social class*, *'race'*, *gender*, *ethnicity*, age, physical disability and so on. Some theorists refer to such inequalities as *social stratification*. There are important differences in the way that the major social theorists theorise social inequalities. Also see *culture*.

Social integration/social solidarity

Sociologists and lay people alike often express concern about how societies work and what holds the different parts together. The underlying assumption of *Durkheimian sociology* is that all societies are integrated – they are cohesive. But, Durkheim argued, there are different kinds of integration, or solidarity. In *traditional societies* people have similar interests and this likeness is a source of social cohesion – what Durkheim called 'mechanical solidarity'. In *Industrial societies*, characterised by the specialised *division of labour*, social cohesion is based on a more complex interdependence – what Durkheim called 'organic solidarity'. See also *functionalism*.

Social sciences

Academic disciplines that systematically analyse the nature and working of societies, and which have their roots in the new definitions of knowledge that emerged at the time of the *Enlightenment*. These include sociology, social anthropology, social psychology, political science, political economy, economics, social administration and social policy. Other disciplines might arguably be included as social sciences – for example, social history and human geography. Many modern areas of academic study, such as business studies and marketing, draw on aspects of the social sciences. The social sciences, are therefore concerned with describing, explaining and evaluating aspects of society.

Social stratification

The hierarchical organisation of society on the basis of social class or some other classification such as 'race' or gender. Some theorists prefer the term *social inequalities* because this indicates that such organisation is based on the power and interests of some groups over those of others.

Social structure

Conceptualisation of the social world as having patterns and regularities, some kind of order that has a deterministic effect on the actions of human beings. The nineteenth-century sociologist, Emile Durkheim, argued that society exists *suis generis* – in itself, and outside particular individuals. Durkheim was attempting to encourage the study of society in its own right, rather than as something that could be reduced to the psychological needs of individuals. In addition, he argued that the various aspects of social structure were interdependent and functional for the operation of the whole (see *functionalism*). The modern sociologist, Anthony Giddens, is less deterministic, and argues for the duality of structure, by which he means that there is both regularity and order, but that at the same time there is movement and change.

Socialisation

The process of becoming social, or learning social *roles* and becoming a *social actor*. The term is sometimes used in a deterministic way to imply that the social constrains the social actor in such a way that s/he has no choice (see *oversocialised view of humankind*).

The state

A modern, centralised nation-state is commonly agreed to be necessary for the development of *industrial* and *capitalist* societies. It is distinguished from traditional societies by the fact that it operates on the basis of an administrative system separate from the ruler's household, and within territorial boundaries. This system is considered to be the legitimate source of power and law. Nationality is the formal, legal category designating a person as having citizenship rights in a particular state.

Structural functionalism

See *functionalism*.

Structuralism

Structuralist approaches to language argue that the structure of language determines how we classify and make sense of our experience because this structure existed before to any particular individual. The Marxist writer, Louis Althusser, makes a similar point concerning *ideology*. Both language and ideology can be understood as systems of signs that symbolise particular cultural meanings. *Post-structuralism* argues, however, that the relationship between the signs (or signifiers) and what they mean (the signified) is not fixed, so, for example, we may interpret a film, or the way someone is dressed, in one of several ways.

Subject/subjectivity

Interpretative social science emphasises the constitution, the creation of the social and *social actors* through cultural and social processes, but at the same time argues that we can only reach an understanding of how society works through the experience that people have and the meaning they ascribe to their experience. At a *commonsense* level, subjectivity is often compared unfavourably with objectivity, which is seen as a method of understanding based on science and the *rational* method. An emphasis on subjectivity indicates that the experience of those involved in social processes can be considered to be just as 'true' as the 'truth' arrived at by objective *positivist/empiricist* methods.

Substantive rationality

Social action which includes consideration of values. See *rationality/rationalisation, social action*.

Superstructure

In *Marxist theory* the system of politics, law, religion, beliefs and values (*ideology*) which rests on or reflects the *economic base/foundation*. Marx argues that *consciousness* or *culture*, the *superstructure* is created through the real economic relations (*relations of production*). But later theorists, in particular Louis Althusser, have stressed the importance of the superstructure in determining the nature of society.

Symbolic interactionism

An approach to the interpretation of *social action* and the formation of *identity* associated with G. H. Mead and Herbert Blumer. Mead argues that the social individual develops through interaction with significant others, and that we learn to distinguish the social 'I' from the individual 'me'. It is the capacity for *reflexivity* that allows us to become social actors. Also see *interpretative social science*.

Symbolic representations

Language is the most obvious example of a set of symbols or signs (letters and words) which have no meaning in themselves but which represent ideas and things. Many everyday and special social rituals and practices contain a whole range of symbolic meanings, meaning more than they appear to on the surface. See also *ideology*.

Theory

A theory is a systematic and logically related set of *concepts*, and contains assumptions and classifications about the relationship between the concepts. It is a way of making sense of what we observe and experience. Human beings cannot operate in the world without using theories, but *commonsense* theories are implicit, whereas those of the natural and social sciences are explicit – they are spelt out and elaborated in a systematic way.

Thick description

See *culture*.

Traditional societies

A vague term referring to societies which are not *industrial* or *capitalist* ones, although they may have sectors which are. Also refers to *pre-literate* societies studied by social anthropologists and characterised by oral rather than written culture, *small-scale*, face-to-face relationships, a relatively unspecialised division of labour, and where social change from generation to generation is relatively slight. Pejoratively, such societies have been called 'primitive' or 'savage', reflecting western European values concerning *culture, 'race'* and *ethnicity*. Traditional societies have been profoundly affected by Western societies through colonialism, and the terms *Third World* or *under-developed* as used to describe some contemporary societies reflects this relationship.

The unconscious

A *concept* largely developed in its modern form by Sigmund Freud and now part of *commonsense* understanding, the *unconscious* refers to those aspects of our thoughts and ideas of which we are not conscious. The techniques of *psychoanalysis*, it is claimed, enable the individual being analysed to bring these unconscious ideas and desires into consciousness. Sociologists such as Anthony Giddens would argue that the unconscious must be included in our understanding of how human actors act.

Value relevance

A *concept* used by the sociologist, Max Weber, who belongs to the *interpretative* or *hermeneutic* tradition in social science, to explain that social scientists only ask questions about society which they perceive as relevant. What is perceived as relevant will differ according to the position and interests of the researcher, and thus the questions asked by social scientists will differ at different times. It is argued increasingly that value relevance also operates in the natural sciences.

Verstehen method
From the German for 'understanding'. Used by the sociologist, Max Weber, to describe the way in which the cultural or social sciences required different methods from those of the natural sciences. The *concept* of *Verstehen* includes the assumption that what is social has meaning for the *social actor* and that as social scientists we are able to search for this meaning because we are human. See also *interpretative social science.*

Weberian sociology
Late nineteenth-century, early-twentieth-century German sociologist, Max Weber, argued that *social science* knowledge could be only partial. He also argued that, because its subject matter was different, social science could not simply replicate the methods of the natural sciences, but must use methods that took account of the fact that social life involved the creation of meaning. See *social action, capitalism, rationality, interpretative social science, Verstehen method.*

Bibliography

ABBOTT, P. and SAPSFORD, R. (1987) *Women and Social Class* (London: Tavistock Publications).

ABERCROMBIE N., HILL, S. and TURNER, B. S. (1980) *The Dominant Ideology Thesis* (London: Allen & Unwin).

ABERCROMBIE, N., HILL, S. and TURNER, B. S. (1986) *Sovereign Individuals of Capitalism* (London: Allen & Unwin).

ALLEN, S. and WOLKOWITZ, C. (1987) *Homeworking: Myths and Realities* (London: Macmillan).

ALTHUSSER, L. (1971) 'Ideology and Ideological State Apparatuses' (first published 1969), in *Lenin and Philosophy and Other Essays* (London: New Left Books).

ANDERSON, B. (1983) *Imagined Communities: Reflections on the Origins and Spread of Nationalism* (London: Verso).

APPADURAI, A. (1990) 'Disjuncture and Difference in the Global Cultural Economy', *Theory, Culture and Society*, vol. 7, no. 2–3, pp. 295–310.

APPADURAI, A. (1993) 'Disjuncture and Difference in the Global Cultural Economy', in P. Williams and L. Chrisman (eds), *Colonial Discourse and Post-Colonial Theory* (London: Harvester Wheatsheaf).

ARDENER, S. (ed.) (1993) *Defining Females. The Nature of Women in Society* (Oxford: Berg).

ARMSTRONG, D. (1987) 'Bodies of Knowledge: Foucault and the Problem of Human Anatomy', in G. Scambler (ed.), *Sociological Theory and Medical Sociology* (London: Tavistock).

AUDEN, W. H. (1976) 'Thanksgiving for a Habitat' (1962), in W. H. Auden, *Collected Poems*, (ed.) D. Mendelson (London: Faber & Faber).

BARLEY, N. (1989) *Native Land: The Bizarre Rituals and Curious Customs that Make the English English* (Harmondsworth: Penguin).

BARTHES, R. (1983) *Selected Writings* (London: Fontana).

BAUMAN, Z. (1993) *Modernity and the Holocaust* (Oxford: Polity Press).

BBC RADIO 4 (FM) (1995) 'A New Respect for St Paul's, 29 August.

BELL, C. and NEWBY, H. (1971) *Community Studies* (London: George Allen & Unwin).

BERGER, P. L. (1973) *Invitation to Sociology: A Humanistic Approach* (Harmondsworth: Penguin).

BERGER, P. L. and KELLNER, H. (1979) 'Marriage and the Construction of Reality', in P. L. Berger (ed.), *Facing up to Modernity* (Harmondsworth: Penguin).

BERGESON, A. (1990) 'Turning World-System Theory on its Head', *Theory, Culture and Society*, vol. 7, no. 2–3, pp. 67–81.

BEURET, K. and MAKINGS, L. (1987) ' "I've Got Used to Being Independent Now": Women and Courtship in a Recession', in P. Allatt. T. Keil, A. Bryman, and B. Bytheway (eds), *Women and the Life Cycle. Transitions and Turning-points* (London: Macmillan).

BILLIG, M. (1991) *Ideology and Opinions: Studies in Rhetorical Psychology* (London: Sage).

BILLIG, M. (1992) *Talking of the Royal Family* (London: Routledge).

BILLINGTON, R. STRAWBRIDGE, S., GREENSIDES, L., FITZSIMONS, A. (1991) *Culture and Society: A Sociology of Culture*, (London: Macmillan).

BLAND, L. and MORT, F. (1984) ' "Look Out For the 'Good Time Girl' ": Dangerous Sexualities as a Threat to National Health', in Formations Editorial Collective, *Formations of Nation and People* (London: Routledge & Kegan Paul).

BLOCH, M. and PARRY, J. (1983) *Death and the Regeneration of Life* (Cambridge University Press).

BLUMER, H. (1969) *Symbolic Interactionism* (Englewood Cliffs, NJ: Prentice-Hall).

BOLOGH, R. W. (1990) *Love or Greatness: Max Weber and Masculine Thinking – A Feminist Inquiry* (London: Unwin/Hyman).

BOSKIN, J. (1986) *Sambo: The Rise and Demise of an American Jester* (Oxford University Press).

BOURDIEU, P. and PASSERANT, J. C. (1977) *Reproduction in Education, Society and Culture* (London: Sage).

BRANNEN, J. and MOSS, P. (1991) *Managing Mothers: Dual Earner Households after Maternity Leave* (London: Unwin/Hyman).

BRITISH PSYCHOTHERAPISTS (1995) Letter in *Free Associations*, vol. 5, 3, no. 35 (London: Process Press).

BROWN, T. (1981) *Ireland: A Social and Cultural History 1922–79* (London: Fontana).

BUNTON, R., NETTLETON, S. and BURROWS, R. (1995) *The Sociology of Health Promotion* (London: Routledge).

BURAWOY, M. (1979) *Manufacturing Consent: Changes in the Labor Process under Capitalism* (London: University of Chicago Press).

BURR, V. (1995) *An Introduction to Social Constructionism* (London: Routledge).

CABEZALI, E., CUEVAS, M. and CHICOTE, M. T. (1990) 'Myth as Suppression: Motherhood and the Historical Consciousness of the Women of Madrid, 1936–9', in R. Samuel and P. Thompson (eds), *The Myths We Live By* (London: Routledge).

CALHOUN, C. (1994) 'Nationalism and Civil Society: Democracy, Diversity and Self-Determination' in C. Calhoun (ed.), *Social Theory and the Politics of Identity* (Oxford: Blackwell)

CAMPLING, J. (ed.) (1981) *Images of Ourselves: Women with Disabilities Talking* (London: Routledge & Kegan Paul).

CAPLAN P. (1987) *The Cultural Construction of Sexuality* (London: Tavistock).

CASEY, C. (1995) *Work, Self and Society: After Industrialism* (London: Routledge).

CHARLES, N. and KERR, M. (1988) *Women, Food and Families* (Manchester University Press).

CHINOY, E. (1955) *Automobile Workers and the American Dream* (Garden City, New York: Doubleday).

CHODOROW, N. J. (1978) *The Reproduction of Mothering* (Berkeley, Calif.: University of California Press).

CHODOROW, N. J. (1994) *Femininities, Masculinities, Sexualities: Freud and Beyond* (London: Free Association Books).

CLARKE, J. and CRITCHER, C. (1985) *The Devil Makes Work: Leisure in Capitalist Britain* (London: Macmillan).

COATES, K. and SILBURN, R. (1970) *Poverty:The Forgotten Englishmen* (Harmondsworth: Penguin).

COCKBURN, C. (1983) *Brothers: Male Dominance and Technological Change* (London: Pluto).

COCKBURN, C. (1991) *In the Way of Women: Men's Resistance to Sex Equality in Organizations* (London: Macmillan).

COCKBURN, C. and ORMROD, S. (1993) *Gender and Technology in the Making* (London: Sage).

COHEN, A. P. (ed.) (1982) *Belonging: Identity and Social Organisation in British Rural Cultures* (Manchester University Press).

COHEN, A. P. (ed.) (1986) *Symbolising Boundaries: Identity and Diversity in British Cultures* (Manchester University Press).

COHEN, P. (1980) 'Subcultural Conflict and Working Class Community', in Hall, S. Hobson, P., Lowe, A. and Willis, P. (eds), *Culture, Media Language* (London: Hutchinson).

COLEMAN, G. (1991) *Investigating Organisations: A Feminist Approach*, Occasional Paper 37 (University of Bristol, School for Advanced Urban Studies).

COLLINS, R. (1985) '"Horses For Courses": Ideology and the Division of Domestic Labour', in P. Close and R. Collins (eds), *Family and Economy in Modern Society* (London, Macmillan).

COLLINSON, D. (1992) *Managing the Shopfloor: Subjectivity, Masculinity and Workplace Culture* (Berlin: Walter de Gruyter).

COLLINSON, D. and HEARN, G. (1994) 'Naming Men as Men: Implications for Work, Organization and Management', *Gender, Work and Organization*, vol. 1, no. 1, pp. 2–22.

COLLINSON, D., KNIGHTS, D. and COLLINSON, M. (1990) *Managing to Discriminate* (London: Routledge).

CONNELL, R. W. (1991) 'Live Fast and Die Young: The Construction of Masculinity among Young Working-class Men on the Margin of the Labour Market', *Australian and New Zealand Journal of Sociology*, vol. 27, no. 2, pp. 141–71.

COURT, M. (1994) 'Removing Macho Management: Lessons from the Field of Education', *Gender, Work and Organization*, vol. 1, no. 1, pp. 33–49.

COWARD, R. (1989) *The Whole Truth: The Myth of Alternative Health* (London: Faber & Faber).

COYLE, A. (1984) *Redundant Women* (London: Women's Press).

CRITCHER, C. (1979) 'Sociology, Cultural Studies and the Post-war Working Class', in Clarke, J. Critcher, C. and Johnson, R. (eds), *Working Class Culture: Studies in History and Theory* (London: Hutchinson).

CROMPTON, R. and SANDERSON, K. (1990) *Gendered Jobs and Social Change* (London: Unwin / Hyman).

CUNNISON, S. (1986) 'Gender, Consent and Exploitation among Sheltered Housing Wardens', in K. Purcell, S. Wood, A. Waton and S. Allen (eds), *The Changing Experience of Employment: Restructuring and Recession* (London: Macmillan).

DAVIDOFF, L. and HALL, C. (1987) *Family Fortunes: Men and Women of the English Middle Class, 1780–1850* (London: Hutchinson).

DAVIDSON J. O. and LAYDER, D. (1994) *Methods: Sex and Madness*, (London: Routledge).

DE SWAAN, A. (1990) *The Management of Normality* (London: Routledge).

DEETZ, S. (1992) 'Disciplinary Power in the Modern Corporation', in M. Alvesson and H. Wilmott (eds), *Critical Management Studies* (London: Sage).

DENNIS, N., HENRIQUES, F., and SLAUGHTER, C. (1969) *Coal is Our Life*, first published 1956 (London: Tavistock Publications).

DEX, S. (1985) *The Sexual Division of Work: Conceptual Revolutions in the Social Sciences* (Brighton: Harvester/Wheatsheaf).

DEX, S. (1988) *Women's Attitudes Towards Work* (London: Macmillan).

DOCHERTY, T. (1993) *Postmodernism. A Reader* (London: Harvester/ Wheatsheaf).

DODDS, E. R. (1951) *The Greeks and the Irrational* (Berkeley, Calif.: University of California Press).

DOUGLAS, M. (1966) *Purity and Danger* (Harmondsworth: Penguin).

DOYAL, L. (1995) *What Makes Women Sick?* (London: Macmillan).

DOYAL, L. and ELSTON, M. (1986) 'Women, Health and Medicine', in V. Beechey and E. Whitelegg (eds), *Women in Britain Today* (Milton Keynes, Open University Press).

DOYAL, L., with PENNELL, I. (1979) *The Political Economy of Health* (London, Pluto Press).

DU GAY, P. (1996) *Consumption and Identity at Work* (London: Sage).

DURKHEIM, E. (1915) *The Elementary Forms of the Religious Life* (London: George Allen & Unwin).

DURKHEIM, F. (1952) *Suicide: A Study in Society* (Glencoe, Ill.: Free Press).

DURKHEIM, E. (1982) *The Rules of Sociological Method and Selected Texts on Sociology and its Method* (London: Macmillan).

DURKHEIM, E. (1984) *The Division of Labour in Society* (London: Macmillan.

EGGLESTON, J. (ed.) (1974) *Contemporary Research in the Sociology of Education* (London: Methuen).

EHRENREICH, B. and ENGLISH, D. (1979) *For Her Own Good: 150 Years of the Experts' Advice to Women* (London: Pluto).

ELDRIDGE, J. E. T. (ed.) (1971) *Max Weber: The Interpretation of Social Reality* (London: Nelson).

ELDRIDGE, J. E. T. and CROMBIE, A. D. (1974) *A Sociology of Organisations* (London: George Allen & Unwin).

ELKINS, S. (1959) *Slavery: A Problem in American Institutional and Intellectual Life* (Chicago: University of Chicago Press).

ELLIS, M. N. (1994) *Free Associations*, vol. 4, pt 4, no. 32 (London: Process Press).

ELLISON, R. (1976) *Invisible Man* (Harmondsworth: Penguin).

FAGIN, L. AND LITTLE, M. (1984) *The Forsaken Families* (Harmondsworth: Penguin).

FANON, F. (1970) *Black Skins White Masks* (London: Paladin).

FEATHERSTONE, M. (1990) 'Global Culture: An Introduction', *Theory, Culture and Society*, vol. 7, no. 2–3, pp. 1–14.

FINEMAN, S. (ed.) (1993) *Emotion in Organizations* (London: Sage).

FISCHER, E. (1973) *Marx in His Own Words* (Harmondsworth : Penguin).

FOSTER, S. and KELLY, R. (1990/1) 'Citizenship: Perspectives and Contradictions', *Talking Politics*, vol. 3, no. 2.

FOUCAULT, M. (1973) *The Birth of the Clinic* (London: Tavistock).

FOUCAULT, M. (1974) *The Archaelogy of Knowledge* (London: Tavistock)

FOUCAULT, M. (1979) *Power/Knowledge: Selected Interviews and other Writings 1972–1977*, trans. C. Gordon (Brighton: Harvester).

FOUCAULT, M. (1981) *The History of Sexuality: Volume One, An Introduction*, (Harmondsworth: Penguin).

FOX, N. (1993) *Postmodernism, Sociology and Health* (Milton Keynes: Open University Press).

FRANSELLA, F. and DALTON, P. (1990) *Personal Construct Counselling in Action* (London: Sage).

FREIRE, P. (1972) *Cultural Action for Freedom* (Harmondsworth: Penguin).

FREUD S. (1977) *On Sexuality*, Pelican Freud Library, vol. 7 (Harmondsworth: Penguin).

FREUD, S. (1984) *On Metapsychology: The Theory of Psychoanalysis*, Pelican Freud Library, vol. 11 (Harmondsworth: Penguin).

FRIEDAN, B. (1982) *The Feminine Mystique*, first published 1963 (Harmondsworth: Penguin).

FRIEDMAN, J. (1990) 'Being in the World: Globalization and Localization', *Theory, Culture and Society*, vol. 7, no. 2–3, pp. 311–28.

FROSH, S. (1995) 'Unpacking Masculinity: From Rationality to Fragmentation', in C. Burck and B. Speed (eds), *Gender, Power and Relationships* (London: Routledge).

GALLIE, W. B. (1956) *Proceedings of the Aristotelian Society*, vol. 56.

GARMARNIKOW, E., MORGAN, D., PURVIS, J., TAYLORSON, D. (eds) *The Public and the Private* (London: Heinemann).

GATES, H. L. (1995) *Colored People* (London: Viking).

GEERTZ, C. (1974) 'From the Native's Point of View: On the Nature of Anthropological Understanding', reprinted from *Bulletin of the American Academy of Arts and Sciences*, vol. 28, no. 1, in Geertz, C. (1993) *Local Knowledge* (Glasgow: Fontana).

GEERTZ, C. (1993) *The Interpretation of Cultures,* first published 1973 (London: Fontana).

GEUSS, R. (1981) *The Idea of a Critical Theory: Habermas and the Frankfurt School* (Cambridge University Press).

GIDDENS, A. (1984) *The Constitution of Society* (Cambridge: Polity Press).

GIDDENS, A. (1989) *Sociology* (Cambridge: Polity Press).

GIDDENS, A. (1991) *Modernity and Self-Identity: Self and Society in the Late Modern Age* (Cambridge: Polity Press).

GIDDENS, A. (1992) *The Transformation of Intimacy: Sexuality, Love and Eroticism in Modern Societies* (Cambridge: Polity Press).

GILLIGAN, C. (1982) *In a Different Voice: Psychological Theory and Women's Development* (Cambridge, Mass.: Harvard University Press).

GILROY, P. (1987) *'There Ain't No Black in the Union Jack': The Cultural Politics of Race and Nation* (London, Hutchinson).

GLYPTIS, S. (1989) *Leisure and Unemployment* (Milton Keynes: Open University Press).

GOFFMAN, E. (1971) *The Presentation of Self in Everyday Life* (Harmondsworth: Penguin).

GOLDTHORPE, J. H., LOCKWOOD, D., BECHHOFER, F., PLATT, J. (1968–9) *The Affluent Worker in the Class Structure,* 3 vols (Cambridge University Press).

GRAHAM, H. (1987) 'Women, Health and Illness', *Social Studies Review,* vol. 3, no.1, pp. 15–20.

GRAY, J. (1993) *Men are from Mars, Women are from Venus: A Practical Guide for Improving Communication and Getting What You Want from Relationships* (London: Thomsons).

GRIFFIN, C. (1987) 'Broken Transitions: From School to the Scrap Heap', in P. Allatt T. Keil, A. Bryman and B. Bytheway (eds), *Women and the Life Cycle. Transitions and Turning-points* (London: Macmillan).

GRINT, K. (1991) *The Sociology of Work: An Introduction* (Cambridge: Polity Press).

HABERMAS, J. (1984) *The Theory of Communicative Action,* vol. 1 (London: Heinemann).

HALL, S. (1983) 'Citizenship, Society and the State, in D. Held *et al.* (eds) *States and Societies* (Oxford: Martin Robertson)

HALL, S. (1992) 'The West and the Rest: Discourse and Power', in S. Hall and B. Gieben (eds), *Formations of Modernity* (Milton Keynes: Open University/Polity Press).

HALL, S. (1995) 'New Ethnicities', in B. Ashcroft, G. Griffiths and H. Tiffin (eds), *The Post-Colonial Studies Reader* (London: Routledge).

HALL, S. AND GIEBEN, B. (eds) (1992) *Formations of Modernity* (Milton Keynes: Open University/Polity Press).

HAMILTON, P. (1983) *Talcott Parsons* (London: Ellis Horwood/Tavistock).

HAMILTON, P. (1992) 'The Enlightenment and the Birth of Social Science', in S. Hall and B. Gieben (eds), *Formations of Modernity* (Milton Keynes: Open University/Polity Press).

HANNAY, D. (1980) 'The "Iceberg" of Illness and "Trivial" Consultations', *Journal of the Royal College of General Practitioners*, vol. 30, pp. 551–4.

HANNERZ, U. (1990) 'Cosmopolitans and Locals in World Culture', *Theory, Culture and Society*, vol. 7, no. 2–3, pp. 237–51.

HARGREAVES, J. (1986) *Sport, Power and Culture* (Cambridge: Polity Press).

HARLAND, R. (1987) *Superstructuralism:The Philosophy of Structuralism and Post-Structuralism* (London: Methuen).

HARRIS, C. (1987) 'The Individual and Society: A Processual Approach', A. Bryman B. Byethway, P. Allatt, and T. Keil (eds), *Rethinking the Life Cycle* (London: Macmillan).

HART, C. W. M. and PILLING, A. R. (1964) *The Tiwi of North Australia* (New York:, Holt).

HAYWOOD, L. KEW, F., BRAMHAM, P. (1989) *Understanding Leisure* (London: Hutchinson).

HEARN, J. SHEPPARD, D. L., TANCRED-SHERIFF, R., BURRELL, G. (eds) (1989) *The Sexuality of Organization* (London: Sage).

HELD, D. (1992) 'The Development of the Modern State', in S. Hall and B. Gieben (eds), *Formations of Modernity* (Milton Keynes: Open University/ Polity Press).

HELMAN, C. (1984) 'Feed a Cold, Starve a Fever', in N. Black, D. Boswell, A. Gray, S. Murphy, J. Popay (eds), *Health and Disease: A Reader* (Milton Keynes: Open University Press).

HELMAN, C. (1990) *Culture, Health and Illness* (Oxford: Butterworth Heinemann).

HERTZ, R. (1960) *Death and the Right Hand*, first published 1907 (New York: Free Press).

HIGGONET, M. R. and JENSON, J. (1987) *Behind the Lines: Gender and the Two World Wars* (London: Yale University Press).

HILLIER, S. (1991) 'The Limits of Medical Knowledge', in G. Scambler (ed.), *Sociology as Applied to Medicine* (London: Bailliere Tindall).

HITE, S. (1989) *The Hite Report* (London: Pandora).

HITE, S. (1990) *The Hite Report on Male Sexuality* (London: Macdonald, Optima).

HOCKEY, J. (1990*) Experiences of Death. An Anthropological Account* (Edinburgh University Press).

HOCKEY, J. (1993) 'The Acceptable Face of Human Grieving? The Clergy's Role in Managing Human Emotional Expression During Funerals', in D. Clark (ed.), *The Sociology of Death* (Oxford: Basil Blackwell).

HOFFMAN, E. (1989) *Lost in Translation: Life in a New Language* (London: Minerva).

HORNE, J., JARY, D. and TOMLINSON, A (eds) (1987) *Sport, Leisure and Social Relations* (London: Routledge & Kegan Paul).

HOWARD, M. C. (1993) *Contemporary Cultural Anthropology* (New York, HarperCollins).

HUMPHREYS, L. (1975) *Tearoom Trade: Impersonal Sex in Public Places* (Chicago: Aldine).

HUNT, P. (1989) 'Gender and the Construction of Home Life', in G. Allan and G. Crow (eds), *Home and Family: Creating the Domestic Sphere* (London: Macmillan).

HUNTINGTON, R. and METCALF, P. (1979) *Celebrations of Death: The Anthropology of Mortuary Ritual* (Cambridge University Press).

ILLICH, I. (1975) *Medical Nemesis: The Expropriation of Health* (London: Marion Boyars).

JAHODA, M. (1982) *Employment and Unemployment: A Social–Psychological Analysis* (Cambridge University Press).

JAHODA, M., LAZARSFELD, P. F., ZEISEL, H. (1971) *Marienthal: The Sociography of an Unemployed Community* (London: Tavistock).

JAMES, A. (1996) 'Cooking the Books: Global or Local Identities in Contemporary British Food Cultures', in D. Howes, (ed), *Cross-Cultural Consumption: Global Markets, Local Realities* (London: Routledge).

JAMES, A. and PROUT, A. (1990) *Constructing and Re-constructing Childhood* (London: Falmer).

JAMES, N. (1989) 'Emotional Labour: Skill and Work in the Social Regulation of Feelings', *Sociological Review*, vol. 37, pp. 15–42.

JAMES, N. (1993) 'Divisions of Emotional Labour: Disclosure and Cancer', in N. Fineman (ed.), *Emotions in Organizations* (London: Sage).

JEFFERY, P. (1979) *Frogs in a Well: Indian Women in Purdah* (London: Zed Books).

JORDANOVA, L. (1989) *Sexual Visions. Images of Gender in Science and Medicine between the Eighteenth and Twentieth Centuries* (London: Harvester/Wheatsheaf).

KARASAK, R. A. and THEORELL, T. (1990) *Healthy Work* (New York: Basic Books).

KEESING, R. M. (1981) *Cultural Anthropology* (New York: Holt, Rinehart & Winston).

KELVIN, P. and JARRETT, J. (1985) *Unemployment: Its Social Psychological Effects* (Cambridge University Press).

KITZINGER, C. (1987) *The Social Construction of Lesbianism* (London: Sage).

KONDO, D. K. (1990) *Crafting Selves: Power, Gender and Discourses of Identity* (London and Chicago: University of Chicago Press)

KUBLER-ROSS, E. (1970) *On Death and Dying* (London: Tavistock)

LA FONTAINE, J. (1966) *Chisungu* (London: Faber).

LACAN, J. (1949) 'The Mirror Stage', in (1977) *Ecrits: A Selection* (London: Tavistock).

LAING, R. D. (1965) *The Divided Self* (Harmondsworth: Penguin).

LANDY, R. J. (1993) *Persona and Performance* (London: Jessica Kingsley).

LARKIN, P. (1974) 'This Be the Verse', in *High Windows* (London: Faber & Faber).

LASCH, C. (1977) *Haven in a Heartless World* (New York: Basic Books).

LAWRENCE, D. H. (1964) 'Chaos in Poetry', in A. Beal (ed.), *Selected Literary Criticism*, (London: Mercury).

LEE, D. and NEWBY, H. (1983) *The Problem of Sociology: An Introduction to the Discipline* (London: Hutchinson).

LEE, L. (1969) *As I Walked Out One Midsummer Morning* (Hamondsworth: Penguin)

LEONARD, D. (1980) *Sex and Generation. A Study of Courtship and Weddings* (London: Tavistock).

LÉVI-STRAUSS, C. (1966) *The Savage Mind* (London: Weidenfeld & Nicolson).

LEWIS, G. (1986) 'Concepts of Health and Illness in Sepik Society', in C. Currer and M. Stacey (eds), *Concepts of Health, Illness and Disease* (Oxford: Berg).

LISTER, R. (1991) 'Citizenship Engendered', *Critical Social Policy*, no. 32.

LONDON, L. and YUVAL DAVIS, N. (1984) 'Women as National Reproducers: The Nationality Act (1981)', in Formations Editorial Collective, *Formations of Nation and People* (London: Routledge & Kegan Paul).

LONG, J. (1989) 'A Part to Play: Men Experiencing Leisure through Retirement', in B. Byetheway, T. Keil, P. Allatt and A. Bryman, (eds), *Becoming and Being Old. Sociological Approaches to Later Life* (London: Sage).

LYOTARD, J. F. (1984) *The Postmodern Condition: A Report on Knowledge*, first published 1979 (Manchester University Press).

LYOTARD, J. F. and THEBAUD, J. L. (1985) *Just Gaming* (Manchester University Press).

MACDONELL, D. (1986) *Theories of Discourse: An Introduction* (Oxford: Basil Blackwell).

MACFARLANE, A. (1978) *The Origins of English Individualism* (Oxford: Basil Blackwell).

MACPHERSON, C. B. (1962) *The Political Theory of Possessive Individualism: Hobbes to Locke* (Oxford University Press).

MARCUSE, H. (1972) *Negations* (Harmondsworth: Penguin).

MARKS, E. and COURTIVRON, I. DE (1981) *New French Feminisms: An Anthology* (Brighton: Harvester).

MARS, L. (1989) 'Coming of Age among Jews: Bar Mitzvah and Bat Mitzvah', in P. Spencer (ed.), *Anthropology and the Riddle of the Sphinx*, ASA Monographs (London: Routledge).

MARSDEN, D. and DUFF, E. (1975) *Workless: Some Unemployed Men and their Families* (Harmondsworth: Penguin).

MARSHALL, G., ROSE, D., NEWBY, H., VOGLER, C. (1988) *Social Class in Modern Britain* (London: Unwin/Hyman).

MARSHALL, T. H. (1983) 'Citizenship and Social Class' (first published 1950), in D. Held, J. Anderson, B. Gieben, S. Hall, L. Harris, P. Levis, N. Paster, B. Turok (eds), *States and Societies* (London: Martin Robertson).

MARTIN, E. (1987) *The Woman in the Body: A Cultural Analysis of Reproduction* (Milton Keynes: Open University Press).

MARTIN, J. (1990) 'Deconstructing Organizational Taboos: The Suppression of Gender Conflict in Organizations', *Organization Science*, vol. 1, no. 4, pp. 339–59.

MARTIN, J. and ROBERTS, C. (1984) *Women and Employment* (London: Department of Employment).

MARX, K. (1950a) 'Preface to the Critique of Political Economy', in K. Marx and F. Engels, *Selected Works*, vol. 1 (London: Lawrence & Wishart).

MARX, K. (1950b) *The Eighteenth Brumaire of Louis Bonaparte,* in K. Marx and F. Engels, *Selected Works*, vol. 1 (London: Lawrence & Wishart).

MASTERS, W. H. and JOHNSON, V. E. (1966) *Human Sexual Response* (Boston, Mass.: Little, Brown).

MCFARLANE, G. (1986) 'It's Not As Simple As That': The Expression of the Catholic and Protestant Boundary in Northern Irish Rural Communities', in A. P. Cohen (ed.), *Symbolising Boundaries: Identity and Diversity in British Cultures* (Manchester University Press).

MCLEOD, J. (1996) 'Working with Narratives', in R. Bayne, I. Horton and J. Bimrose (eds), *New Directions in Counselling* (London: Routledge).

MCNAY, L. (1992) *Foucault and Feminism* (Cambridge: Polity Press).

MCNEILL, M. (ed.) (1987) *Gender and Expertise* (London: Free Association Books).

MEAD, G. H. (1962) *Mind, Self and Society from the Standpoint of a Social Behaviourist*, (ed.) C. W. Morris (University of Chicago Press).

MEARNS, D. and THORNE, B. (1988) *Person-Centred Counselling in Action* (London: Sage).

MIES, M. (1983) 'Towards a Methodology for Feminist Research', in G. Bowles and R. D. Klein (eds), *Theories for Women's Studies* (London: Routledge & Kegan Paul).

MILES, A. (1991) *Women, Health and Medicine* (Milton Keynes: Open University Press).

MILGRAM, S. (1974) *Obedience to Authority* (London: Tavistock).

MINSKY, R. (ed.) (1996) *Psychoanalysis and Gender. An Introductory Reader* (London: Routledge).

MITCHELL, J. (1975) *Psychoanalysis and Feminism* (Harmondsworth: Penguin).

MOORHOUSE, H. F. (1984) 'American Automobiles and Workers' Dreams', in K. Thompson (ed.), *Work, Employment and Unemployment* (Milton Keynes: Open University Press).

MORLEY, R. E. (1984) *Intimate Strangers* (London: Family Welfare Association).

MORRIS, C. (1973) *The Discovery of the Individual 1050–1200* (New York: Harper & Row).

MORRIS, J. (1991) *Pride Against Prejudice; A Personal Politics of Disability* (London: Women's Press).

MORRISON, T. (1993) *Playing in the Dark: Whiteness and the Literary Imagination* (London: Picador)

MUMBY, D. K. and STOHL, C. (1991) 'Power, and Discourse in Organisation Studies: Absence and the Dialectic of Control', *Discourse and Society*, vol. 2, no. 2, pp. 313–32.

MURGATROYD, L. (1985) 'The Production of People and Domestic Labour Revisited', in P. Close and R. Collins (eds), *Family and Economy in Modern Society* (London: Macmillan).

NAVARRO, V. (1976) *Medicine under Capitalism* (New York: Prodist).

NICHOLSON, B. (1995) 'Domestic Production and the Market: Where Status and Contract Meet', *Sociology*, vol. 29, no. 2, pp. 221–39.

O'CONNOR, N. and RYAN, J. (1993) *Wild Desires and Mistaken Identities: Lesbianism and Psychoanalysis* (London: Virago).

OAKLEY, A. (1974) *The Sociology of Housework* (Oxford: Martin Robertson).

OAKLEY, A. (1984) 'Doctor Knows Best', in N. Black, D. Boswell, A Gray, S. Murphy J. Popay (eds), *Health and Disease: A Reader* (Milton Keynes: Open University Press).

OCHBERG, R. L. (1987) 'The Male Career Code and the Ideology of Role', in H. Brod (ed.), *The Making of Masculinities: The New Men's Studies* (London: Allen & Unwin).

OKELY, J. (1983) *The Traveller Gypsies* (Cambridge University Press).

OSBORNE, K. (1991) 'Women's Work... Is Never Done', in J. Firth-Cozens and M. A. West (eds), *Women at Work: Psychological and Organizational Perspectives* (Milton Keynes: Open University Press).

PAHL, R. E. (1984) *Divisions of Labour* (Oxford: Basil Blackwell).

PARKER, R. and POLLOCK, G. (eds) (1987) *Framing Feminism: Art and the Women's Movement 1970–1985* (London: Pandora).

PARKES, C. M. (1972) *Bereavement. Studies of Grief in Adult Life* (London: Tavistock)

PARSONS, T. (1951) *The Social System* (London: Routledge & Kegan Paul).

PATEMAN, C. (1987) 'Feminist Critiques of the Public/Private Dichotomy', in Phillips, A (ed.) *Feminism and Equality* (Oxford: Basil Blackwell).

PHILLIPS, S. K. (1986) 'Natives and Incomers: The Symbolism of Belonging in Muker Parish, North Yorkshire', in A. P. Cohen (ed.), *Symbolising Boundaries: Identity and Diversity in British Cultures* (Manchester University Press).

PHILLIPSON, C. (1982) *Capitalism and the Construction of Old Age* (London: Macmillan).

PHIZACKLEA, A. (1990) *Unpacking the Fashion Industry: Gender, Racism and Class in Production* (London: Routledge).

PLUMMER, K. (1995) *Telling Sexual Stories: Power, Change and Social Worlds* (London: Routledge).

POLLERT, A. (1981) *Girls, Wives, Factory Lives* (London: Macmillan).

PORTER, R. (1983) 'The Language of Quackery', *Bulletin of the Society for the Social History of Medicine,* vol. 33, p. 68.

PORTER, R. (1987) *Disease, Medicine and Society in England 1550–1860* (London: Macmillan).

POWLEY, D. (1992) 'Moments of Grace: Order in Chaos', in *Dramatherapy,* Spring.

PURCELL, K., WOOD, S., WATON, A., and ALLEN, S. (eds) (1986) *The Changing Experience of Employment: Restructuring and Recession* (London: Macmillan).

PURVIS, T. and HUNT, A. (1993) 'Discourse, Ideology, Discourse Ideology, Discourse, Ideology...', *British Journal of Sociology,* vol. 44, no. 3, pp. 473–99.

PUTNAM, L. L. and MUMBY, D. K. (1993) 'Organizations, Emotion and the Myth of Rationality', in S. Fineman (ed.), *Emotion in Organizations* (London: Sage).

RAWLS, J. (1973) *A Theory of Justice* (Oxford University Press).

REID, I. (1978) *Sociological Perspectives on School and Education* (Shepton Mallet: Open Books)

REINISCH, J. and BEASLEY, R. (1991) *The Kinsey Institute New Report on Sex* (Harmondsworth: Penguin).

RICHARDS, A. (1956) *Chisungu: A Girls' Initiation Ceremony among the Bemba of Northern Rhodesia* (London: Faber).

RICHARDSON D. (ed.) (1996) *Theorising Heterosexuality* (Buckingham: Open University Press).

ROBERTS, H. (1981) 'Male Hegemony in Family Planning', in H. Roberts (ed.), *Women, Health and Reproduction* (London: Routledge & Kegan Paul)

ROJEK, C. (1985) *Capitalism and Leisure Theory* (London: Tavistock).

ROJEK, C. (ed.) (1989) *Leisure For Leisure: Critical Essays* (London: Macmillan).

ROPER, M. (1991) 'Yesterday's Model: Product Fetishism and the British Company Man, 1945–85', in M. Roper and J. Tosh (eds), *Manful Assertions: Masculinities in Britain since 1800* (London: Routledge).

ROSE, M. (1975) *Industrial Behaviour: Theoretical Development Since Taylor* (London: Allen Lane).

ROSE, N. (1989), *Governing the Soul: The Shaping of the Private Self* (London: Routledge).

ROWAN, C. (1984) 'For the Duration Only: Motherhood and Nation in the First World War', in Formations Editorial Collective, *Formations of Nation and People* (London: Routledge & Kegan Paul).

SAMPSON, E. (1993) *Celebrating the Other: A Dialogic Account of Human Nature* (Hemel Hempstead: Harvester/Wheatsheaf).

SAMUEL, R. and THOMPSON, P. (1990) 'Introduction', in R. Samuel and P. Thompson (eds), *The Myths We Live By* (London: Routledge).

SAUSSURE, F. DE, (1974) *Course in General Linguistics*, first published in *1916* (London: Fontana).

SAYERS, S. (1988) 'The Need to Work: A Perspective from Philosophy', in R. E. Pahl (ed.) *On Work: Historical, Comparative and Theoretical Approaches* (Oxford: Basil Blackwell).

SCAMBLER, G. (1991) *Sociology as Applied to Medicine* (London: Bailliere Tindall).

SCHEFF, T. (1994) 'Emotions and Identity: A Theory of Ethnic Nationalism', in C. Calhoun (ed.), *Social Theory and the Politics of Identity* (Oxford: Basil Blackwell).

SCHON, D. (1987) *Educating the Reflective Practitioner* (London: Jossey-Bass).

SCHULLER, T. (1989) 'Work-Ending: Employment and Ambiguity in Later Life', in B. Bytheway T. Keil, P. Allatt and A. Bryman (eds), *Being and Becoming Old: Sociological Approaches to Later Life* (London: Sage).

SCOTT, P. (1983) 'The Year of the Bomb', editorial, *The Times Higher Education Supplement*, January.

SEABROOK, J. (1982) *Unemployment* (London: Paladin).

SEIDLER, V. (1994) *Unreasonable Men: Masculinity and Social Theory* (London: Routledge).

SELLERS, S. (ed.) (1989) *Delighting the Heart. A Notebook by Women Writers* (London: Women's Press).

SHARPE, S. (1984) *Double Identity: The Lives of Working Mothers* (Harmondswoth: Penguin).

SHOTTER, J. (1993) 'Rhetoric and the Roots of the Homeless Mind', *Theory, Culture and Society*, vol. 10, no. 4, pp. 41–62.

SHOWALTER, E. (1987) *The Female Malady; Women, Madness and English Culture, 1830–1980* (London: Virago).

SILVERMAN, D. (1970) *The Theory of Organisations* (London: Heinemann).

SMITH-ROSENBERG, C. (1984) 'The Hysterical Woman: Sex Roles and Role Conflict in Nineteenth-Century America', in N. Black, D. Boswell, A. Gray, S. Murphy, J. Popay (eds) *Health and Disease: A Reader* (Buckingham, Open University Press).

SNELL, B. (1982) *The Discovery of the Mind: In Greek Philosophy and Literature* (New York: Dover).

STACEY, M. (1988) *The Sociology of Health and Healing* (London: Routledge).

STAINTON ROGERS, W. (1991) *Explaining Health and Illness* (Hemel Hempstead: Harvester/Wheatsheaf).

STOLLER, R. (1991) *Pain and Passion: A Psychoanalyst Explores the World of S & M* (New York: Plenum Press).

STOREY, J. (1993) *An Introductory Guide to Cultural Theory and Popular Culture* (Hemel Hempstead: Harvester/Wheatsheaf).

STRATHERN, A. (1971) *The Rope of Moka* (London: Cambridge University Press).

STRAWBRIDGE, S. (1993) 'Rules, Roles and Relationships', in J. Walmsley, J. Reynolds, P. Shakespeare and R. Woolfe (eds), *Health, Welfare and Practice: Reflecting on Roles and Relationships* (London: Sage/Open University Press).

STRAWBRIDGE, S. and WOOLFE, R. (1996) 'Counselling Psychology: A Sociological Perspective in R. Woolfe and W. Dryden (eds) *Handbook of Counselling Psychology* (London: Sage).

STUBBS, C. (1989) 'Property Rites? An Investigation of Tenure Changes in Middle Age', in B. Bytheway T. Keil, P. Allatt, A. Bryman (eds), *Being and Becoming Old. Sociological Approaches to Later Life* (London: Sage).

STURROCK, J. (ed.) (1979) *Structuralism and Since: From Levi- Strauss to Derrida* (Oxford University Press).

TANNEN, D. (1995) *Talking from 9 to 5 . . .* (London: Virago).

TAYLOR, C. (1992) *Sources of the Self: The Making of the Modern Identity* (Cambridge University Press).

TERKEL, S. (1974) *Working* (New York: Pantheon).

THANE, P. (1983) 'The History of Provision for the Elderly to 1929', in D. Jerrome (ed.), *Ageing in Modern Society* (London: Croom Helm).

THE TIMES (1995) 21 August and (1997) 8 Sept.

THOMSON, A. (1990) 'The Anzac Legend: Exploring National Myth and Memory in Australia', in R. Samuel and P. Thompson (eds), *The Myths We Live By* (London: Routledge).

THOMPSON, P. (1983) *Living the Fishing* (London: Routledge & Kegan Paul).

TOWNLEY, B. (1994) *Reframing Human Resource Management: Power, Ethics and the Subject of Work* (London: Sage).

TOWNSEND, P. and DAVIDSON, N. (1982) *Inequalities in Health* (Harmondsworth: Penguin).

TURNER, B. (1987) *Medical Power and Social Knowledge* (London: Sage).

TURNER, V. (1969) *The Ritual Process. Structure and Anti-structure* (Chicago: Aldine).

TURNER, V. (1974) *Dramas, Fields, and Metaphors* (Ithaca, New York: Cornell University Press).

VAN GENNEP, A. (1960) *The Rites of Passage*, first published 1908 (London: Routledge & Kegan Paul).

WAGNER, P. (1994) *A Sociology of Modernity: Liberty and Discipline* (London: Routledge).

WAJCMAN, J. (1991) *Feminism Confronts Technology* (Cambridge: Polity Press).

WALTER, T. (1996) 'A New Model of Grief: Bereavement and Biography, *Mortality,* 1, 1 (7–25)

WATSON, T. J. (1994) *In Search of Management: Culture, Chaos and Control in Managerial Work* (London: Routledge).

WEBER, M. (1978) *Selections in Translation,* (ed.) W. G. Runciman (Cambridge University Press).

WEBER, M. (1983) 'Politics as a Vocation' first published 1970, in D. Held, A. Anderson, B. Gieben, S. Hall, L. Harris', P. Loris, N. Parker, B. Turok (eds) *States and Societies* (Oxford: Martin Robertson).

WEEKES, J. (1985) *Sexuality and its Discontents: Meanings, Myths and Modern Sexualities* (London: Routledge & Kegan Paul).

WEEKES, J. (1986) *Sexuality* (London: Tavistock).

WESTWOOD, S. (1984) *All Day Every Day: Factory and Family in the Making of Women's Lives* (London: Pluto).

WESTWOOD, S. and BHACHU, P. (EDS) (1988) *Enterprising Women: Ethnicity, Economy and Gender Relations* (London: Routledge).

WHEELOCK, J. (1990) *Husbands at Home: The Domestic Economy in a Post-Industrial Society* (London: Routledge).

WILEY, N. (1994) 'The Politics of Identity in American History', in C. Calhoun (ed.), *Social Theory and the Politics of Identity* (Oxford: Basil Blackwell).

WILKINSON, R. G. (1994) *Unfair Shares. The Effects of Widening Income Differences on the Welfare of the Young* (Ilford: Barnardo's).

WILLIAMS, C. (ed.) (1993) *Doing "Women's Work": Men in Non-traditional Jobs* (London: Sage).

WILLIAMS, R. (1965) *The Long Revolution* (Harmondsworth: Penguin).

WILLIS, P. (1978) *Learning to Labour: How Working Class Kids Get Working Class Jobs* (Aldershot: Gower).

WILLIS, P. (1979) 'Shop-floor Culture, Masculinity and the Wage Form', in J. Clarke C. Critcher and R. Johnson, (eds), *Working Class Culture: Studies in History and Theory* (London: Hutchinson).

WILLIS, S. (1991) *A Primer For Daily Life* (London: Routledge).

WILTON, T. (1995) *Lesbian Studies: Setting an Agenda* (London: Routledge).

WINSHIP, J. (1987) *Inside Women's Magazines* (London: Pandora).

WORSLEY, P. (ed.) (1987) *The New Introducing Sociology* (Harmondsworth: Penguin).

WRIGHT, P. (1985) *On Living In An Old Country: The National Past in Contemporary Britain* (London: Verso).

WRONG, D. (1961) 'The Oversocialized Conception of Man in Modern Sociology', reprinted from *American Sociological Review* in R. Bocock, P. Hamilton, K. Thompson and A. Waton (eds) (1980), *An Introduction to Sociology* (Fontana/Open University Press).

WRONG, D. (ed.) (1970) *Max Weber* (Englewood Cliffs, NJ: Prentice-Hall).

WUTHNOW, R. (1989) *The Restructuring of American Religion* (Oxford: Princeton University Press).

WUTHNOW, R., J. D. HUNTER, A. BERGESON, E. KURZWEIL (1984) *Cultural Analysis: The Work of Peter L. Berger, Mary Douglas, Michel Foucault and Jurgen Habermas* (London: Routledge & Kegan Paul).

ZARETSKY, E. (1976) *Capitalism, the Family and Personal Life* (London: Pluto).

ZARETSKY, E. (1995) 'The Birth of Identity Politics in the 1960s: Psycho-analysis and the Public / Private Division', in M. Featherstone, S. Lash, and R. Robertson, (eds), *Global Modernities* (London: Sage).

ZOLA, I. (1966) 'Culture and Symptoms: An Analysis of Patients' Presenting Complaints', *American Sociological Review*, vol. 31, pp. 615–30.

ZOLA, I. (1975) 'In the Name of Health and Illness', *Social Science and Medicine*, vol. 9, pp. 83–8.

Name Index

280

Subject Index